AMERICA AT NIGHT

AMERICA AT NIGHT

THE TRUE STORY OF TWO ROGUE CIA OPERATIVES,
HOMELAND SECURITY FAILURES, DIRTY MONEY, AND
A PLOT TO STEAL THE 2004 U.S. PRESIDENTIAL
ELECTION—BY THE FORMER INTELLIGENCE AGENT WHO
FOILED THE PLAN

LARRY J. KOLB

RIVERHEAD BOOKS | a member of Penguin Group (USA) Inc.

NEW YORK | 2007

RIVERHEAD BOOKS
Published by the Penguin Group
Penguin Group (USA) Inc., 375 Hudson Street, New York, New York 10014,
USA • Penguin Group (Canada), 90 Eglinton Avenue East, Suite 700, Toronto,
Ontario M4P 2Y3, Canada (a division of Pearson Penguin Canada Inc.) •
Penguin Books Ltd, 80 Strand, London WC2R 0RL, England • Penguin
Ireland, 25 St Stephen's Green, Dublin 2, Ireland (a division of Penguin Books
Ltd) • Penguin Group (Australia), 250 Camberwell Road, Camberwell, Victoria
3124, Australia (a division of Pearson Australia Group Pty Ltd) • Penguin Books
India Pvt Ltd, 11 Community Centre, Panchsheel Park, New Delhi–110 017,
India • Penguin Group (NZ), 67 Apollo Drive, Mairangi Bay, Albany,
Auckland 1310, New Zealand (a division of Pearson New Zealand Ltd) •
Penguin Books (South Africa) (Pty) Ltd, 24 Sturdee Avenue, Rosebank,
Johannesburg 2196, South Africa

Penguin Books Ltd, Registered Offices:
80 Strand, London WC2R 0RL, England

Library of Congress Cataloging-in-Publication Data

Kolb, Larry J. (Larry Jackson), date.
  America at night : the true story of two rogue CIA operatives, homeland security
failures, dirty money, and a plot to steal the 2004 U.S. presidential election—by
the former intelligence agent who foiled the plan / Larry J. Kolb.
    p.   cm.
  Includes bibliographical references and index.
  ISBN-13: 978-1-59448-900-6
  ISBN-10: 1-59448-900-9
  1. Intelligence officers—United States. 2. Conspiracies—United States—
History—21st century. 3. Presidents—United States—Election—2004.
4. Kolb, Larry J. (Larry Jackson), date. I. Title.
  JK468.I6K64   2007   2006027011
  973.931—dc22

Printed in the United States of America
10 9 8 7 6 5 4 3 2 1

BOOK DESIGN BY GRETCHEN ACHILLES

FOR K.P. AND J.

The Summer is over,
the harvest is in,
and we are not saved.

Jeremiah 8:20

Politics in a literary work are a pistol-shot in the middle of a
concert, deafening and out of tune, though impossible to ignore.
We are about to speak of very ugly matters.

STENDHAL, *The Red and the Black*

CONTENTS

AMERICA AT NIGHT

1. HOW I SPENT MY SUMMER VACATION

Unfortunately, this is a true story. It begins in a hotel suite in the Hollywood Hills in the last week of May 2004. I'd just checked in and, outside my windows, birds were singing, trees were flowering, it was a fine sunny day—and my first day away from home in too long. I remember parting the billowing white inner curtains in a corner of the bedroom, opening a window wider, sticking my face outside, and then just standing like that for a moment, thinking there was something wonderful about the air, how it could be cool and warm, just cool enough and just warm enough, at once.

L.A. New scenery, a change of direction. I'd been looking forward to this. For the past two years I'd been at home in Florida, locked up in a single room, writing a great swirling devil of a book that, for too many months, I'd never quite been able to bring to an end. That book, *Overworld*, was the story of my life so far. The story of how I grew up all over the earth as the son of a senior American intelligence official, a spymaster; how the CIA recruited me when I was twenty-two, but I said no thanks; how, after my father's death, I became a close friend of Muhammad Ali, traveled all over the world, especially the Third World, with him, and became so well connected in Middle

Eastern capitals that I was soon irresistible to a certain CIA co-founder, Miles Copeland. And how Miles recruited me, trained me in what ways of spies I hadn't already picked up from my father, and then steeped me in Miles's specialty: covert political operations—at which no American intelligence officer was ever better than Miles. I mention all of this because, when the facts have been laid out and we get to the part about how I connected the dots and saw a plot to use Al-Qaeda to subvert the American presidential election of 2004, you will need to understand that, when it comes to covert political operations, I was trained by the master.

Miles Copeland had engineered the CIA's first coup d'état and a few more after that. He'd rigged elections, been friend and confidant to Egyptian strongman Gamal Abdel Nasser, the Shah of Iran, and various American presidents. In the 1960s, when Miles wrote a bestseller, no less than the most famous spy in the world, the British traitor Kim Philby, had stepped out of the shadows to proffer his opinion of it. "I've known that intriguer for twenty years," Philby said live on Radio Moscow, "so I can say with authority that Miles Copeland's book, *The Game of Nations,* is itself a move in the CIA's monstrous game."

Overworld recounts some of my experiences, under Miles's direction, in places like Beirut, Riyadh, Islamabad, Managua, Washington, and ends with an account of a covert political operation that, near the end of Miles's life, I ran for the Indian prime minister Rajiv Gandhi. When Rajiv, my friend and protector, was assassinated, his political enemies came after me, stranding me in a safe house on a beach in Florida. After living most of my life overseas, that felt to me like exile. Thrice the United States government refused to extradite me to India.

But spying and covert operations were things that, more often than not, I'd only done reluctantly, and I hoped that by writing about them I'd gotten them out of my system. The book was finished. There were no more passages to rewrite, no more page proofs to correct. The U.S. hardcover edition was in production. Foreign rights had been sold. Movie rights had been sold. It was time for me to take it easy. That was what I'd come here for, and to hang out with old friends, and meet some new ones—the movie producers who bought the rights to my book. After ten years on the beach in exile, and two more writing, I was finally free. Just then, almost anything seemed possible.

Anything except that I would ever again live a covert life. By writing about it, I had intentionally blown my cover. Once the book was published, spying would no longer be a career option for me, and thank God for that.

So, back to the twenty-seventh of May 2004, and my suite in The Argyle on the edge of the Hollywood Hills. During my long forced march through the first and second drafts of *Overworld,* I'd lived almost entirely inside the memories I was writing about. It was only during the past couple of months, while I'd worked on final revisions, that I'd begun to reconnect with what was going on in the world. Every day, two subjects dominated the news: the war in Iraq and the presidential election campaign. The war wasn't going quite as well as the administration had projected. For most of the past month, the Pentagon and the White House had been reeling from revelations about American soldiers abusing Iraqi prisoners at Abu Ghraib. President George W. Bush, who'd led us into Iraq, was standing for re-election. It was likely that his opponent in November would be Democratic senator John Kerry. But I was more interested right now in taking care of a little business and then beginning my frolic through Los Angeles.

I hadn't worn a suit in ages, so it took me a while to get ready for lunch. I remember a struggle with my tie. There'd been entire decades in which I lived in suits and ties. So how many attempts could it take me to form a simple four-in-hand knot? In this case, the answer was six. It wasn't that I couldn't get the basics right. But I kept having symmetry problems. Then I found I'd brought no cuff links. I had to change shirts, which I managed to accomplish without completely re-tying my tie. And my shoes were brand new, still in the box.

I had to lace them, and while I did, seated on the Art Deco sofa in the living room, by then I had all the curtains and floor-to-ceiling windows open, and I spent a time listening to birdsong and street sounds and looking toward the top of the green hill that stretched out above me—at stilt houses, Andalusian mansions with red barrel-tiled roofs, cantilevered houses, Cape Cods, among impossibly tall palm trees, stands of eucalyptus, cedars, telephone poles. A hillside of people who made their livings buying and selling dreams. Lately, I'd been considering the possibility I'd begin spending a lot more of my time out here. It felt so good to be here.

First stop, lunch at The Palm with an old friend, a Washington attorney. I got up from the sofa in my new shoes and headed down-stairs and out into that lovely cool-warm air and found a taxi to take me down the hill to the lunch where it all began. What happened after that, I thought I would never tell anyone. It's an ugly story, ex-cept for the girl; and it's not the sort of truth you'd think you could expose and survive. So what I did about it, up to a point, I did anony-mously, intending to disappear when I finished. But then my identity was exposed, or, if you prefer the intelligence jargon: I was blown—by a careless act from on high. And suddenly, unambiguously, I saw that the more people who knew exactly what I'd discovered, and what I'd done about it, the less reason anyone would have to silence me, the less likely I'd be to wind up with a tag on my toe, or in protective cus-tody somewhere. Incommunicado either way.

Vince was late for lunch, and I wish he'd never shown up. But, then again, all indications are if Vince hadn't sucked me back into the secret world, somebody else would've. So I don't hold it against him. Vince Messina. Washington tax and immigration attorney, international dealmaker, bon vivant. Based on what I know of his background, he has to be as old as the hills. But somehow he doesn't seem it. Bald on top, short dark hair on the sides, olive skin, smiles a lot, constantly on the move. Vince is on the up-and-up, but spends much of his time in strange lands working for mysterious clients.

He was heading soon to Libya, where I had some experience and good business contacts, and he wanted to pick my brain. Which was all right by me, and simple enough. Things to do and people to see in Libya had already been exhausted as a topic before we got our main course—sitting across a white linen tablecloth from each other in a brass-railed wooden booth, fan blades slowly spinning overhead. Over my small steak and Vince's big red plate of linguine with clam sauce, we had plenty of time to chat about all sorts of other things.

Vince is prone to sudden recollections that launch him into epic stories. Fascinating digressions beautifully told, and usually drawn from his own experiences. In the middle of a conversation about a business deal, you might get, for instance, a detailed and nuanced firsthand account of subterranean Washington warfare back in the fifties between HUAC and Senator Joe McCarthy, or an FBI campaign some years later to squeeze the Mob out of Vegas. He's also so well read that, listening to Vince, you never know when you might find yourself, say, watching a man on horseback beside the banks of the Tigris, galloping away from certain death. And Vince telling it so well, as if it happened just last month and he'd been eyewitness to it, recalling every movement, every expression, that you're surprised when he tells you it's only something he read, it happened centuries ago.

But on that day Vince said he was getting over a touch of flu. So maybe he just didn't have the energy to work up any narrative momentum.

Or maybe if we'd just ordered dessert I wouldn't be telling you this story. It took, they say, only the taste of a single cookie, dunked in tea by Marcel Proust, to unlock a memory so vivid it yielded a flood of memories requiring multivolumes and thousands of printed pages to contain them all. If Vince had tasted the chocolate cake, things might've turned out very differently for me and a lot of others. Take, for example, the body count. Had lunch somehow ended on a different note, there are certain persons still living and breathing who very probably wouldn't be, and at least one other, now dead, who would still be alive. But we skipped dessert. We'd asked for the check and were down to our last dregs of coffee when, an afterthought, Vince casually said, "Oh, Larry, I should ask you—because these days I try to ask everyone I know who's ever been involved in intelligence—you don't happen to know a guy by the name of Bob Sensi, who used to work for the CIA, do you?"

"As a matter of fact, I do," I said, a little startled by the question, and Vince looked quite surprised himself, sat up straighter, said in a year and a half of his asking dozens of people, I was the first person who'd answered yes.

Then Vince asked me to tell him what I knew of Bob Sensi, and not long after I started doing that, Vince stopped me, brought out his cell phone, and called his nephew Gary so he could hear too. Gary was one of the highest-ranking officers in the Department of Homeland Security; in fact, he was in control of what was supposed to be our government's most comprehensive database on all known bad guys, and Bob Sensi was a bad guy, yet it was already coming clear that I knew more about him than the combined databases of the several security agencies of the United States government.

It was all fresh in my mind because I'd written about it in *Overworld*. And just a few weeks earlier, I'd gone through my Sensi files again in some detail with one of my publisher's attorneys during their strenuous vetting of my manuscript. This, in essence, is what I told Vince and Gary:

Early in 1985, in a secret meeting in the White House that I attended with Muhammad Ali and others, Vice President George Bush asked Muhammad to use his credibility in the Muslim world to start a covert dialogue with the Ayatollah Khomeini to try to procure release of the American, British, Kuwaiti, and Saudi hostages then being held in Beirut. In the course of that meeting, the Vice President gave me the business card of Robert M. Sensi—*Chairman, The Ambassador's Club, Republicans Abroad, c/o The Republican National Committee*—and informed us Sensi actually worked for the CIA and would provide whatever support Muhammad needed for the mission.

When we met Sensi, he told us he was being run directly by CIA director Bill Casey, in close concert with Vice President Bush. Sensi also said he worked, nominally, for Kuwait Airways, and the Kuwaiti royal family would be funding our operation.

Sensi was raised in Chicago and, when among Americans, he pretended to be a bit of a rube—but he could speak five languages, fluently, and could blend into a crowd like nobody I'd ever seen before. Sensi's primary mission for the CIA was engineering a covert opening to moderates within the Iranian power structure. His primary mission for the Republican Party was running an offshore financing operation, collecting political contributions from American interests overseas.

Over the next few weeks, Sensi orchestrated meetings in London between Muhammad—accompanied by me and certain others—and a tag team of friendly Persian gentlemen in French suits. They had their own big white house in Belgravia and were said to be Iranian government commodities-trading officials. But they seemed to be representatives of an Iranian intelligence service.

After several meetings in London, we went to Beirut, at the height of the Lebanese Civil War, open season on Americans, and there, in a safe house, in the middle of the night, we met secretly with Ibrahim Amin, political leader and deputy chief of Hizballah; and Muhammad procured the release of one American hostage—a fact reported only by the Arab press.

Months later, Sensi was arrested in London and extradited to the United States, to stand trial on charges of embezzling from Kuwait Airways. Sensi's defense was that he worked for the CIA, and the expenditures for which he was being prosecuted were part of a CIA mission knowingly paid for by the Kuwaiti royal family. During the proceedings, a CIA representative appeared and stipulated that Sensi had been affiliated with the CIA, but also that the expenditures specified in the charges were not part of any CIA operation. Sensi was convicted and sent to federal prison.

Sometime after his release, Sensi was arrested, tried, convicted, and reincarcerated by the federal government for his involvement in a Nigerian Letters fraud operation.

But, until I told all this to Vince and Gary, virtually the only things they'd been able to find out about Sensi, the only facts about Sensi not purged from the government's records, were that he once worked for the CIA and that he now was a con man who claimed he still worked for the CIA.

"Oh shit!" I said when I saw the time. "Sorry, guys, I've got to go." I stood up to leave for my next appointment—with the movie guys who'd recently paid me a handsome sum and were threatening to pay me a lot more sometime soon. It was free money, for work I'd already done while writing the book, and this was a concept I found quite charming.

So I already liked these guys a lot, though I'd never actually met them, and I'd been looking forward to this meeting. But, when I got there, I found I couldn't keep my mind off my lunch with Vince. As I left the restaurant, Vince had followed me out with his cell phone, and Gary had said to me, "Look, Larry, I can't tell you a lot about why this is so important to us, except that it involves national security and Al-Qaeda. There's a guy who's working as Sensi's partner. Together they're friggin' in the riggin' of a very sensitive situation. Sensi's partner is a lawyer going by the name of Richard Marshall. You don't know him, do you?"

I'd said, "I don't think so." And thought that was the end of that.

But now, as I sat in the boardroom of the burled-wood offices of Atmosphere Entertainment MM LLC, chatting about the complexities of adapting my book into a screenplay, I found my palms beginning to sweat. I *did* know a lawyer named Richard who'd worked with Sensi before. That Richard's last name wasn't Marshall, but he was a very bad guy and capable of almost anything. Perhaps I did know who "Richard Marshall" was, and, if I was right, and he and Sensi were working together again, and it involved Al-Qaeda—it would not end well.

———

That night, I had drinks in The Argyle's bar with my friends Malcolm Venville and Dave Morrison. Malcolm's a director and lives in London. I remember we talked for a while about Malcolm's hero of heroes, Muhammad Ali, until Malcolm downed his second drink and announced he had a plane to catch in the morning, that it was time for him to go. Then Dave drove me, at unforgettable speed, like there were hellhounds on our trail, gaining on us, down Sunset, through Beverly Hills and beyond, up to the tip-top of Bel-Air.

There, he lived in a Space Age house with slate floors, vintage sixties furniture, plasma screens and art on the walls, fantastic views out the huge rear windows. A matched pair of beautiful, vigilant Great Danes was patrolling the perimeter.

Enter: Dave's wife, Sarah-Jane Wilde—American passport, British accent, Parisian education. Deep mysterious beauty. Sarah-Jane served us champagne, salad, risotto, and crème brûlée. And she kept the table talk flowing beautifully while the three of us ate, interrupted occasionally by walk-on performances by the boy pharaoh, Dave and Sarah-Jane's son—who spoke to me in a special dialect of English translatable only by his parents, and was wearing footed pajamas but didn't seem to want to stay in his crib.

If either of them had foreseen the shit storm I was heading into, probably Dave would've done his best to get me so ridiculously drunk that I couldn't move the next morning, or Sarah-Jane would've tried harder to convince me to stay in town another five nights for the party she proposed to organize in my honor, complete with film stars, eccentric artists, supermodels—*for you, Larry, the works!* Just five nights. Shouldn't have been a problem, since I had so many more friends in town to see, and so much more I'd planned to do before leaving L.A.

But it was no use. Already the challenge was beginning to possess me. And by the next morning, I barely had time to go out and send flowers and a thank-you note to Sarah-Jane, and then, well, fuck it, I was checking out of the hotel and Vince was driving me to LAX, briefing me all the way there—because there were certain things I was going to need to know if I was going to hit the ground running when I got to where I was going to try to help the government of the United States of America solve the mystery of just who the hell Richard Marshall was, and what he was up to, and why.

2. PULP NONFICTION

When I went to Beirut in February 1985, with Muhammad Ali and Bob Sensi on that covert mission sanctioned by George Bush from inside the Reagan White House, one of Muhammad's friends who made the trip with us was an attorney from Charlottesville, Virginia, by the name of Richard Hirschfeld. Though I'd never met him in person until then, I'd never liked Hirschfeld. The three or four times I'd had to talk to him on the phone, he'd started out charming and ended up screaming at me. I knew enough assholes already. No need to become acquainted with Hirschfeld.

But I couldn't resist Beirut at the peak of the Lebanese Civil War with the only traveling companion almost guaranteed to keep my skinny white American ass out of trouble. So when I heard Hirschfeld would be going too, I decided I'd just have to put up with him.

Listening to his thunderous voice on the phone, I'd always pictured Hirschfeld a big, barrel-chested fellow. But when I met him he was, not quite elfin, but slight. Five-six at the most, in a gray flannel suit. With bright white teeth, a receding hairline, and a pleasant, fragile smile—along with that voice. I hated him on sight, and, when I wrote about the Beirut trip in *Overworld,* I found that over time I'd blocked

Hirschfeld out of nearly all my memories of the trip. But one episode I did remember, from what had to be my first or second day in Beirut.

It began down in the lobby of the remarkably intact, beachfront, five-star-deluxe Summerland Hotel, where we stayed, while marveling and wincing at the everyday soundtrack of Beirut in the littoral zone. Bombs exploding in the distance, the whistling of cannon shells in flight, squalls of automatic-weapons fire. And, during the long lulls between booms, birds singing on the balconies, and gentle surf. I was on my way from the coffee shop to the elevators when a reporter stopped me.

He asked me why Muhammad had come to Beirut, rather than going to Tehran to meet with Khomeini. That was what Muhammad had announced he was doing when he left the United States. And, the reporter went on, was Muhammad really paying for all of this himself? Well, those were tricky questions given certain facts.

Such as the fact that, while Muhammad had spoken with Khomeini on the phone from London, and after that one of Khomeini's many factotums had instructed us to go to Kuwait and wait there until a plane was sent to take us to Tehran, Muhammad had also spoken with reporters in London and told them he'd already asked Khomeini for help. That, coupled with the release of American hostage Jeremy Levin soon thereafter, could be made to look like proof that Iran was behind the kidnappings in Beirut. Consequently, word had come down to Muhammad in Kuwait that he'd be wasting his time in Tehran—Iran had absolutely nothing do with the hostages. *But,* the Ayatollah's representative had added helpfully, perhaps you should go to Lebanon to meet directly with the parties who *are* involved in this matter. And, if you do, and if Allah blesses us, perhaps we may be of some small assistance from behind the scenes. That was how we came to be in Beirut.

And the fact that, hell no, Muhammad wasn't paying for any of this. The CIA was, through some impenetrable off-the-books arrangement between the White House and someone in the Kuwaiti royal family.

I told the reporter none of that. I said I'd get the facts from Muhammad and let the reporter know the next time I saw him.

Sometime later that day, upstairs in the living room of Muhammad's suite, Muhammad and I were sitting together chatting when I remembered the reporter and his questions.

"What should I tell him?" I said to Muhammad. "I think we're going to have to think this through a little better than what you said in London."

And on hearing that, Hirschfeld, who'd been sitting across the room quietly talking with his fast new friend Bob Sensi, and listening to Muhammad and me, rose out of his chair, while curling his lip into something ugly for emphasis, and snarled at me: "The man can speak for himself."

Hirschfeld could be preternaturally calm or ferociously angry. Those seemed to be his only two waking states. At the moment, he was standing right in front of me and his face was turning pink. He said it again, bellowing now. "The *man* can speak for him*self*." And what I realized then was he was jealous. He'd never seen Muhammad and me with our heads together, just the two of us talking, didn't understand we spoke about delicate things all the time, that, in my own way, I was just as tight with Muhammad as Hirschfeld was. Right there and then, Richard Hirschfeld wanted to tear into all six feet six inches of me. I stood up.

So did Muhammad. And he inserted first his size-13EEE foot and his hip, and then his arms, between us like a referee breaking up a clinch. "Richie," said Muhammad, staring down into Hirschfeld's eyes now, *"be cool, fool!"*

A rebuke, and one of his favorite throwaway lines, all in one. And by that simple measure Muhammad dealt, for the moment, with one of the essential complications of his life—regularly, routinely, he compartmentalized his friends and allegiances. He was never in one place for long, and that made it simpler. He was as kind and gentle a man as I had ever known, and I loved Muhammad like a brother. But if it meant I was going to have to deal much more with Richard Hirschfeld, I might have to rethink my plans.

From what I'd heard, Muhammad was under Hirschfeld's spell. Crisscrossing the globe with him in pursuit of lavish business deals that came heartbreakingly close but never quite seemed to come off. Staying often at Hirschfeld's farm in Virginia. Riding horses together there every day, like country squires. Riding Hirschfeld's Rolls-Royce around Charlottesville and Washington, seeing and being seen. Muhammad had allowed himself to become Hirschfeld's means of ascent, and, while Hirschfeld appeared to be racking up some dough, so far Muhammad hadn't gotten much more than free horseback riding out of it. But he wasn't ready to pull the plug.

Still, he had just stood up for me, shut Hirschfeld down. *Be cool, fool!* Hirschfeld walked out of the suite without another word, and didn't reappear for some time. In fact, in my memory, he walked out of Beirut forever.

Probably he did go with us—Muhammad, Sensi, me, a couple of others in our party, and our guide, the original American mujahideen, Isa Abdullah Ali—into the netherworld of nighttime Beirut, the soukhs, the mosques, the cafés and safe houses, the meetings with certain very clever, very dangerous, very security-conscious, nearly invisible men who ran terrorist organizations. But I found while writing the book that the next place I actually remembered seeing Hirschfeld was in Cyprus, which was where we spent the night when we finally had the good sense to get the hell out of Lebanon while we still could.

After that, the only other time I ever spent with Hirschfeld was one weekend in Cairo, in 1986. I flew in from Jiddah to meet with Muhammad. He hadn't told me Hirschfeld was with him. Once I arrived, all I could do was make the best of it.

My heart sank when I saw Hirschfeld pop out of a door right behind Muhammad. And as they walked up to me, both smiling, I was struck all over again by just how short Hirschfeld was. He was in his late thirties then, and in the year and some since I'd seen him he'd gone a little soft and pudgy. Packaged and produced by the same studio that gave you the midlife Mickey Rooney.

Waiting is both art form and business necessity in the Middle East. Muhammad was waiting for Hirschfeld's client, the Saudi wild man–tycoon Mohamed Al-Fassi—who'd registered his first blip on the American cultural radar a few years earlier by buying a mansion on Sunset Boulevard in Beverly Hills and painting the genitalia of the lawn statuary Day-Glo orange and pink and lime. *That* Sheikh Al-Fassi. Somehow or other, Hirschfeld had roped Ali, and his manager Jabir Muhammad and his assistant Abuwi Mahdi, into coming to Cairo to meet with Al-Fassi, who supposedly had agreed to fund a deal that would engorge them all for years.

Muhammad and Jabir and Mahdi and Hirschfeld had already been in Cairo for three or four days when I arrived, and they hadn't even seen Al-Fassi yet. He was, however, putting them up in a fine Old World hotel on the Nile, and had provided them a stretched white Mercedes limousine, with driver, which, on the dusty, torrid streets of Cairo, looked like something right out of a James Bond movie. To make a deal in the Middle East, you had to wait. Sometimes, if you waited long enough, good things actually happened.

In Jiddah, I'd once waited with Muhammad in King Fahd's palace for seventeen days before we saw the King. Each day a royal protocol officer had informed us we should stay close at hand because His Majesty would likely see us within hours. And each day, for the first sixteen days, nothing happened. This was not a slight, nor gamesmanship. It was just the Middle East, a timeless place.

So, in Cairo, for three days—before I bid everyone *Ma'a-salaama* and headed off to the airport in Dr. No's snow-white stretched limo—I waited too. And being around Hirschfeld wasn't all that bad, actually. He was on good behavior, told jokes, did uncanny Ali impressions, and could be rather charming.

The key to having Richard Hirschfeld like you, I discovered, was to make sure he understood you appreciated his genius. And truly that was not difficult. He was a very bright man, intellectually gifted— and one sorry sack of shit.

Witness: One day while we waited, I was sitting in the living room of Muhammad's suite all by myself when the phone rang. I answered, and on the other end of the line was Ferdinand Marcos, the deposed president of the Philippines, calling from exile in Hawaii. Muhammad was in his bedroom praying, I said, and couldn't be disturbed. But could he call you back?

And when Muhammad did call back he made sure Jabir, Mahdi, Hirschfeld, and I were all listening in on extensions—for the sheer entertainment value of it. We were all a little bored.

Marcos told Muhammad he had a couple billion dollars in gold hidden away, and transportable by ship, and he wanted Muhammad's help converting the gold into cash, perhaps in a nice Muslim port somewhere Muhammad had lots of influence. In exchange, Muhammad would receive a piece of the action. Muhammad declined to participate.

But some few weeks after the long wait for Al-Fassi ended inconclu-
sively, Hirschfeld, without Muhammad's approval, slunk off to Hawaii
and introduced himself to Marcos as Muhammad's emissary. Hirschfeld
had the gift of appearing perfectly normal and sane. Dependable. He
was really, really good at what he did. In short order, he made a deal,
whereunder President Marcos retained Hirschfeld as his attorney and
entrusted him to make certain discreet arrangements in his behalf.

Three simple tasks. The first was obtaining foreign passports for
Marcos. The U.S. government had taken his Philippine passport and
confined him to the island of Oahu; these restrictions were really
rather annoying for a man of Marcos's vision. The second was the
purchase of sufficient quantities of arms to support Marcos's plan to
invade the Philippines, landing near his power base in Ilocos Norte to
reunite with ten thousand loyal troops, who, with Marcos, would
fight their way south and retake Manila. Third, since Marcos was going to need some working capital to pull this off, he needed a loan of
twenty million dollars, of his own money.

That is, Marcos said he had plenty of cash stashed in various banks
throughout the world, but he couldn't be seen to have that money. So
what he needed was someone trustworthy to give, say, twenty-five million dollars to, and for that trustworthy person to take five million off
the top for his trouble, and then to "loan" Marcos the remaining
twenty million. Hirschfeld said he knew just the man for the job.

From Honolulu he went to Cairo. There Hirschfeld met with his
client Mohamed Al-Fassi, who, after cooling his attorney's heels for a
suitable time, said yes, he would participate in a sham loan to Marcos. Next, Hirschfeld visited with representatives of certain banana
republics and other jurisdictions, who indicated that, yes, for the
right consideration, they would grant citizenships and issue passports
to Mr. Marcos.

Hirschfeld bounced back and forth for weeks between Cairo and Honolulu, making arrangements, negotiating. He set up a complex deal under which Marcos's bank would transfer Al-Fassi the twenty-five million dollars, then Al-Fassi would take his five million off the top, giving the remainder to Hirschfeld. And this was the point at which it would become a classic Hirschfeld deal—the sacred moment in which, without benefit of clergy, Hirschfeld would transsubstantiate himself from attorney acting in someone else's interest to principal acting for himself. Unbeknownst to Al-Fassi, Hirschfeld, through a shell company he secretly controlled, would keep the twenty million dollars, in cash, while giving Marcos bank credits that only seemed to be worth twenty million, and actually were worth nothing.

In the end, Marcos wouldn't receive a single dime of his twenty-five million dollars. But he would have his faithful attorney Richard Hirschfeld by his side, commiserating with him and vowing revenge against the scalawags who'd stolen Marcos's money.

Or—if, at the last minute, Hirschfeld judged that he couldn't make that work, well, there was always Plan C. And that, too, was a hallmark of a classic Hirschfeld deal. At every step along the way, he increased his options. At some point, precisely when was not clear, Hirschfeld went to Manila, met with high officials, and told them he had Marcos's trust and soon he would know the locations of certain of Marcos's hidden assets. Another deal was struck. The People Power government of Corazon Aquino irrevocably promised to pay Richard Hirschfeld, of Charlottesville, Virginia, a five-percent commission on any assets he helped them locate and recover. Hirschfeld didn't actually plan to help the Aquino government recover any of Marcos's money, not if he could steal it for himself. But he was keeping his options open. Five percent for betraying Marcos was better than nothing.

However—before he managed to bring all this to critical mass, Hirschfeld was informed by the FBI that they knew what he was doing and he had two choices: go to jail, or they would own him for the duration of his dealings with Marcos.

Under the control of the FBI, Hirschfeld went back to Honolulu—with an old friend and business partner of his, Robert Chastain, playing the role of arms dealer—equipped to record Marcos. They met in Marcos's living room next to a television set, and Marcos kept turning up the volume on *Leave It to Beaver* to foil audio surveillance. But he also kept leaning closer and closer to Hirschfeld, and his briefcase, which contained a recording device, and Hirschfeld got it all on tape. The cash, the gold, the passports, the arms, the invasion plan.

Then a stroke of luck for Hirschfeld—the FBI determined it didn't want to compromise its sources by revealing it had learned of Hirschfeld's dealings with Marcos. As soon as he realized this, Hirschfeld managed to turn himself into a hero. Plan D. He left out the part about the FBI catching him and turning him, and he also failed to mention he was a swindler, when he testified, rather breathlessly, at a sensational House Foreign Affairs subcommittee hearing about Marcos's wicked plans and Hirschfeld's own selfless role in bringing them to the attention of the Congress. For hours, he answered questions from the panel and played his tapes. *Hirschfeld rising.*

Or something like that. It was all rather vague in my memory. During the trial of Adnan Khashoggi and Imelda Marcos in New York in 1990, I'd researched the whole affair in some detail for Adnan's attorneys. But I hadn't looked at my Hirschfeld file in years.

I did still remember that, as a result of his performance at the hearing, Hirschfeld had found he had ready access on Capitol Hill. And he quickly began building working relationships with senators and key members of their staffs. He developed a particularly close friendship with Orrin Hatch, Republican senator from Utah.

Soon enough—it was in 1988, if I remembered right—Hirschfeld came close to conning a majority of the U.S. Senate into enacting a private bill under which he and Muhammad would've collected fifty million dollars from the U.S. government for Muhammad's "wrongful conviction" on Vietnam-era draft-evasion charges.

How did Hirschfeld do that? Telephonically.

Night after night, he called senator after senator, at home— calling not as Richard Hirschfeld, but as Muhammad Ali.

Hirschfeld's brass-balled impersonation was so convincing that dozens of senators, including Hatch, Strom Thurmond, John Warner, Arlen Specter, and Ted Kennedy, suddenly believed Muhammad was their new best friend and happened to have time to call them almost every night. Just to chew the fat for a while, then offer to support their favorite initiatives, and ask them to support the aforesaid private bill. Ted Kennedy actually credited Muhammad with brokering the bipartisan compromise that led to passage of a landmark fair housing act. Orrin Hatch actually proposed the bill that would've benefited Muhammad and Hirschfeld by the sum of fifty million dollars. But the whole thing was scuttled when a reporter named Dave Kindred of *The Atlanta Journal-Constitution* exposed it.

Richard Hirschfeld was a brilliant man with a rotted soul. Things began unraveling for him after the Kindred story hit the wires. The last I'd heard about Hirschfeld was around 1992, when Muhammad told me Hirschfeld was in federal prison for tax evasion.

What I was thinking as we climbed out of LAX and headed east was: What if "Richard Marshall" is Richard Hirschfeld?

————

I may as well tell you right now that I was not on my way to some top-secret, state-of-the-art Homeland Security counterterrorism center. I was on my way back to my house. Back to my files, and the desk and computer terminal I'd been hoping I'd seen the last of for quite some time. It was in my home office that I would attempt to solve the mystery the CIA, the FBI, the DEA, the BCIS, and the Department of Homeland Security hadn't quite managed to solve in two years of trying. According to Gary Messina, I was probably better equipped than they were to actually get to the bottom of it. And if that doesn't scare you, well, it should.

In the parking lot outside the terminal, the air felt like a hot, wet blanket. Even though it was approaching midnight. Welcome to Florida. Where they count the votes real slowly. Where the 9/11 terror pilots learned to fly. Where the air is never cool and warm at once.

No one seemed to follow me home, and when I got there, after I'd kissed my wife and hugged my son, walked my black dog, Guinness, and seen them all off to bed, I waded into my files in the closet in the back of my office. There was way too much stuff in there. It was a walk-in closet, but not as big as the one in the room I'd used as my home office until the arrival of my son.

Yet, behind its louvered mahogany door I'd stuffed as much as I'd had in the last closet, and more: five gray-steel four-drawer file cabinets, full; stacks and stacks of white cardboard document boxes; stationery; reams of paper; my father's sad and astonishing Dachau photo album; magic supplies, silks, ropes, appearing canes, rising decks, gossamer threads, a fez, relics of the magic act I used to do with Muhammad; piles of FedEx airbills and envelopes, UPS airbills and envelopes; a chunk of the Berlin Wall I'd never quite figured out what to do with; two amorphous bundles of bubble wrap; a pair of briefcases I'd semi-retired; a boomerang; maps; software disks; dubs, on tape and DVD, of archival video footage; dog-eared *Overworld* drafts complete with editorial marks. It was a mess, because there just wasn't enough space inside the closet to neatly organize everything I might want access to but didn't want cluttering my workspace. For years, my wife, Kim, had been trying to get me to throw more stuff out. Probably she was right. On the other hand, it's because I'm a pack rat that I still had files on Sensi and Hirschfeld. After twenty minutes of searching, I spotted them and dug them out of a cardboard box.

Two battered redrope accordion files. One marked in black Sharpie, in big block letters, in my own hand—SENSI. The other, R. M. HIRSCHFELD.

The first thing I got out was the card. "ROBERT M. SENSI/ Chairman, The Ambassador's Club"—printed in flat dark-gray ink in a sans serif font on milk-white card stock. Slightly edgeworn, despite the varying degrees of care I'd taken to preserve it over the years.

To the left of Sensi's name and title was a logo. A red, white, and blue elephant centered within curving blue lines representing a globe. Below that, in the same font and gray ink, "Republicans Abroad c/o Republican National Committee/310 First Street S.E., Washington DC 20003/tel: (202)662-1390/telex: 701144 RNC.RNC."

I sat down at my computer keyboard, Googled the phone number, and got: *Republicans Abroad International.* Same address and phone number as all those years ago. Below that, this text: *The Republicans Abroad association provides up-to-date briefings on issues of national importance to Republicans living overseas in diplomatic, personal, and professional capacities.*

No mention of Sensi, or his special talents raising offshore campaign contributions. Let alone his felony convictions. No mention of The Ambassador's Club. Which perhaps never existed at all, except as a cover for Sensi's operations.

I scanned Sensi's card, saved the image on my hard drive as a JPEG file, attached the file to an e-mail message, and sent it out through the ether to Vince and Gary.

Next I pulled from the SENSI file two pages of biographical information Miles Copeland had obtained for me years ago. A man's entire life, to the age of thirty-five, distilled to just a few paragraphs:

Robert Mario Sensi. Born November 22, 1950, in Blue Island, Illinois. Parents, Stephen and Frances Sensi. Two brothers, Ulisse and Edgar; no sister. K–7th grade, St. Joaquin School, Chicago. Grades 8–11, schools in Detroit, New York, and Rome. In Rome studied opera and Italian, while living with his grandparents. By age 17, had forsaken a future as an opera singer and was back in Illinois. 1968, graduated from New Trier High School, Northfield, Illinois. Attended Fordham University in New York and Loyola University in Chicago, obtaining Bachelor's degree in Political Science from Loyola 1970, just two years after high school.

Sensi's first job after college was as a repo man for CIT Financial Corp. in Chicago. Within months, moved on to positions as tour guide and incentive sales director for Travel Headquarters, a Chicago travel agency. 1973, left to work in Chicago sales office of Air France. Within a year was assistant district manager. 1976, moved to Gulf Air, opening Gulf's Chicago office with title Midwest Sales Manager. Developed reputation among diplomats and other Arab VIPs as the guy who could get things done for them in Chicago—a fixer, adept at solving problems with INS, customs, local police, just the guy to arrange theater tickets and private shopping tours for wives on a moment's notice, or to discreetly procure prostitutes or about anything else for their husbands once the wives were out on the town.

1977, left Gulf Air and took job in Washington office of Kuwait Airways. There, reported directly to Kuwaiti ambassador, and began performing services not only for the airline's VIP travelers but also for

the ambassador and visiting members of the Kuwaiti royal family. Excelled in obtaining visas, residency, prestigious university enrollments,
medical treatment, and other dispensations for prominent Kuwaitis and
their friends. Also excelled in procuring prostitutes, covering up arrest
records, bribing professors to improve grades and doctors to amend
records of embarrassing diagnoses. Proved so adept at extraordinary
services that he was soon given expanded responsibilities and control of
a multi-million-dollar Kuwait Airways slush fund to cover his operating
expenses.

Also in 1977, Sensi met and befriended then relatively unknown fre-
quent flyer Yasir Arafat, PLO Chairman. Arranged Arafat's first U.S. media
interviews. By then was fluent in Italian, French, Spanish, English, learning Arabic and Farsi. With these special talents and high-level access to
prominent Arabs, Sensi was talentspotted and recruited by CIA. He has
ready access to DCI Casey and is a regular visitor to White House. Guards
there reportedly wave Sensi through on sight, without requiring creden-
tials. He travels frequently to Europe, the Mideast, West Africa, Latin
America in fundraising role as Chairman, Ambassador's Club, Republicans
Abroad division of RNC.

There were another couple of paragraphs after that, about Sensi's
two failed marriages, one in Chicago and one in Washington, his
now-teenaged daughter who lived with her mother back in Chicago,
his son soon to be born in Washington, out of wedlock, to Sensi's
off-and-on girlfriend. Then a closing paragraph about how Sensi's
many talents had made him a very useful intelligence asset. I had no
doubt about that. Sensi could go into a revolving door behind you
and come out ahead of you. But the paragraph about Casey and Republicans Abroad was what I'd been looking for.

To hear Bob Sensi tell it—and I'd heard him tell it over a glass of whisky one night in June of 1986 in a hotel bar in Washington, D.C.—Republicans Abroad got its start as a player in the secret world in 1980, during the summer of the presidential campaign. President Jimmy Carter versus Governor Ronald Reagan. Reagan's campaign manager was one William J. Casey—who'd been an OSS officer during the Second World War, after that an attorney in private practice, then a big-shot investment banker on Wall Street, and then chairman of the Securities and Exchange Commission. Still, he was "Mumbles" to those who worked for him and faced the day-to-day problem of trying to make out what he was saying when he spoke to them. But never "Mumbles" to his face.

What Bill Casey did in that summer of 1980, it had long been alleged, was engineer the October Surprise. It was said that, upon learning the mullahs running Iran were ready to order the release of the fifty-two American hostages who'd been held in Tehran since the previous year, and realizing that that would swing the election to President Carter, Casey had taken it upon himself to meet secretly in Paris and Madrid with Iranian government representatives to promise them arms and other consideration if they would delay the release until after the election. And that whatever flummeries and enticements Casey had mumbled to the Iranians had carried the day, and the election. A very dirty trick, if it was true. And without quite saying it, Sensi seemed to be telling me it was true.

That was one of the decades in which I lived in suits and ties, especially if tuxedos count as suits. As incongruous as it seems to me now, back then I wore a tuxedo about one night a week. That night in Washington, Bob Sensi and I were both wearing black tuxedos. I was thirty-two, but still occasionally getting carded in bars. Sensi was thirty-five, but he looked older, and a bit exotic. With his olive skin, rich brown hair and mustache, he could've convinced you he was an

Arab dictator, a Persian arms dealer, an Italian businessman, a Latino, an American. We'd been to a charity dinner with Muhammad. Afterward we'd gone for a midnight walk past the Vietnam Veterans Memorial—the Wall, all those names and missing faces. Then we'd seen Muhammad back to his hotel and bed, and now it was just Sensi and me down in the bar off the lobby. Deep-brown ultrasuede covered the walls, and recessed lighting was casting long, theatrical shadows around the room.

"The Republican National Committee opened a secret channel to Iran in the summer of 1980," Sensi said, setting down his drink. By that night, of course, I'd already been to Beirut with him and he knew I knew his card said Republicans Abroad but his real employer was the CIA. He also knew about my father's career and that Miles Copeland and I had been spending a great deal of time together. Sitting there with him that night, I thought that was why Sensi was confiding in me. Though it is axiomatic of intelligence operations that the members of one cell don't know the identities of the members of any other cell, he knew enough about me that he figured we were playing on the same team.

But it turned out I was wrong about his motivation. All Sensi was doing was singing to me the opening bars of a song he'd soon be singing to anyone who'd listen. What I didn't know, but Sensi apparently had begun to suspect, was that he had become expendable. The Iran-Contra mess hadn't quite boiled over into the headlines yet, but was already roiling under the surface inside the CIA and the White House. Bill Casey was up to his eyeballs in damage control, and in ill health—he'd be dead of a brain tumor in less than a year. With everything else going on, Casey, who'd looked out for Sensi in the past, wasn't going to be able to protect Sensi this time.

Sensi didn't tell me *why* the Republican National Committee had opened a covert dialogue with Iran during the runup to the 1980 election—though that seemed obvious. But he did tell me Casey was involved from the beginning, as was Robert Carter. In 1980, Robert Carter was deputy chief of the Reagan campaign. And in 1986, when Sensi was telling me this, Robert Carter was the president of Republicans Abroad, and Bill Casey had for the past five and a half years been about the wiliest Director of Central Intelligence anyone had ever seen.

From the start of his tenure in Langley, Casey had recognized the benefit of continuing the clandestine dialogue he'd started with Iran. And the value of using Republican Party business as cover. "Republicans Abroad is a great drawing card," Sensi told me. "It gives us access to embassies and a lot of people we would've had a hard time getting to without the cachet of representing the ruling party in the United States." And, of course, in this world in which almost nothing is for free, the quid pro quo for the Republicans was that they had their own in-house team of covert operatives, as capable of conducting espionage and sabotage for the Republican Party as for the CIA. It seemed the Republicans were still doing what they'd been caught doing during Watergate. Spying on and sabotaging the Democrats. Ratfucking, as the Republican operatives called it. Coming just a few years after the Watergate national Passion Play and all it had put our country through, this seemed flagrant and foul, like sleaze squared. And like politics-as-usual. What Sensi told me that night didn't surprise me much, but the next afternoon, back in my apartment in New York, I'd written it up and sent it to Miles—across the Atlantic, in Oxfordshire, via our usual circuitous channel. Now, eighteen years later, here was a copy of that report sitting on my desk in Florida.

If I hadn't been so possessed, if I'd paid a bit more attention to the auguries scattered so liberally throughout the Sensi file, I might've realized I was traveling straight into that shit storm I mentioned earlier, I might've seen the wisdom of turning back. But that never even occurred to me. I was busy—to use the intelligence jargon Miles had taught me—reading myself into the case. And as anxious as I was to skip ahead to the Hirschfeld file, I knew Miles would've told me it was only my supposition that Hirschfeld was involved in this somehow. The only known player was Sensi, so I should start with him. I pulled out another sheaf of papers and read on.

Between four and five in the morning is the Burglar's Hour, when most humans are sleeping deepest, and least likely to be alert and capable of resistance. This makes it the hour during which enlightened burglars prefer to burgle. And the hour during which enlightened policemen prefer to arrest potentially dangerous suspects.

Bob Sensi was arrested at a quarter past four in the morning on the twenty-second of August 1986, in the Gloucester Hotel in Kensington in London. Two plainclothes officers from Scotland Yard knocked once on his door, opened it, woke him, restrained him, ordered him to dress quickly, handcuffed him, put him in a Black Maria, and told him they were acting upon a request from the FBI—that he was charged with embezzling two and a half million dollars from Kuwait Airways.

Wait just a goddamned minute! Sensi said. *I was following orders— from the CIA. With the full knowledge and approval of the Kuwaiti Ambassador to the United States. And members of the Kuwaiti royal family. I'm not going to be the fall guy.* And then, in high operatic dudgeon, he began to sing. When he'd sung to them of everything he'd informed me of that night, only seven weeks earlier in Washington, he was just clearing his throat. Under arrest, the new and expanded Sensi libretto also included facts about how he'd begun running the CIA's Iran initiative in 1982—using Kuwaiti money to establish front companies in Washington and London, cover for talentspotting, recruiting, and running Iranian spies.

And how the Kuwaitis were more than happy to provide him a few million dollars for a covert operation targeting Iran. The Kuwaitis were scared shitless that any day now hordes of Iranian fanatics were going to roll in and take over Kuwait. The money the Kuwaitis gave me for this, Sensi said, is nothing compared to the ten billion dollars a month they're sending to Saddam Hussein to fight Khomeini's army.

This isn't about stolen money, Sensi said. This is a Kuwaiti cover-up, damage control. All because it had emerged in Arab newspapers that Sensi had gone with Muhammad Ali to Israel, for discussions with Prime Minister Shimon Peres, using Kuwaiti money.

Sensi went on, about how he'd been a friend of Casey since the seventies, but that didn't mean this operation started and stopped within the CIA. A whole wrecking crew of characters in the White House was also involved. Including Reagan, Bush. *I'm not going to be the fall guy,* Sensi said again. But maybe he was. Because the CIA soon sent someone to London to shut him up.

By acknowledging Sensi had worked for the CIA, but denying they knew anything at all about the Kuwaiti money or the Iran initiative, and refusing to say anything more—on national security grounds—they quite effectively forestalled his defense. So Sensi did time.

And if you're looking for motivation for what he's done since, I'm no psychoanalyst, but—sitting there at my desk in Florida, reading in a little pool of light at half past two in the morning—it certainly seemed to me that in his first trial Sensi was framed, and everything he did afterward must've carried inside it at least a small measure of revenge.

Another piece of paper came out of the file. It said Sensi's last known address, as of whenever I'd checked, was "517 SW 2nd Street,

Oklahoma City, OK 73109." Cross-reference that with property records and you find the name on the deed: "Oklahoma Halfway House, Inc." Where Sensi lived, or was supposed to live, for three years after his second stretch in a federal penitentiary. That time for participating in a Nigerian Letters financial scam. *What the hell was that all about, Bob?*

Maybe it was more than just revenge. Maybe one day in jail, in England or Virginia, Sensi decided that, as he couldn't rely on his government, he was going to do whatever he had to to survive. Intelligence operatives are licensed con men. Poseurs, illusionists, charmers— trained in the dark art of conning other humans out of information, access, documents, trust, money, sanctuary, whatever it is the operative wants at the moment. In theory, intelligence professionals deploy these talents only for the purposes of the governments that trained them and sanctioned them. But once you've crossed the line and knowingly conned law-abiding citizens out of their savings, for no one's benefit but your own—if the money or other incentives were right, would it be all that hard to sell out to Al-Qaeda?

I pulled out another sheaf of papers from the Sensi file. A transcript of Hirschfeld's testimony at the first criminal trial of Robert Mario Sensi. Another Hirschfeld masterpiece, as I recalled. I set it aside to read it in the morning.

My watch was still set on L.A. time. About twelve hours had passed since Vince dropped me off at LAX. Outside my window, in the night heat, a million cicadas were droning in unison. I called Gary's office number in Washington and left him a voicemail message asking him to e-mail me a photograph of Richard Marshall and whatever information Homeland Security had about Marshall's address and background. Next I shut my office door and crept into my son's room to watch him sleep for a moment. It was the second day of his summer vacation. Mine was

already over. I went upstairs and slid into bed beside Kim, gently bur-
bling in her sleep. "Hair row," she said. "Hello," I whispered back.

I slept like shit, and when I came to, bright sunshine in the room,
way too hot, I threw off the covers and picked up the phone to check
my voicemail. There was a message from Gary. "No," he said, "unfortunately, I can't send you a picture of Marshall. We don't have one.
There've been plenty of times we've known where he was. I've even sat
down and talked with him. But his comings and goings are always
unpredictable, and whenever we've gotten someone positioned to
photograph him, he either never showed up or by then he was gone.
We also don't know his address. Or his background."

Richard Marshall was a wraith.

Above all, I was hot. I took a cool shower, put on some cargo shorts
and slides, and took Guinness out for a walk. The original name of
the county we live in was Mosquito County. Each day at sunset, thick
clouds of mosquitoes rise out of the grass into the evening heat.
Which isn't all that different from the morning heat Guinness and
I were walking through now under loblolly pines, oaks hung with
Spanish moss, a blistering blue sky. There's a twenty-acre wood behind
my property. At night it sounds like Africa. Prehistoric-looking birds,
raccoons, possums, armadillos, foxes, cats, boars—screeching and chit-
tering. Frogs lamenting. Cicadas.

Guinness is half schnauzer, half cocker spaniel, a purebred
schnocker spaniel—and ferociously loyal. In this wood in the morn-
ings, she likes finding and smelling whatever was killed in the night
and hasn't been eaten or dragged off yet. Walk another mile or so to
the river, and on a day like that day you'd see dozens of alligators, sun-
ning themselves on the banks.

Sensi and Hirschfeld hit it off real well from the beginning. It wasn't long after we all got back from Beirut that Muhammad told me Bob and Richie were spending a lot of time together. Doing business. Whatever the hell that meant.

All these years later, *Sensi and Hirschfeld ride again!* Could it possibly be true? Sensi and Hirschfeld *and Al-Qaeda*? I knew enough about Hirschfeld to know that if he did get involved with terrorists he'd find a way to skip the middlemen and go *straight* to the top. Sensi and Hirschfeld *and Osama bin Laden*? Could that be? What's the going rate for signing up with jihadists bent on washing the streets of your own country with blood? And what could Al-Qaeda want from guys like Sensi and Hirschfeld? Insiders' knowledge of how America's intelligence and counterintelligence services work. Security protocols. Access to information from high-level sources in Washington. Cover. Financial expertise. It was hard to guess. And I found it hard to believe Sensi would cooperate with Al-Qaeda. Hirschfeld was another story.

I was sweating, Guinness was done smelling things, then peeing on them, and we were walking home now. When we got there, I jumped into my pool and swam for a few minutes, to cool off again. Then Guinness dozed at my bare feet in my office while I got back to work.

Once when I was a kid asking questions, trying to get details from my father about his glamorous job, he told me, "The soul of every intelligence organization is its registry, its files." In Germany, the world capital of espionage, in the sixties, at the height of the Cold War, I used to go to his office with him on weekends, when he said he needed to squeeze in a little work before we went to the golf course. By then, I'd learned enough to know that there were Communist agents everywhere out there, GRU, KGB, Stasi—spies, saboteurs, disinformation artists, provocateurs, tunnelers, infiltrators, exfiltrators,

fixers, seducers, elicitors, buggers, bagmen, assassins. We were surrounded by talentspotters, listeners, recruiters, cutouts, handlers. And
how did the great spymaster deal with them all?

He sat at his desk reading his way through mountains of files.
Some of them marked CLASSIFIED, some SECRET. A few: TOP SECRET.
As my father read, now and then he underlined passages in red grease
pencil—while I sat in the visitor's chair in front of his desk and read
comic books. Occasionally, he looked up from his files and smiled at
me, and I looked up from *Sgt. Fury and His Howling Commandos* and
smiled back.

Miles, too, had impressed upon me just how prosaic most intelligence work really is. Reading files, and writing reports to add to the
files. It's all about files.

So why didn't Homeland Security have anything useful in its files
on a couple of Renaissance men as bad and multitalented as Sensi and
Marshall? Gary had access to CIA files, FBI files, DIA files, and more.
Nothing.

I had the contents of the two scuffed and dented accordion files
atop my desk, and whatever else I could remember or dig up. I got
busy. Making notes, reading and rereading old documents. Searching
the Internet.

On my first try, Google found me a U.S. Department of Justice
press release, dated October 7, 1994, about the indictment of Sensi
and six others on the Nigerian Letters fraud charges. If I could find
that so easily, why couldn't Homeland Security? There wasn't much
else about Sensi on the Internet.

There was a bit more about Hirschfeld, but most of it I already
knew. The most recent hits about Hirschfeld were various versions of
a widely published 1999 wire-service story about a lawsuit Ali had
brought against Hirschfeld and Ali's former manager, Jabir Muham-

mad, seeking to nullify a contract Ali had signed in 1988 giving Hirschfeld and Jabir, allegedly for free, forty percent of the rights to Ali's life story. That was news to me, as was the fact, buried deep in the fullest version of the news story, that in 1996, one year after he was released from prison, facing new federal charges, Hirschfeld had fled the United States and taken up residence in the Canary Islands. *Hirschfeld as fugitive.*

For the first time in years, I read the thick U.S. Government Printing Office document titled PLAN TO INVADE THE PHILIPPINES, which included Hirschfeld's testimony on July 9, 1987, the day he'd sold his client Ferdinand Marcos down the river to the House Committee on Foreign Affairs. Next I read Hirschfeld's testimony of March 15, 1988, at the first, but not the last, criminal trial of Robert M. Sensi. And this was Hirschfeld at his shapeshifting best. He'd started out in the case as an attorney, a member of Sensi's defense team. But when the defense couldn't find a witness willing to testify to just what Sensi needed someone to testify to, Hirschfeld, a truly versatile fellow, dropped out of the case as an attorney and became a key witness.

On the stand, the learned Mr. Hirschfeld presented the case against his friend as a sort of cross-cultural comedy of errors and misunderstandings in three acts—with a tragic, almost Shakespearean, turn at the end.

The first element of the comedy was that, as improbable as it might seem to Americans who had no experience with the hilarious folkways of Arab potentates, Sensi's story that Kuwaiti royals had given him two and a half million dollars without any written authority or instructions was actually quite typical of the way Arab kings and princes do business. Believe it or not, Your Honor, and ladies and gentlemen of the jury, they just don't bother to put such things in writing. For a billion dollars maybe, but not for a couple of million in petty cash.

During my extensive travel in the Middle East, Hirschfeld said, I have observed that their business practices simply are not like ours. In my law practice, I represent a member of the Saudi Arabian royal family. In fact, I happen to have here bank statements showing his wire transfer of one million dollars into my Citibank account in September 1982. I also have here a copy of my letter to this member of the Saudi royal family, providing him no details but merely confirming I have followed his *oral* instructions as to disbursement of the money. In my experience, and may I humbly say I have a great deal of experience in this arcane field, Arab royals do not leave a paper trail in matters such as these.

The second element of the comedy was the way the prosecutor kept portraying Bob Sensi as small beer. Why, not long after I met Mr. Sensi, Hirschfeld said, we were together in his hotel suite in the Carlton Hotel, right here in Washington, when Mr. Sensi received a telephone call from Vice President George Bush himself, calling Mr. Sensi to give him advice and instructions on how to conduct the dangerous but all-important mission he was about to lead us on in Beirut. It's not many CIA operatives that take their instructions directly from the Vice President of the United States. And when I remember that phone call and all the amazing contacts Mr. Sensi made for us in Beirut and Tel Aviv, it's really very funny to hear the prosecutor calling Mr. Sensi nothing more than a marginal player for the CIA.

In the third act, the villain appeared. And the way Hirschfeld framed it, it was clear he wanted everyone to understand that the villain was not a Kuwaiti prince, nor the American prosecutor. The villain was prejudice itself, and prejudice was the principal adversary of civilization. Blinded by their irrational hatred of Israel, and unused to the spirit of transparency with which the press had uncovered Sensi's mission to Tel Aviv, the Kuwaiti royals denied they'd ever authorized Sensi to spend their money on anything. And then the prosecutor, a well-meaning man and a good American, but without experience in the ways of Arabs, misunderstood Sensi's honest admission that he had no written authorization for his use of the funds, took it as a sign he was a crook. That was a tragedy, because the brave but humble humanitarian Bob Sensi was an American patriot, whose life itself was a contribution to the American ideal of freedom everywhere.

Damn, Hirschfeld was good. But even after his performance, and after Robert Carter broke ranks with the government and testified that he had met at the White House and again at CIA headquarters with Bob Sensi and Bill Casey to discuss the Iran initiative, Sensi was convicted.

And though it never came out in court, Hirschfeld's testimony—like much of the rest of his life—was predicated upon a lie. The "member of the Saudi royal family" who Hirschfeld testified had transferred a million dollars into his Citibank account was Sheikh Mohamed Al-Fassi. *Sheikh,* not *Emir.* VIP, not prince. Mohamed Al-Fassi was not Saudi royalty. A fine distinction, of the sort Hirschfeld had lived off for years.

What I needed now was a picture of the son of a bitch. Gary had told me "Marshall" was shortish, fit, prone to smirk. That could be Hirschfeld.

But I couldn't find a picture of him. Not with Google, Overture, Ask Jeeves, HotBot, Excite, Dogpile, Mamma, Lycos, or any of the other search engines I tried with. It was as if every image ever published of Hirschfeld had been systematically wiped off of the Internet. And my Hirschfeld file contained not a single picture of Hirschfeld. Come to think of it, there were a lot of things I remembered putting in my Hirschfeld file that weren't there now.

For example: "The Man and the Voice"—Dave Kindred's exposé of Hirschfeld's attempt to con the U.S. Senate out of fifty million dollars. Where the hell was my copy of the Kindred article? And for that matter, where the hell was Kindred? I tried all his old numbers, but they were disconnected. I tried finding a new phone number for him using WhoWhere.com, WhitePages.com, Yahoo.com, Infobel.com. I even dialed 411. Then gave up.

"Come on, girl," I said to Guinness, attaching a lead to her collar. "We've gotta go see a man about a dog."

Over lunch, at the counter at Yianni's, it occurred to me that the voice was Hirschfeld but the man was Muhammad. Probably, "The Man and the Voice" had migrated into my Ali files. I had a few hundred pounds of those. Boxes and boxes of them, stacked to the ceiling of my office closet. That afternoon I spent hours lifting and opening boxes, sifting through their contents for anything mentioning Hirschfeld—resulting in a little stack of paper on my desk.

The sky blackened outside my window while I read. The frogs and cicadas started up. After I'd been through everything once, I made another pass, dating and numbering each document in red pen in the top left corner, then rereading, and, one by one, logging them into the Hirschfeld file.

Item: Typewritten notes of my first conversation with Hirschfeld. August 8, 1983, at the urging of Jabir Muhammad, I'd phoned to discuss a Hirschfeld penny-stock deal Jabir wanted to hear my opinion on. Con men like to control the patter, the effects, the lighting, the dramatic timing; they get nervous when someone from the audience is wandering around in the wings, checking out the props. I'd asked so many questions that Hirschfeld started screaming at me. To the right of the final paragraph—marginalia, furiously scrawled in blue fountain pen, in my hand: "What an asshole!"

Item: Faded Lexis/Nexis extract, dot-matrix-printed on three thumbed and foxed sheets of continuous-feed paper, still connected, sprocket holes still attached—the text of an October 30, 1974, story in *The New York Times*. Headline: "Virginia Bank Calls Off Unusual Stock Offering." Lead: "The Hirschfeld Bank of Commerce, a bank being organized in tidewater Virginia with ambitious plans to raise as much as $76 million in initial capital, has run into a storm of opposition from corporate executives and regulators." Hirschfeld's eponymous bank—and his first great adventure in the national spotlight—was going to revolutionize the banking industry like it'd never been revolutionized before. And what an investment opportunity it was. But the problem with that, according to the SEC, was the bank had offered five million shares of stock at twelve dollars per share without registering the offering. Also, according to state securities regulators, the offering "contained allegedly fraudulent material, including a copy of an article about Mr. Hirschfeld that had appeared in the Virginian-Pilot in Norfolk so edited by the bank as to conceal material facts." Attorneys for Lockheed Aircraft, Hughes Tool, and twenty other public companies said the bank had somehow obtained lists of their shareholders and sent them circulars implying a relationship between the bank and those companies when none, in fact, existed. The extract contained no photo, but a caption was duly noted: "Top officials of the Hirschfeld Bank of Commerce are Richard M. Hirschfeld, left, chairman, and James A. Milby, president. The Virginia bank has been delayed in its ambitious plan to raise up to $76 million in capital." Hirschfeld had sent prospectuses to three hundred thousand shareholders of big public companies and had bought full-page ads for his bank's stock offering in *Time, Newsweek, U.S. News & World Report,* and *Sports Illustrated.* Before he was stopped, he'd already raised more than two million dollars in stock subscriptions. According to Hirschfeld, it was all a big misunderstanding, and the money received from investors would be returned. Not all of it was, however, and I learned later that money wasn't the only thing that wasn't returned. Before he blew out of town and moved to Las Vegas, the bank's twenty-seven-year-old founder and chairman made off with his partner's wife. Thus did Loretta Milby become Loretta Hirschfeld.

Item: Text of *The Washington Post* story dated October 29, 1984, detailing SEC efforts to enjoin further public sale of shares of Champion Sports Management, Inc. "The company's working capital so far had come entirely from loans, and they had been used to purchase, among other things, an 11-seat Sabreliner Model 60 jet from Lockheed for $733,125, a $65,000 1983 Stutz Bearcat company car, and the down payment on a $1.7 million, 88-acre estate in Virginia Beach." U.S. District Judge Robert J. Ward halted sales of the stock and ruled the company's founder and promoter Richard Hirschfeld had attempted to defraud investors by failing to disclose the note purported to be the company's principal asset was issued by a worthless shell entity controlled by Hirschfeld and an accomplice who happened to reside in a prison in Utah.

Item: Yellowed, torn, and slightly faded original newsprint clipping of June 22, 1985, *The New York Times* story quoting, in order, former President Jimmy Carter, former Secretary of State Dr. Henry Kissinger, veteran of Beirut hostage negotiations Richard Hirschfeld, and Reverend Jesse Jackson, calling on Americans to support President Reagan in his efforts to obtain release of the forty American hostages being held by Hizballah terrorists aboard a hijacked TWA aircraft. Both Mr. Hirschfeld's client Muhammad Ali and Reverend Jackson, the story noted, pledged to use all their contacts in the Muslim world to gain release of the hostages. No photo included.

Distasteful details I should never have forgotten, but had, were coming back to me. But "The Man and the Voice" I still couldn't find. And Dave Kindred, once the leading authority on the crimes and misdemeanors of Richard Hirschfeld, had moved, no longer worked in Atlanta.

I went back to Google and eventually found an e-mail address for Kindred at *The Sporting News,* where he was now the lead columnist. I sent him an e-mail message, then went to bed, without a picture of Hirschfeld.

Sunday morning, false dawn. Back to my desk. My head hurt, my neck ached, and I couldn't sleep but was only half-awake. I popped two Tylenol and a Vioxx, chugged a Red Bull, and went to work. A couple of hours later, at 7:48 A.M., to be precise, an e-mail message appeared in my Inbox. "From: dave/To: L.J. Kolb/Subject: Kindred here!"

Dave's message said he and his wife had moved from Georgia to Virginia in 1997. And that, as it happened, he was busy now writing a dual biography of Muhammad Ali and Howard Cosell, how their lives intertwined. He said he'd recently come across some old notes of our conversations and wondered how he could get in touch with me. He gave me his home phone number and said he'd be out all day, but to feel free to call that evening.

I poked around in my closet for a few minutes, then went back to bed. I was getting sleepy, very sleepy.

Elicitation, one of the core techniques of espionage, is a gentle conversational approach that, used correctly, will get you the information you need without the target even knowing he or she has been interrogated. It helps if you keep it casual and give as much information as you're getting. I know Muhammad well and I knew Cosell. In fact, I'd known Cosell even before I met Muhammad. That evening on the phone with Dave Kindred, I spent almost an hour answering a lot of questions, and not asking many.

Dave gave me his home address, and I promised to overnight him several items from my Ali files. I asked him if he remembered interviewing me for "The Man and the Voice," and Dave said, yes, of course.

"You don't happen to have a copy of that article lying around, do you?" I said. "I was looking for my copy of it the other day and couldn't find it."

Dave said, yes, he thought he did, and he would find it and e-mail it to me "soonest."

Bingo!

But what Dave e-mailed me half an hour later was the original compositor's text file of the article, not a scan of the article itself. No pictures—but tantalizing instructions to the layout editor, including this one: *Photo: Mug of Richard M. Hirschfeld.* God in his wisdom did not want me to come by a photograph of Hirschfeld easily.

The next morning, I called Dave and thanked him for sending the article, didn't mention yet my disappointment that I didn't get the illustrated version. We talked and talked, and I answered questions about the great and good. Eventually, I steered the conversation away from Ali and Cosell and round to Hirschfeld. And eventually Dave told me that last night he'd checked his file and the most recent record he had on Hirschfeld was seven years old.

"In 1997," Dave said, "someone writing in English with, if you will, a Cuban accent, e-mailed me. He said he was a Cuban reporter writing from Havana to request help with a story. I've looked and I can't find the e-mail now, Larry, but I think he said his name was Pelletier. Or that he worked for Pelletier News Service. Something like that. I'll keep looking for the e-mail. Anyway, this reporter said Richard Hirschfeld was living now in Havana, in an apartment filled with photographs of himself with Muhammad Ali. He said he thought Hirschfeld was working on a scam involving Ali, in Cuba, and asked me for background information."

"Did you help him?" I said. "I really would like to talk to that reporter."

"When I got that e-mail," Dave said, "chills went up and down my spine. I'd been rid of Hirschfeld for years. Wanted nothing more to do with him. And besides, I wasn't sure that the 'Cuban reporter' writing me wasn't Hirschfeld himself. How could I know who it really was? With Hirschfeld, anything, *anything*, is possible. For all I know, *you* might not be Larry Kolb on the other end of this phone call. *You* might be Richard Hirschfeld." Dave chuckled a little nervously. "I didn't respond to the message," he said, "but I probably should've."

Not all that funny, one might think. But I was grinning. The information Dave had received fitted nicely with something I'd heard the night before from a government source: Richard Hirschfeld was a fugitive from American justice, possibly sighted in Cuba.

It was primarily in Miami that Robert Sensi and Richard Marshall were now operating, that much Gary Messina had told me. Both of them were claiming to be CIA officers—Sensi saying he was based in Washington, Marshall saying he was based *in Havana*. I was onto something.

3. HOMELAND SECURITY

That same morning, I got busy calling old friends and sources—Washington reporters, high government officials, lowly court clerks, political operatives, archivists, power mavens—wheedling information about Hirschfeld and Sensi out of them. Asking them to check their records, to look things up for me, to ask around, to sleep on it, and call me back if anything came to mind.

Kim saw me for maybe an hour that day, and our son was away at camp. I took Guinness for her walks. Most of the rest of the day, and most of the rest of that week, I was locked up in my office, living on adrenaline and catnaps, obsessing, mining information, building a file on Hirschfeld, trying to figure it all out, sweating. The exhaust fan on my tired old computer put out so much heat that my office was the hottest place in the house. Every time I went up the hall and turned down the thermostat, Kim slipped past it and turned up the temperature. I worked in boxer shorts, or surf baggies, cargo shorts when I was feeling formal; no shirt, no shoes. In the corner of my office stood a tall black pedestal fan, so retro that it looked like a prop you might see in a Hitchcock movie, humming away in the background in an innocent man's office when the femme fatale walked in to rearrange his life forever. I couldn't aim it directly at me. It would've blown all the papers off my desk. But at least it stirred the hot air in part of the room, useful when I was pacing.

Had I known how long it was going to take me to get my hands on a picture of Hirschfeld, I would've done the obvious. Put some clothes on, flown to Atlanta, laid siege to *The Atlanta-Journal-Constitution*'s morgue, and refused to leave until they gave me a nice, clear *Mug of Richard M. Hirschfeld*. But day after day someone credible told me that, by the next day, they'd be supplying me a photograph of Hirschfeld. And next day after next day, something always came up. Lost files, rush orders from Editorial, sick days, not to mention thoroughly modern legal considerations.

Just before noon on Monday, a *Washington Post* archivist e-mailed me a link she said I could use to download the image of the original newsprint version of a 1987 *Post* story. Her message said that she'd just had a look at it and it included a couple pictures of Hirschfeld. But when I downloaded the story, the pictures had been whited out. "Oh, dear, I'm sorry," the archivist said when I called to ask her what had happened. After checking, she called me back and said, "Sugar, I'm sorry to inform you we can't transmit the pictures that were part of that story over the Internet. Because of copyright problems. When we bought the photos, no one had ever heard of the Internet. It existed, I'm told, but no one had ever heard of it. So the paper bought print rights to the photos but not Internet rights. Do you understand?"

At times like that, it felt like a conspiracy to wipe Hirschfeld's face out of the record. But that feeling passed every time I thought about how brilliant I was going to look if I gave the Department of Homeland Security a thousand-page dossier on Hirschfeld, including the first photograph of him I could find, and they glanced at the picture and said *Nope, that's not Marshall, not even close.* But I'd learned from my father you've got to play your hunches.

And that wasn't all he'd taught me. Every time it seemed to me that I should just tell Dave Kindred what I needed, and that it was urgent, and why, my father whispered in my ear, "He doesn't need to know." Then all I had to do was close my eyes or stare at the wall to see and hear the ferocious speech my father gave me one day in Germany about how good people die when someone entrusted with knowledge of intelligence cases tells secrets to those who don't need to know.

So when I did call Dave, and I called him many times that week, I gave more than I received. I mean, in the beginning I did. Getting Dave's Hirschfeld file cost me hours answering questions about Muhammad, and about Cosell, and more hours rooting through my boxes looking for things Dave had never seen. But it was worth it. And I'd always liked Dave, anyway.

Around three on Monday afternoon, I opened MS Word and started cutting out of my *Overworld* manuscript every passage about Muhammad, and pasting them together into a new document file. One hundred forty-seven double-spaced pages. When I finished, I e-mailed it to Dave. Two hours later, he e-mailed me back—"Subject: Ran me out of ink!" An hour and a half later, another message. He'd started reading, and stopped to say, "Subject: Kindred here with Double WOW!" So far, he liked it. And five hours later, he'd finished reading, and wrote: "To sum up, Larry, I'm fired up by reading your stuff. The first fresh material on Ali in years. So much detail. When can we talk again?"

The next morning, Dave and I talked again, and the next afternoon. In between, I e-mailed him the texts of the *Playboy* interview of Cosell and both *Playboy* interviews of Muhammad. Then I overnighted Dave copies of a *Spin* story on Muhammad by Harold Conrad, and a *Jet* story on Muhammad, and a *Life* pictorial on young Cassius Clay, and several other clippings.

I e-mailed Dave a scan of a 1984 *Penthouse* article that described me up front beside Muhammad in his Stutz Bearcat, at loose and at speed on the Santa Monica freeway, while, in the backseat, Muhammad's little Moroccan butler Abdel cowered and cried and begged Muhammad to slow down, and the article's author, Allan Sonnenschein, closed his eyes and prayed.

"Yes," Dave wrote right back, "I've been in the passenger seat when Muhammad was flying in a big ol' Cadillac at 85 mph on a logging road somewhere near Deer Lake."

I sent Dave a rare 1979 photograph of Muhammad in an exhibition fight for children, in a ring in the shadow of the Washington Monument: Muhammad knocking out the fully costumed Mr. Tooth Decay. No comment from Dave on that one.

On Tuesday afternoon, we spent nearly an hour on the phone discussing the mysterious disappearance of Ron Levin—friend of Muhammad, acquaintance of mine—missing since June 1984, presumed dead, at the hands of Joe Hunt, leader of the Billionaire Boys Club. A genial con man killed by a less genial one.

When I told Dave my Jersey Joe Walcott story, my sweetest memory of Muhammad, Dave said, "That's priceless. That's going in the book."

Then something possessed me to give away to Dave my best Ali material of all—at least I'd always thought so. And I'd intended to write about it someday. But it seemed perfect for Dave's book because, being about Ali and Cosell, it was also about television. It was only fitting the story should be told in Dave's book. There was that; plus I was desperate for Dave's help.

It was Muhammad, of course, who first linked the world by television. The Rumble in the Jungle, Muhammad Ali versus George Foreman for the heavyweight championship of the world, on October 30, 1974, was the first event watched live by a global audience. Even man's first walk on the moon had been relegated to a taped clip, delayed until the nightly news, in most of the Eastern Bloc. But not Ali. Not even Ali fighting at four o'clock in the morning, local time, broadcast live from the heart of darkness in a dictator's stadium in a swamp by the banks of the Congo in Kinshasa, Zaire. Foreman was the champion and he seemed invincible, but it was Muhammad the challenger who had the drawing power to assemble the first world-wide live audience. In Europe and the Mideast, millions tuned in in the middle of the night. In Islamabad and New Delhi, in Singapore and Shanghai, it was a morning of fathers and their children playing hooky together in front of televisions. In America, in prime time, Madison Square Garden and sold-out arenas and theaters all across the country projected the closed-circuit feed onto huge screens. People all over the world watched together as, between Round One and Round Two, out of desperation Muhammad invented the Rope-a-Dope, and those millions kept watching as, round after round, Muhammad lay on the ropes absorbing punches and hanging on, and then watched in rapture as, finally, Muhammad came off the ropes and shocked the world.

Naturally, Dave already knew all of that. "But," I asked, "do you know how Muhammad closed the show?"

"You mean something more than K-O, Round Eight?"

"Yes, after that," I said.

"Tell me."

"And after Muhammad fainted for a moment in his corner, which I'm sure you saw. Do you know what Muhammad did after all of that? I don't think you do. Because it's never come out. I've never seen a word about it in any of the articles and books on Muhammad I've read over the years. It's never even been mentioned. Now it's time for you, Dave, to bring it to light."

"Go on."

"After the pandemonium of people spilling into the ring, the hug for Foreman, the jungle drums, the tribal dancers, after Muhammad bragged and brayed for the postfight TV interviewers, he left the ring with his retinue, and somehow a cameraman got right behind him and stayed with him. Up the aisle, through the sea of love, through sixty thousand natives still wailing and chanting—*Ali, boma ye! Ali, boma ye!*—up some stairs, down some stairs, around tight corners, through cordons of black policemen in white helmets, into the gray concrete bowels of the stadium, somehow the camera stayed right behind Muhammad.

"Just imagine it, Dave. *You've* walked with Muhammad. You know: Even with policemen out front, there's so much jostling and shoving. That cameraman had to be one tough muther, holding the camera, keeping it steady, keeping up with Muhammad. And imagine the support team stretched out behind the cameraman, feeding him more and more cable as he snaked his way around corners and down a long gray hallway, right to the door of Muhammad's dressing room. Once he got in the room, Muhammad stopped dead still, ten feet in front of the camera, his back to the cameraman. The cameraman stood at the threshold, taking it all in.

"Most of Muhammad's crew had beaten him into the room, and this was their first moment alone with him since the fight. Everyone was shouting at once and Muhammad raised his fist over his head in triumph. Then he did what I've seen him do every time I've ever seen him walk into a dressing room, Dave. And probably you've seen the same thing too, if you think about it. Satin's hot. Africa's hot as hell, and humid. Boxing's hot, and Muhammad had just boxed eight rounds with a monster. Muhammad had no idea he was still on television. Live. Around the world. He reached down and, in one quick, graceful, almost balletic, movement, stripped off his trunks. Then he just stood there, in nothing but a jockstrap—bare-ass naked from behind.

"Well, the television announcer, some guy with an English accent, had been quite glib throughout this entire parade from the ring to the dressing room. But when Muhammad pulled off his pants, the guy clammed up. Instantly. And Muhammad just stood there with his back and ass to the camera for ten seconds, maybe twenty—it seemed like half an hour—until someone, in a control room in London, or wherever it was they routed the program through before they uplinked it to the world, had the presence of mind to cut the feed. And all around the world at once screens turned to static.

"So *that*," I said, "is how Muhammad ended the first global television event. He mooned the whole fucking world!"

"I watched the fight closed-circuit in Louisville," Dave said. "I don't remember that."

"Yeah," I said. "But you were a reporter. Probably five seconds after Foreman was counted out, you were running to a telephone or a typewriter somewhere. You had to file a story."

"That's right," Dave said.

"Well, I was just a college kid, watching my hero. I took in every last second of it. I *saw* it. In fact, I remember I sat there in the dark in the Great Southern Music Hall in Gainesville, Florida, watching the static, waiting, hoping someone would put Muhammad's pants back on him and send out more live pictures. But then the houselights came up. It was over.

"And though you can be certain they've edited it out of every version of the fight ever released since then, you can bet that somewhere—in a vault in London, or at Big Fights, Inc., in New York, or the National Archives, or the NSA—*somewhere* there's got to be a full-length master tape of the original feed. It's a little piece of lost history, Dave, and Ali mooning the world has got to be a perfect metaphor for something else. I'm not sure what, but it's your book, you'll figure that out. Find that tape and write about it."

"Really?" said Dave. "That *really* happened?"

"Absolutely it happened. And there's got to be a way to find it," I said. "There's this quote I've been keeping on my desk for the last few days, for a reason I'll get to in a moment. This is Dashiell Hammett, from *The House Dick*: 'Since matter cannot move without disturbing other matter along its path, there always is—there must be—a trail of some sort.'"

I'd decided my father was wrong. Or that by now he would've changed his position, sworn Dave to secrecy, and enlisted him in the war. Dave did need to know. Not everything, but at least enough that he'd want to help me find a picture of Hirschfeld with a certain measure of alacrity. "So, Dave," I said. "I can't tell you much, except—*in total confidence, this just cannot show up in a newspaper anytime soon—* I'm working on something for some friends of mine in Homeland Security, something involving Al-Qaeda, and I really, really need the picture of Hirschfeld that appeared in 'The Man and the Voice.' That and anything else on Hirschfeld you can give me."

Dave played me his Hirschfeld tapes. He had a tape of Hirschfeld as Hirschfeld and another of Hirschfeld as Ali. We started with Hirschfeld as Hirschfeld.

Hearing him again, after so many years, was startling. No longer just a loathsome memory, he was coming back to life for me—a real human being again, a voice, an astonishing blend of competence, extravagance, opacity, defiance. And, near the end of this particular tape, fear. *Hirschfeld Agonistes.* Hirschfeld cornered and nearly begging Dave not to write the story that would blow up his fifty-million-dollar score.

> HIRSCHFELD: I don't mind anything you write about me. Because you won't hit anything but scar tissue. But I do mind what you say about Ali. . . . Why don't you do this? Why don't you write a story castigating me, saying I'm a terrible, diabolical, satanic person, if you want to. But leave Ali alone, okay? He's a good person.
>
> DAVE: I have no doubt of that. But he's in the middle of something that—
>
> HIRSCHFELD: He sure is. And you're going to ruin it for him.

But the Ali Hirschfeld was defending wasn't Ali. Which isn't to say that when I heard the beginning of Dave's tape of Hirschfeld as Ali, I didn't almost fall over in shock. There'd been a mistake. The voice on the tape, it *was* Ali.

I knew every shade of Muhammad's voice. For several years of my life, I'd spent, on average, about one day out of every three with Muhammad. I'd sat beside him on twelve-hour flights to Japan and ten-hour flights to the Middle East, talking most of the way. In hotel suites in London and Lagos, Jakarta and Beirut, when everyone else in our group was asleep, I'd sat up with Muhammad talking into the night. One night in New York, after a flight delay, we'd arrived at a hotel so late that they'd given us their only remaining bed. It was king-sized, and Muhammad and I were going to try to sleep in it. But we couldn't sleep, and we ended up lying there in the dark, talking until dawn, like kids at summer camp—talking about God, religion, pussy, money, the many and varied uses of power. I knew Muhammad's voice when he was sleepy and when he was wide awake; when he had taken his medicine and when he hadn't. And I knew how he answered the phone.

So when Dave played me his tape, of a phone ringing and ringing, and someone finally answering, whispery soft, in words made out of high tones and low tones, almost nothing in the midrange—only the hiss of air rushing across his vocal cords—I had no doubt. It *was* Muhammad.

But after a while I realized, no, it wasn't Muhammad. It was better than any impression of him I'd ever heard. Even better than Hirschfeld's dead-on impressions during that long-ago weekend in Cairo. By now, of course, Hirschfeld had had dozens of hours of practice, calling senators, calling Vice President Bush, even trying to call President Reagan, while working his con. He had the voice down.

The voice said, "Hello."

Dave said, "Ali?"

The voice said, "Who's—who is this?"

Dave said, "Dave Kindred."

The voice said, "Dave! Yeah. What can I do for you?"

At that point, and for the next two or three minutes, I would've bet money that the voice was Muhammad. And in two or three minutes Muhammad could've gotten on the phone, said, yes, Dave, it's me making those calls to the masters of the Senate, and, no, Dave, the details of why I'm doing it are none of your business, not yet, and then said he had some people waiting to see him, or a plane to catch, or a nap to take, and hung up. And, with that, Dave's exposé would've been spiked and Hirschfeld might very well have conned the United

States Senate out of fifty million dollars. He was *that* close to pulling it off.

But Hirschfeld was a cocky soul, smarter than almost everyone else, and he knew it. He couldn't resist pretending to be Muhammad for thirty-nine minutes on the phone with Dave. Unlike the senators on Hirschfeld's call list, Dave had known Muhammad for more than twenty years. The longer I listened the more I realized, as Dave had realized during that long call, that the voice may have sounded like Muhammad's but the intellect behind the voice was unmistakably Hirschfeld's.

Dave said he would try harder to find me the Hirschfeld picture. If real life had all the tidiness of a novel, I would've waited until I had that picture. But we are limited here by the facts, and the inconvenient fact is I did not wait. Since I'd left L.A., I'd thought I probably did know who "Richard Marshall" was, but I hadn't been convinced; and, until I was fairly certain, I didn't want to embarrass myself with the professionals of the Department of Homeland Security by hazarding an amateur guess. They, after all, were wearing suits, and I was wearing cargo shorts.

But, in spite of not yet having the photo I wanted, I'd spent the last twenty-four hours trebling the size of my Hirschfeld file. It would no longer fit in one redrope accordion file. People I'd talked with two days earlier were starting to call me back, and e-mail me, send me documents, facts, curious details. Hirschfeld's shit was flowing in from what seemed like all directions. And there was something about the preponderance of evidence, and the smell of it all, that made me send Gary a long e-mail message saying I thought "Richard Marshall"

was Richard Hirschfeld. Assuming other men in suits would ultimately read this message, I began by saying Hirschfeld was as smooth,
relentless, and unpredictable as anyone I'd ever encountered. Then
I outlined what I'd known about Hirschfeld when I arrived in
Florida—including what I'd already told Gary and Vince about the
trip to Beirut for Reagan and Bush. I said it was during the prepara-
tions for that trip that Hirschfeld had met Sensi. I wrote of the Marcos gold, the FBI sting, Hirschfeld and his partner Robert Chastain
returning to Honolulu to implicate Marcos on tape; Hirschfeld as
hero and star witness on Capitol Hill; Hirschfeld's attempt to con the
Senate; his arrest, conviction, and imprisonment for tax evasion and
conspiracy.

After that, I laid out what I'd learned since my return home. This
included:

How, in 1974, Hirschfeld founded and, by popular demand,
shut down the Hirschfeld Bank of Commerce.

How, in 1975, the Securities and Exchange Commission charged
Hirschfeld with looting a company called Atlantic General Corp. and
Hirschfeld signed a consent decree agreeing not to violate securities
laws in the future.

How, in 1976, Hirschfeld's Lincoln Continental limousine,
which he had been so proud to tell everyone had once belonged to
Elvis Presley, was torched, and Hirschfeld left Virginia on the run
from angry investors.

How, in 1977, Hirschfeld filed for bankruptcy in Nevada, declar-
ing debts in excess of five million dollars against assets of less than two
thousand dollars.

How, also in 1977, Hirschfeld moved to Newport Beach, California, where he started a law practice and became the attorney of

record for, among others, John Wayne and Donald Nixon, brother of President Nixon.

How, in 1981, Hirschfeld founded—and in 1983, with all appropriate fanfare, proudly announced the initial public offering of— Hirsch-Chemie Ltd., which was destined to be a pharmaceutical giant, the prospectus made clear, because the company owned the patent to, and would soon introduce to grateful doctors and consumers everywhere, the world's only known cure for herpes. A patent, it later turned out, the company didn't actually own; though that was less relevant finally than the fact that the drug didn't actually work.

How, in 1985, soon after the Beirut trip, Sensi—who didn't yet realize that, when it came to subterfuge, the talented Mr. Hirschfeld already made him look like a novice—recruited Hirschfeld to work occasionally for the CIA, then trained him in the covert arts.

How, in 1986, Hirschfeld was permanently barred from practice before the SEC, for knowingly, recklessly, and repeatedly filing fraudulent stock reports and prospectuses.

How, in 1987, Hirschfeld allegedly took twelve million dollars, packed in suitcases, from Ferdinand Marcos, to be paid to Ronald Reagan to stop the U.S. government from indicting the Marcoses; but the money never quite made it all the way to Reagan, or anyone other than a banker in Switzerland.

How, in 1989, when Hirschfeld was arrested in West Germany for using a phony British passport, while traveling under the name Richard T. Halen, he explained to German authorities that he was working undercover for the U.S. government, attempting to lure a terrorist out of Iran.

How, later in 1989, Hirschfeld's old friend and partner, Robert Chastain, died under mysterious circumstances in a hotel room in

Vienna. Austrian officials ruled the cause of death was suicide; but many found this curious since the death occurred just two weeks after the expiration of the suicide exclusion clause in a five-year-old insurance policy on the life of Chastain. The beneficiary was not Chastain's wife but a certain Richard M. Hirschfeld, who collected four million seven hundred fifty thousand dollars in death benefits from the insurance company. Years later, when the FBI exhumed the body said to be that of Chastain, alleging Hirschfeld and Chastain had faked the death to defraud the insurance company and split the money, forensic testing proved it was indeed Chastain's body.

How, in 1991, soon after his conviction and incarceration for tax evasion and conspiracy to defraud the Internal Revenue Service and the Securities and Exchange Commission, Hirschfeld began filing appeals, but was denied his request for bail pending the outcome of the appeals.

How, in 1993, after a mountain of appellate briefs had been proffered by his attorneys to several courts, Hirschfeld nearly managed to manumit himself—when those incarcerating him received a series of letters from a high official of Habitat for Humanity urging Hirschfeld be let out to participate in Habitat for Humanity's work-release program, for the noble purpose of going to Miami to build homes for Hurricane Andrew victims. And how it wasn't until three years later that federal authorities discovered Habitat for Humanity didn't have a work-release program and the "Habitat for Humanity official," a Dr. Joe Seriani, who signed the letters, was actually a con man and a client of Hirschfeld.

How, in 1996, a federal indictment was unsealed, and it alleged that, during his incarceration for tax evasion and conspiracy, Hirschfeld had plotted to blind the federal judge who'd overseen his conviction, by contracting for acid to be thrown into the judge's eyes. A warrant was issued for Hirschfeld's arrest. But by then Hirschfeld had fled the United States, having first had the foresight to ship his Rolls-Royce to Spain. And how Hirschfeld was arrested in Spain on a fugitive warrant, jailed for a time, then released on thirty-five thousand dollars' bail, just before he fled to Cuba.

Gary thought I was probably right, Richard Marshall and Richard Hirschfeld were the same person. But most of the Feds who were deeply interested in this were not convinced—in fact, were deeply uninterested in my opinion even though I'd sent them a stack of documents on Richard Hirschfeld that was seven inches thick.

Gary was the CIO of the BCIS, which is the Department of Homeland Security's first line of defense against terrorists, and he was its principal liaison with the CIA, the DIA, the DEA, the NSA, DARPA, the IRS, and various other federal agencies. Most of their records showed Hirschfeld was a fugitive living in Cuba. And most of their records were classified. The information I'd provided them was from open sources, unclassified.

In every espiocracy, there's a tendency to believe that unless information is classified it's not worth knowing. So how could I be right and they be wrong? That was the prevailing view at Homeland Security.

Naturally, it was only a few hours after Gary informed me of the government's low opinion of my theory that I received this e-mail message from Dave Kindred: "Larry, in the flurry of notes, I've lost your address. I have, however, found the photo of Hirschfeld (wearing an Orrin Hatch campaign button)." And naturally, even though I wrote Dave right back asking him to scan the picture and e-mail it to me, and he said he would, the next morning the picture remained just out of my grasp.

Extract from Dave's e-mail message to me of 8:11 A.M., Thursday, June 3, 2004: "Larry/I do have a scanner and am able to scan the photo—but the owner's manual doesn't tell me how to attach the photo to an e-mail. If you could talk me through that, I'll do it."

But not everyone is hardwired for the computer age, and though I tried to talk him through it, Dave never quite managed to attach an image of the photo to an e-mail message. In the end, it wasn't until the afternoon of Friday, the fourth of June 2004, eight days after my lunch at The Palm with Vince, that I opened a FedEx package from Dave and finally laid my hands on an old newspaper clipping containing a clearly captioned photograph of Richard M. Hirschfeld, Esq. I scanned the clipping and e-mailed it to Gary and Vince, along with this question: "Is this the guy who calls himself Richard Marshall?"

The answer I received was telling. And what it spoke to most, I thought, was both how desperately bad our government's databases are and how desperately certain government agencies wanted to identify Robert Sensi's partner.

The answer I received was: "YES!!!"

Forty-two exclamation points' worth of desperation—I counted.

And so the newspaper photo was circulated and certain federal agencies were disabused of their position. "Attaboy"s and "We never doubted you"s were lavished on me.

Mystery solved. But—Gary told me, a day later—not all the interested federal agencies were immediately convinced. After all, they didn't have a photograph of Richard Marshall to compare with my photograph of Richard Hirschfeld. And some of them didn't have a single human asset who'd managed to lay eyes on Hirschfeld even once during their more than two years of investigating and fretting over the strange doings of Mr. Sensi and his mystery partner. Worse, now that I'd told them who he was, and Homeland Security had verified it, certain federal agencies still couldn't find any information on Richard M. Hirschfeld. This, Gary informed me, was because certain agencies can't pull data without a Social Security number, and I didn't know Hirschfeld's Social Security number, yet. And to certain other agencies, a Social Security number is useless; they can't pull data without the subject's complete first, middle, and last name, and date and place of birth. And almost none of them can easily get at information from open sources, like I did, because almost all of the federal government's computers are firewalled against external webcast—which means they can't get on the Internet.

Gary explained all this to me, and what a frustration it was to him. Because, as CIO of the BCIS—which before the September 11 attacks was called the INS—as the chief gatekeeper in the war on terror, he was now supposed to have seamless and instantaneous access to the files of the CIA, the FBI, the DIA, the DEA, the IRS, plus several agencies no one has ever heard of, on every known or suspected bad guy in the terror world, the illicit arms trade, the illicit drugs trade, and organized crime. "That's the neat, clean, official version," Gary told me. "In reality, it's a mess."

I called another old friend who worked for Homeland Security, and he told me more. "Even if the FBI could make their computers work," he said, "and that's iffy, at best—they still wouldn't share with us. Because they don't share anything of real value with anybody. Even now."

"But what about the CIA?" I asked him. "Sensi was once employed by them. And Hirschfeld was a CIA asset run by Sensi. They've got to know Hirschfeld. How come they couldn't figure this out?"

"The CIA can't find its ass in a phone booth," said my friend—who was in a position to know.

We kept talking and, a few minutes later, he said to me, "Look at it this way: The War on Terror is being brought to you by the same people who brought you the War on Drugs. Think about it—maybe one time in a thousand they actually catch somebody transporting or selling drugs. Then what do they do? They put that person in a federal facility, which is locked down and guarded twenty-four hours a day by federal officers. And they still can't even keep drugs out of that facility, let alone off our streets, or outside our borders. Now, really, how do you think we're doing in the War on Terror?"

So what curious events in Moscow and Baghdad and Kabul, in Washington, and, most of all, in Miami, had kept the CIA, the DEA, the BCIS, the DIA, the BICE, and the IRS in a lather for the past two years? Now that I'd proven I could be a little bit useful, I was, by degrees, allowed to know what was really going on. Various of our security agencies wanted my help. They had questions galore for me, and as they asked their questions, they filled me in, on—as the saying goes—a need-to-know basis. Call after call, fact after fact, the picture slowly emerged.

Messrs. Hirschfeld and Sensi had been keeping busy, verily they had. No one was quite certain how long Hirschfeld had been back in the United States. Until forty-eight hours earlier, no one had even known Hirschfeld *was* back in the United States. But, for at least the last three years, Sensi and his mystery partner—now positively

identified as Richard Marshall Hirschfeld—had been making themselves a fine living convincing a select cast of clients, mostly Russian
mafia billionaires, that for emoluments ranging from a few hundred
thousand dollars to millions of dollars they could get them off watch
lists that prevented them from entering the United States; they could
get them green cards, maybe even U.S. citizenships—in spite of their
criminal affiliations. For harder cases, Hirschfeld and Sensi offered
certain clients new identities and genuine, but ultimately illegal,
British passports.

And because we are living in an increasingly hectic and complex
world, in which, occasionally, there just isn't time for paperwork, for
special clients who needed to get into and out of the United States in
a hurry to, for example, close a business deal or attend a favorite
niece's wedding, the dynamic duo offered brief but beautiful and un-
scheduled sunset flights from Tijuana to San Diego. Not due north
across the U.S.-Mexican border, for that would elicit interdiction.
These flights took off from a grass strip in Tijuana, flew west out over
the Pacific, then turned north, then back east, flying *around* the border, and then landed on a grass strip in San Diego no more than ten
minutes after takeoff. Even if the Border Patrol ever bothered to figure this out and send someone to try to apprehend the arriving passengers, within two minutes of landing, America's latest VIP visitors
were inside vehicles, on their way to a freeway, and about to be swal-
lowed up into the belly of the great American beast, and the plane
was already in the air and on its way back out into the haze and
around the border.

Oh, it was as impressive as hell to the clients. And on the cocktail
party circuit in the Lenin Hills and certain yacht harbors in Odessa
and Saint-Tropez, word spread from oligarch to oligarch, yielding
more clients. For fugitive billionaires already in the United States, but

facing deportation proceedings, Messrs. Sensi and Hirschfeld offered to, for a sum certain, make their immigration problems go away. "But how can you do this?" the clients wanted to know.

"It's really very simple," Richard Marshall told them. "We work for the CIA. For a special branch of the CIA that does things so important and clandestine that not even our congressional oversight committees can be allowed to know of them. No oversight. No written budgets. And thus, accordingly, no congressional appropriations to fund our operations. So we look to people such as yourselves— good people whom we've carefully screened and determined aren't really bad, but are misunderstood, by Interpol and others. To you, we offer certain of our agency's clandestine resources and capabilities, in exchange for money that funds our special operations."

"That's their pitch," Gary told me during our second conversation of the day after I sent him a picture of Hirschfeld. "It's all a grand illusion. Even CIA's managed to determine that Sensi and Marshall— excuse me, Sensi and Hirschfeld—aren't really working for them. But they get away with it because, to an extent, they can deliver. Not because they have the government's cooperation. But because they're more than clever enough to work the angles and beat the system. It's like a bad novel," Gary added, "except it's true."

Take, for example, the dream journey of Boris Birshtein. Born in the Soviet Union. Emigrated to Israel. Moved on to Switzerland. Now living in Canada. According to an FBI report I possess, Boris Iosifovich Birshtein hosted a summit meeting of all the leading Russian organized crime figures at his compound in Tel Aviv in October 1995. Sort of the Apalachin Conference of Russian mobsters, if you will. It is alleged that, among other things, Birshtein controls almost all of the aluminum in all of the former Soviet Union, and he controls the Central Bank and almost everything else in the Republic of Moldova—all from his home base in Toronto.

But where he really wants to live, of course, is the United States. And who doesn't? Bring me your tired, your poor, your huddled masses yearning to breathe free. Sensi and Hirschfeld offered Birshtein a green card, but added that, because he had a particularly ugly record—all of it due to misunderstandings, of course—it was going to cost him rather a lot. "How do I know you can do this for me?" Birshtein asked.

"Allow us to give you a little demonstration," Sensi said, "for a greatly reduced fee."

Think of it as a special introductory offer. And what an amazing deal Sensi and Hirschfeld gave Birshtein: For the merest of sums, one hundred thousand dollars, he flew into Washington in his private jet, was quickly processed through immigration, greeted at the airport by a high government official, and then delivered to the White House for a meeting with our president, George W. Bush.

"How the fuck did they do that?" I asked Gary—though I should point out I didn't hear this story first from Gary. But he did confirm it to me, after I'd heard it from someone else.

"First of all," Gary said, "Sensi befriended me. Took me to lunch a few times over several months. Then one day he invited me to another lunch, and we agreed I'd meet him in his office and we'd walk from there. But when I showed up for lunch, Sensi tapped his palm on his forehead and said, 'Oh, shit! I forgot. I'm supposed to make a run to the airport. Come with me. There's something I've got to talk to you about that shouldn't wait. We'll grab sandwiches downstairs, and then we can eat and talk on the way. I'm sorry. You don't mind, do you?'

"Well, what could I say?" Gary went on. Then he told me he was already pretty much a hostage in Sensi's car by the time he figured out they weren't going to Reagan National Airport but to Dulles International. But Sensi kept it pleasant all the way there, in his charming way. When they got to Dulles, they went to the private jet terminal. Sensi led Gary inside and stopped just a few steps away from the immigration counter. And a moment later, Boris Birshtein stepped up to the counter and handed his passport to the man on duty.

The immigration officer ran Birshtein's passport, and, in a moment, on his computer screen a red flag was flashing: "OC" . . . "OC" . . . "OC" . . . "OC" . . . "OC." Which meant Organized Crime. But, on the other hand, Mr. Birshtein had just arrived on a twenty-million-dollar jet, bearing a valid forty-eight-hour visa specially sponsored by a U.S. congressman, and an invitation to attend a conference at the White House with the Congressman and the President. And—holy shit!—that was Assistant Director Messina standing over there apparently waiting to greet Mr. Birshtein. Who had never been deported from the United States. Or blacklisted. He was merely on a watch list. It was a judgment call. The immigration officer took one more quick look at the paperwork, and then another at the Assistant Director, and then decided, in his best judgment, to immediately stamp Mr. Birshtein's passport and welcome him to the United States of America.

Gary was shaking Birshtein's hand before he even knew who he was. And, later that day, Sensi was delivering Birshtein to the White House and a meeting with President Bush. Gary wasn't sure whether Sensi actually accompanied Birshtein into the White House and into the meeting with the second President Bush. Or whether political contributions were paid or promised in exchange for Birshtein's special reception in Washington. But I was sure it was through the second

President Bush's father that I met CIA operative and Republican bag-man Robert Sensi.

As you might imagine, Gary was royally pissed off by the time he got back to his office from Dulles. He'd figured out how he'd been used. And, some months later, when, still pissed off, Gary learned the rest of the story from a source who heard it firsthand in Toronto, the central highlight was this: The day after his meeting with the President, not wishing to waste his forty-eight hours in the United States by spending the entire time in just one city, Birshtein flew to New York. There, he met with Sensi's partner Richard Marshall. And, true believer now, Birshtein gave Marshall a small suitcase con-taining four hundred thousand dollars—a down payment for Birsh-tein's green card. That exchange took place in a Manhattan building which had a helipad on top. And once Sensi's partner had possession of the suitcase, he said, "Come on, Boris, let's take a ride upstairs." Before they got into the elevator, Sensi's partner pulled out his cell phone and made a quick call. At the top floor, according to Birshtein, they got out and took the stairs to the roof. Upon which, moments after they got there, a black helicopter landed and out stepped a man in a black suit. Sensi's partner handed the suitcase to the man in the black suit. Then Sensi's partner said, "See you, Boris. We'll be in touch."

And with that, Sensi's partner—that would be Richard Marshall Hirschfeld—climbed into the helicopter with the man in the black suit and the money and flew off into the New York sky, and Boris Birshtein was suitably impressed by the capabilities and resources of the special branch of the CIA. Of course they were from the CIA. They had to be. But Birshtein never saw Hirschfeld again. And Bir-shtein seemed to be genuinely surprised months later when a BCIS officer told him there was no way he could ever receive a green card.

"Why don't you arrest these clowns?" Gary asked his CIA liaison contact a few days after he heard the report from Toronto.

"Sensi used to be one of us," said the CIA representative, a woman Gary had known for years. "We don't like to go after people like that."

"But what about Marshall?" Gary said.

"We had a look at him," she said, "and we don't know who he is."

Next Gary asked the FBI to make the arrests, but the FBI also declined.

Gary didn't push it. In the secret world, it's not all that unusual for security agencies to decline to arrest bad guys. Quite often, instead, they like to watch the bad guys and see where they might lead them.

I was getting warmer. But still, I'd left LAX in mortal fear for the fate of the planet Earth if Sensi and Hirschfeld were somehow involved with Al-Qaeda. And in spite of all the questions various Feds had asked and I had answered, I hadn't been deemed to need to know a single thing about Al-Qaeda.

But soon there were more questions. Interesting new questions, with a decidedly different slant. Questions such as: *Do you know of any prior relationships between Sensi and any Israeli government official or intelligence asset?* And: *Do you remember the names of any Iranian nationals Sensi or Hirschfeld had contact with when you knew them?* And: *Do you remember the names—and we're talking true names or work names now, Larry—of any Libyan intelligence officers or agents Sensi or Hirschfeld had contact with? Or how about Syrian intelligence officers?* Then: *Did Sensi, or Hirschfeld, have anything at all to do with your trip to Islamabad and Peshawar, Pakistan, in 1987?* Interesting questions these were, pregnant with possibilities, and along with the questions, I was finally deemed to need to know enough to be told just what was really going on that had so many federal agencies concerned.

First Gary e-mailed me a photo of Richard "Marshall." There he was, all these years later, the new, remodeled Richard Hirschfeld. Shorter hair, tanner, a bit leaner, just as smug as ever. I wanted to slap his face as soon as I saw the picture. And, speaking of the picture, first they hadn't had one of him. Now, *presto,* they did. What was that all about? And was this taken before or after I'd identified Marshall as Hirschfeld? I knew better than to ask.

Then, little by little, Gary and others told me about the Turk, and the Turk was at the center of everything. It came out in fragments, each fact wrapped in a question. Gary told me parts of it. Others, nameless others, nameless to you here but even to me then, filled in the gaps. Gradually, the story took shape.

It seemed that in Miami there lived a niche-marketing genius of a Turk by the name of Engin Yesil. Mr. Yesil was not only a Turk, but a Muslim Turk with a slightly shady past, and he lived now in a most impressive house in Miami, which he'd recently purchased for fifteen million dollars, reportedly the highest price ever paid for a single-family residence in Miami. All of this—his nationality, his religion, his one prior conviction for a youthful offense, his obvious wealth, and the nature and scope of his latest niche-marketing success—made the Turk an obvious target. Though, it was the considered assessment of those in the know inside the many federal agencies that had recently investigated the Turk up the wazoo that years ago he'd seen the error of his ways and gone straight, and had since then been on the up-and-up. Which made it extremely unfortunate for the Turk that he had, during the past few years, come to know, quite well, a pair of gentlemen named Sensi and Marshall. Who worked for the CIA.

While he was a student at the University of Florida in the 1980s, the Turk had received a fifty-thousand-dollar commission for introducing a cocaine dealer he barely knew to another cocaine dealer he barely knew. He'd bought himself a slick car with the money and never had anything more to do with drugs. Bolivian Marching Powder was in his past, he thought.

After graduating from college, he'd founded a company called Lens Express, and at first he'd run it out of a tiny Fort Lauderdale apartment. He'd hired former *Wonder Woman* star Lynda Carter to appear in ads for the business, which sold contact lenses at a discount by mail order, and the business had taken off. But then he'd been arrested and convicted on federal charges of aiding and abetting distribution of a controlled substance, cocaine, for the niche-marketing deal he'd made back in college. The prosecutors had recommended leniency, probation but no jail time. Instead, the judge had sentenced the Turk to six years in prison. He'd run Lens Express from a minimum-security federal prison camp, mailing long lists of instructions to his management team each morning and meeting with them almost every weekend during visiting hours. Then, on appeal, his sentence was reduced to time served, twenty months, and he'd been released with no requirement of probation. Not long after his release, he'd sold the company for forty million dollars.

With those proceeds, the Turk, or "Mr. Yesil," as one of the nameless Feds I spoke with insisted on calling him, had founded several companies, including, most prominently, iPrepay.com and Radiant Telecom. Businesses he'd founded were generating so much cash that he now also owned hundreds of millions of dollars in publicly traded stocks.

iPrepay.com had developed a new generation of touch-screen ATM and financial services machines, and it owned and operated several thousand of those machines, which were now deployed in retail locations throughout the United States.

Radiant Telecom was a telecommunications company and we would come back to it in a moment, said the nice young Fed who'd been briefing me ever so dryly until now. Then he dropped the neutral tone and finally said something human enough for me to write it all down. I recall thinking that maybe his boss had just walked out of his office.

"This guy Yesil's fucking amazing," he said. "Everything he touches turns to money. And it's a testament to his business talents that he managed to start these companies while fighting a deportation action brought against him by the INS before he came out of prison. He fought back, took it all the way to the Supreme Court, and won. Meanwhile, in his spare time, he built huge companies. And you should see the guy's wife! Is she ever beautiful, holy shit! We all figure the guy's gotta be a great lover. I mean, he's forty-two years old and not bad looking, but his wife is twenty-something and easily one of the five most beautiful women on the face of the earth. You should see the surveillance photos. So you figure, well, he's forty-two and rich and living in the most expensive house in Miami, this babe's with him for his money. But, no, we checked, and her father's a billionaire. Which means our boy Engin Yesil's gotta have a wart on the head of his dick."

Then his boss strolled back into earshot, or such a nice young nameless fellow just didn't have it in him to be glib about national security issues, because now he retreated soberly into the heart of the matter.

Radiant Telecom, he told me, was the second-largest wholesaler in the United States of prepaid telephone calling cards. The company sold more than a hundred thousand calling cards every day, generating revenues in excess of two hundred fifty million dollars per annum.

Prepaid telephone calling cards are sold at a multitude of retail locations all over the United States and throughout most of the world, for cash, without any identification, credit application, or background check required. Once you have a prepaid calling card, you can use it to place calls to almost anywhere, anonymously, with no record of the caller's identity and little record even of the numbers the calls were placed from. This made Radiant Telecom inadvertently the telephone company of choice for Al-Qaeda operatives working in the United States. Mohamed Atta's suicide cells had used Radiant prepaid calling cards on several occasions while planning and coordinating the September 11 attacks.

Radiant, I was told, had also, through an affiliated company, developed and recently introduced state-of-the-art money-transfer technologies, including an automated vending system for prepaid credit cards. This, I was told, not only suited the legitimate needs of many in the general public, but was also ideal for Al-Qaeda's anonymous money-transfer needs, and those of the illicit drugs industry.

All these factors, as well as Mr. Yesil's background, had made Radiant and Mr. Yesil, unbeknownst to him, the subject of ongoing CIA, DEA, BCIS, and IRS investigations, which were coming to a head.

Gary took up the story from there.

Unaware of the extent to which federal agencies were encircling him, what the Turk now craved more than anything else was respectability and acceptance. And those were precisely the things Sensi and Hirschfeld had offered him. They'd already convinced him that they, not his attorney, Vince Messina, were the unseen reason he'd prevailed in his Supreme Court challenge to the deportation order issued against him by the INS. They'd further convinced the Turk that they had so much juice in Washington that they would someday be able to arrange for him to obtain a pardon for his drug conviction, then U.S. citizenship, and other consideration and honors. Mr. Engin Yesil, formerly of Istanbul, Turkey, was now under the extreme undue influence of Messrs. Sensi and Hirschfeld, and seldom made a business move without first obtaining their advice and blessing.

He had allowed them full access to his facilities and offered them call logs, traffic analyses, transaction data, and sophisticated trapping and eavesdropping capabilities over all of the eight hundred million minutes per month of traffic generated through his proprietary switches. He thought they would pass these patriotic gifts on to the CIA and the FBI.

And, through funds provided by another affiliate, he and one of his partners had set his two new friends up in business, providing Messrs. Sensi and Hirschfeld the working capital and the equipment and expertise necessary to establish their own telecommunications company. The previous year—in 2003—Sensi and Hirschfeld's company, GlobalNet, had conned Paul Bremer into granting them what they said was an exclusive contract to provide mobile satellite phone service to military, government, and civilian customers throughout Iraq. And GlobalNet had celebrated the contract, with much attendant publicity, by distributing a few hundred handheld satellite phones to American fighting men and women in Iraq, so that they could make free calls to loved ones in the United States through Valentine's Day.

With every fact I received, I also got a question. The CIA and the FBI were wondering who the hell, if anyone, was really getting the call logs and traffic analyses—since they weren't getting them. The CIA was also concerned about technology transfers to the governments of some of the foreign markets in which certain of Radiant's highly sophisticated switches and nodes were deployed. They asked if I knew anything, anything at all, which might help them find an-

swers. The DEA and IRS were concerned about money laundering
through Radiant's financial network. And, I was told, in addition to
its concerns about the logs and reports, the FBI was thoroughly concerned about a recent diaspora of computer geniuses and their rabbis
from Israel to Radiant's headquarters in Miami. What the FBI was
wondering was: Are any of them Mossad?

But the BCIS didn't give a shit about that; the Israelis all had
valid visas. What the BCIS was concerned about was why they
couldn't get anyone to arrest these two motherfuckers, "Marshall"
and Sensi, who were running around telling OC figures they had the
BCIS in their pockets and, for the right bribes, could get them visas,
green cards, passports, anything they wanted.

It was soon very clear to me that it is the nature of our present
system that outside of their unique spheres of responsibility, their
own bailiwicks, none of our national security agencies gives a damn
about anything else. As a result, nobody sees the big picture. The
United States government had no more idea than I did what Sensi
and Hirschfeld were really up to.

4. PATTERN RECOGNITION

That should've been the end of it. I'd done my duty for Homeland Security, answered every question put to me, and I was free now to return to Los Angeles or wherever I wanted to go. But I'm the curious sort, and they were very curious facts I'd recently come to possess. Plus I was still running on adrenaline, and not inclined to stop at the moment. Just because no one else could see the big picture didn't mean that I couldn't. Not if I tried. Not if what I did next was what I used to watch my father do.

I cleared off the tops of my desk and the credenza behind it and started laying out all my files. On: Sensi; Hirschfeld; our trip to Beirut; our London meetings with the mysterious Iranians; my trip to Islamabad and Peshawar with Muhammad; Muhammad's trip with Sensi and Hirschfeld to Israel; the name of the company I happened to remember Hirschfeld used to open accounts in the Cayman Islands branch of BCCI; the legendary Mossad figures Miles Copeland and Adnan Khashoggi had introduced me to; every public record item I'd found on Boris Birshtein, Roi Azim, Lev Chernoy, and various Russian businessmen who thought they'd availed themselves of the special services of a special branch of the CIA; my files on the Turk, Engin Yesil; his Israeli partner, Arik Meimoun; Arik's computer boffins, suspected of Mossad ties; all their known associates and affiliates; my notes on everything I'd recently been told by, or inferred from, Homeland Security and other agencies about their case.

There were a lot more files to go. I was just getting started. Then Guinness stirred at my feet, stood up, cocked an ear, and bolted out of the room yipping and growling and barking all the way to the front door.

Someone knocked. Twice.

Guinness started wailing.

I went to the door and opened it a crack. I'd been expecting FedEx all morning, a package that was going to require my signature. Still, I didn't unchain the door before I pulled it open a couple of inches.

It was steamy hot out there. On my doorstep stood a man in black trousers, a salmon-colored dress shirt, black wing tips, cracking with age, and a flowered tie. They were tiny flowers, in a discreet pattern, something out of the seventies rather than the sixties. A step behind him was his wife. Blonde, overbosomed, wearing a blouse that was slightly too tight.

She wasn't holding a FedEx package either.

The man's face was right in front of mine now, and he was wearing glasses with gold frames, a gold wedding band, and a gold-plated watch, maker's mark indistinct. In the last couple of years, my vision had gone from terrific to so bad that, at certain distances, such as the distance from my eyes to his wrist, I could make out almost no detail. He was holding, *fuck,* a Bible. Not that I mind reading the Bible. Not at all. But I really would prefer to do it on my own time, thank you.

He said, "I'd like to read you a passage from Psalm 27." Then he read me a passage from Psalm 27. Then he told me his interpretation of the passage from Psalm 27: "I believe it is God's vision for a world without evil, and it is clearly what we need to solve the problems of the world today."

I had the door open about five inches now, still chained. Guinness was still wailing and growling, but she'd also entered a new propulsive phase. She was dying to leap out onto the doorstep and attack.

"I'm sorry about my dog," I said, not really sorry at all.

"What breed is he?" the man asked.

"*She*," I said.

Guinness kept barking. "I'm sorry," I said again, "and I'm afraid that—"

"That's okay," he interrupted me. "We've got bichons ourselves. If you know what they are."

"Uh-huh," I said. "I do."

I was about to add, "Bichon *frises*." But I stopped myself. *Don't engage.*

I looked past the man to his wife, still a step behind him, smiling at me in the tight red blouse and black skirt. She had nice calves and was standing on incongruously high heels in black patent leather. The authentic shoes of a church lady?

His hair was black, with tinges of gray. Perfectly parted. Like he'd worked on it for quite a while earlier that day. He was maybe fifty. He never stopped smiling. He opened his black vinyl case and pulled out two copies of *The Watchtower.*

Jehovah's Witnesses. Oh shit! This could take forever. Time to enter the Witness Protection Program. I nudged Guinness with my foot.

She barked louder. I said, "I'm sorry. But I've really got to go. I was working when you knocked, and I've got to get back to it. But I do promise to read my Bible."

"We can accept donations, if you like," said the man.

"Is there an address in here I can send one to?" I held up the copy of *The Watchtower* he'd given me. "I'd rather read this first, and then decide if I want to give you support. All right?"

"Okay," said the man, pointing now to the pamphlet I was holding. "We'll check back with you and see what you thought about that."

I nodded and smiled and pushed the door shut. The woman smiled a sexless smile at me through the last crack of daylight I saw between the jamb and the door as it closed. I locked the deadbolt.

Guinness kept growling. She still wasn't happy, and I was feeling a little hinky myself. Back in my office, I went through *The Watchtower* looking for anything stuck between the pages. There was nothing. It was just a pulp pamphlet.

I ran it through my shredder. Relax, I told myself. They're probably real Jehovah's Witnesses.

Ten minutes later, I took Guinness out for a walk. Four houses down from mine and across the street, my recent visitors were standing earnestly on another doorstep, opening their hearts to one of my neighbors. That made me feel better. But, then again, if they were a surveillance team and any good at it, they *would* maintain their cover for at least a while after they left my house, wouldn't they?

I arranged more folders atop my desk. My files on: the great and mythical Muhammad Ali Motor Car Company, to be built in Brazil by Richard M. Hirschfeld and partners; the great and mythical nostrums of Hirsch-Chemie Ltd.; Republicans Abroad; Bill Casey's secret channel to Iran; Ferdinand Marcos's Ship of Gold; the Hirschfeld Bank of Commerce; Mohamed Al-Fassi; the curious death and exhumation of Robert Chastain; Hirschfeld and Ottimo Stabilimente

Immobiliere; Hirschfeld and Pan Nordic Corporation, reputedly a conduit for illegal shipments of arms to Panama and Chile; Industrias Cardoen Limitada, reputedly a conduit for secret sales of arms from Chile to Saddam Hussein's army; Sensi's recent affiliation with the Washington consulting firm of Jefferson Waterman International, ex-spies all; an unconfirmed report of Senator Orrin Hatch visiting Richard Hirschfeld in prison; inmate Richard Marshall Hirschfeld's prison friendship with inmate Joseph Matthew Gaffney II, incarcerated for diving from a ship in Sicily in 1985 to fake his death and collect on a life insurance policy; FBI Intelligence Section report dated August 1996 headed "SEMION MOGILEVICH ORGANIZA-TION EURASIAN ORGANIZED CRIME RING"; "Defendant Sensi's Proposed Stipulation Regarding CIA Witnesses and Classified Material." And more; there was a lot more by the time I finished arranging it all on my desk and credenza.

I read each file carefully, then copied every page and combined all the files into one big file and read it through in chronological order, twice, slowly, meticulously, as my father used to do. I made notes along the way. I lost track of time. I looked up at what I thought was the gray light of evening and, to my surprise, saw instead that it was dawn. I kept sifting facts, and cross-referencing. I charted dates, people, places, events. I looked for anomalies. I looked for links. I diagrammed relationships and commonalities. This is what intelligence professionals refer to as constructing matrices. And what the popular media refers to as connecting the dots.

Month after month, day after day, we do not stop them. Honest-but-illegal immigrants, criminals, smugglers and spies, terrorists and traffickers—we do not stop them. We cannot stop them. I imagined them coming over, under, and around the border in waves, entering

America on little cat feet. I imagined Hirschfeld and Sensi sitting at meetings with their pigeons, not saying much of anything to each other, communicating in that special telegraphic way a good catcher works with a pitcher. Racking up money, sure. But what else were they doing? What were they really up to?

Hirschfeld would do anything he thought he could get away with, would stop at nothing, ever, short of his own glory or demise, I'd always known that. Sensi had always seemed to me more of a follower than a leader. A good soldier. But not a visionary. I could barely believe that, as had been reported to me, Hirschfeld, a federal fugitive, was eating openly in the picture windows of the best restaurants in Miami, tooling around town in a black Mercedes, even flying often to Washington and New York for meetings—not unless he had somebody big, a lot bigger than Sensi, watching his back. Who? And why?

I kept reading.

Patterns were beginning to emerge. Comprised of things I'd known all along and other things I'd glossed over or missed during my mad rush to throw together for Gary and his friends a quick bio of Richard Hirschfeld, and find and supply a reference photo of him.

Some patterns looked promising at first, then lost direction, or trickled off into nothingness. In other words, they ceased to be patterns.

For nearly half a day, I focused on the disappearance of Abuwi Mahdi—best man, in December 1986, at Muhammad's wedding to his current wife, Lonnie. Mahdi was an American black man, originally from Mississippi, Baptist-born, but by the early 1980s he was a Muslim preacher and traveling often with Muhammad. Along the way, Mahdi became friend or acquaintance of Arab potentates and intelligence chiefs, plus, of course, Hirschfeld and Sensi. Come to think of it, the last time I'd actually seen Sensi was with Mahdi at a charity gala called The Banquet of the Golden Plate, in Washington, D.C., in the last week of June 1986.

I remembered how happy I'd been that night to run into my old golf buddy Alan Shepard, decked out in dress whites, an admiral now. I remembered waiting until he was surrounded by a whole crowd of illustrious admirers to give him shit for once missing, on the final hole of a match, a two-foot putt that had cost us fifty dollars each. To be more precise, what I'd said was "You know, for a hot-stick Navy test pilot, astronaut, moonwalker, All-American hero, you sure swing a golf club like a pussy." At that same party a few minutes later, I'd met Steven Spielberg and Chuck Yeager.

When it came time for dinner, I'd found myself seated at a big round table that included, among others, Shirley Temple Black, Mahdi, and his guest Sensi. It was that same night, after the gala, that Sensi and I had sat together in tuxedos in the bar of the J. W. Marriott Hotel on Pennsylvania Avenue in Washington, while Sensi told me about Republicans Abroad, Bill Casey, and the Iran initiative—just weeks before Sensi's arrest.

No one I knew admitted to seeing Mahdi or hearing from him since 1992. But my suspicion that he'd left the country and was working now for an Arab *mukhabarat,* perhaps with Hirschfeld and Sensi, died when, after hours of phone calls and searches on the Internet, I finally discovered that Mahdi had for some years now been in prison in California. For what I wasn't sure yet, but it was a state charge, not federal, so it wasn't espionage.

I looked for links—beyond the known link to Boris Birshtein—between Sensi and Hirschfeld and associates of the Semion Mogilevich branch of the Russian mafia, or any other branch of the Russian Mafia that might be willing and able to sell weapons or nuclear matériel to Al-Qaeda. For hours, I was fixated on this passage in an FBI report:

Semion Mogilevich attended a summit meeting of Russian OC figures in Tel Aviv, Israel, from October 10–19, 1995. Participants included Sergei Mikhailov, Viktor Averin, Boris Birshtein, Vadim Rabinovich, Leonid Bilounov, and Arnold Tamm. The subjects met in Boris Birshtein's office in the diamond center of Tel Aviv. The subject of the meeting was the sharing of interests in Ukraine. While in Israel, the group traveled around the country, including a visit to a shooting range. The INP obtained telephone coverage of the hotel rooms, detecting phone calls to Russia, Hungary, and Paris.

The use of cellular and regular telephones by the Semion Mogilevich Organization is common. Organization members did not appear to practice communications security, freely discussing business over the telephone. However, this may change as Mogilevich has become aware of the investigations targeting his organization.

And this passage of the same report:

The BIS and SBU indicate that criminal groups under Semion Mogilevich's domain in the Czech Republic are involved in the trafficking of illegal weapons, radioactive materials, and precious gems. They are also involved in prostitution and assassinations.

If Sensi and Hirschfeld were facilitating the illegal entry of Mogilevich associates into the United States, were they also, say, orchestrating the sale of a nice little Soviet nuclear warhead to Osama bin Laden? I didn't know. There was a whole lot I didn't know.

So much data. What is signal and what is noise? How do you winnow possibility from fact? And what was I to make of *this*? A source inside the Department of Homeland Security told me of a meeting in 2003 in Albany, New York. The meeting was called by a DEA official based in New York City. The subject, he said, was too sensitive to discuss anywhere in Manhattan, there was too much chance of being noticed there. So: an ill-lit motel room in Albany.

In addition to the DEA's representative, the meeting was attended by an official of the CIA and an official of the BCIS. Plus a mystery guest: a young Arab man who lived in South Florida and was providing the DEA intelligence on Engin Yesil and Radiant Telecom. What the DEA wanted to know from the BCIS was "Can you give this man an American passport? He's risking his life to further vital national security interests of the United States." The CIA representative was there to back up the DEA's request.

This was the rub: After the meeting, when the BCIS man went back to Washington and got into the paperwork, following through, he discovered that the young Arab confidential informant had been introduced to the DEA by none other than "Richard Marshall."

Did that mean Hirschfeld was working for the DEA, or the CIA, or both? And did someone inside the government know "Richard Marshall" was actually the fugitive Richard Hirschfeld? These were complicated questions. Miles used to tell me the essence of epistemology and the essence of intelligence analysis were the same question: *How can I know that what I think I know is what I really know?*

What was I looking for? I didn't even know that. But it had to be here somewhere. I sipped a Red Bull and kept reading.

———

In the end, only one pattern gained strength the more I searched for connections. It started in the White House:

January 1985. Behind closed doors in the office of the Vice President, George H. W. Bush told us Sensi would provide Muhammad whatever resources he needed in his attempts to negotiate with Khomeini. Sensi's cover job, Bush said, was working for an offshore arm of the Republican Party. Sensi's real job, Bush said, was working for the CIA.

July 1987. In Room 2172 of the Rayburn House Office Building, in Washington, D.C., on the occasion of the testimony of Richard M. Hirschfeld before the House Committee on Foreign Affairs, Subcommittee on Pacific Affairs, regarding Ferdinand Marcos's Plan to Invade the Philippines, Hirschfeld brought with him, as his attorney of record for the hearing, one Jerris Leonard. Mr. Leonard had been appointed by, and served as Assistant Attorney General of the United States for Civil Rights under, President Richard M. Nixon. Since leaving government and entering private practice, Mr. Leonard's most prominent client had been President George H. W. Bush.

Hirschfeld also brought with him to the hearing both Robert Chastain, soon to be mysteriously dead, and Robert Sensi, soon to be convicted on six counts of mail fraud, four counts of first-degree theft, and eleven counts of interstate transportation of stolen securities. In his testimony, Hirschfeld said it was Sensi who had recommended Hirschfeld contact Congress about this matter and arrange this hearing. Hirschfeld further testified that, when Marcos asked his help in obtaining foreign passports, before Hirschfeld agreed, he wrote to Vice President Bush to ask if he had any objections. When asked by the subcommittee chairman, Congressman Stephen Solarz, why on earth he would contact the Vice President about such a matter, Hirschfeld conferred off the record with Jerris Leonard, then very cautiously stated that Vice President Bush was involved in the planning of the Beirut operation, and that it had been organized and run by Sensi.

October 1987. In the civil matter of Kuwait Airways Corporation versus American Security Bank, N.A., and First American Bank, N.A., the witness Robert M. Sensi was represented by Vice President Bush's friend and attorney Jerris Leonard, Esquire.

June 1988. In the netherworld of Washington at night, when Hirschfeld began impersonating Muhammad on the phone, of all the senators he struck up friendships with, only one of them, Ted Kennedy, wasn't a Republican.

August 1988. In New Orleans, in the Superdome, at the Republican National Convention, Hirschfeld was photographed wearing a campaign button of his own design: "BUSH IN '88/HATCH IN '96." And when Muhammad was shown on national television sitting beside Barbara Bush while her husband delivered his "Thousand Points of Light" acceptance speech, Muhammad spent most of his time chatting not with Mrs. Bush but with another occupant of the Bush family box, Richard Hirschfeld.

December 1988. In Washington, when the Ali impersonation fell apart and Hirschfeld came under fire, his new attorney was Judah Best. For a while, that name kept eating at me. I'd heard it somewhere before. Or had I? Oh, hell yes, I'd even met him! Judd Best was what his friends called him, but his card said Judah Best. And what had I been told about him? Judd Best: Republican partisan and problem-fixer, whose most famous accomplishment was cutting the nolo contendre deal that kept Spiro Agnew out of prison when he stepped down as vice president. Then, during Watergate, Judd Best had served as Charles Colson's attorney.

Extend the line again, to *January 1992*. Hirschfeld was in prison now, and according to *The Virginian-Pilot*, a Norfolk, Virginia, newspaper, his appellate team included none other than arch-Republican jurist Robert Bork:

> Add the name of Robert H. Bork to the rich, famous and powerful who have been associated with Richard M. Hirschfeld—a list that includes Muhammad Ali, Sen. Orrin G. Hatch of Utah, various Saudi princes and assorted celebrities. Bork, the would-be Supreme Court justice, is on the defense team appealing Hirschfeld's conviction and 6-year-sentence for tax and securities fraud last year. Hirschfeld, the lawyer from Virginia Beach best known for wheeling and dealing and political intrigue, is in the federal prison in Petersburg and could not be reached for comment. His appeal to the 4th Circuit Court of Appeals in Richmond is scheduled to be heard Feb. 3. The outspoken Bork, a former U.S. solicitor-general and federal appellate judge, was rejected for Supreme Court by the Senate in 1987. He is with the conservative American Enterprise Institute and does limited courtroom work, mostly in the areas of anti-trust and constitutional law. Bork declined to identify the "mutual friend" who recruited him for Hirschfeld's defense team.

One name that kept popping up in the known lifeline of Richard Hirschfeld was Bush, along with a strong supporting cast of highest-level Republican functionaries. Now that I was looking for it, it was easy to see. In Sensi's case, the trail was fainter. There was the record of Jerris Leonard appearing once as Sensi's attorney. But in all the public records and lurid press reports of Sensi's life and career, his trial and incarceration, and his role in the CIA, I had found not a single reference to Sensi's role for the Republican Party. And that, I realized, might make the business card Vice President Bush once handed me a very unique and telling artifact. *1985*: "Robert M. Sensi, Chairman, The Ambassador's Club, Republicans Abroad, c/o The Republican National Committee."

2002: Robert M. Sensi, Boris Birshtein's ticket to the White House and the second President Bush.

I could connect the dots now almost to the present, and I was beginning to consider the possibility that Sensi and Hirschfeld weren't working just for themselves, or for foreign or American intelligence interests—they were working for the Republicans. Or maybe even just for the Bushes.

But was this really going anywhere?

Miles had taught me to do everything I could to push the timeline forward, to look for the big picture. Only once you're thoroughly familiar with the known facts and all of the timeline can you begin to see the nuances and develop an intuitive feel for what might be happening next. For the Republicans and the Bushes, of course, what was happening next was political warfare—the 2004 presidential election was just less than five months away. And for Hirschfeld and Sensi and their favorite client, Mr. Yesil, the Turk, what was happening next was he was in deep shit but didn't know it, and they were manipulating him. Most recently, I'd been told, they'd induced him to enter into a reverse merger agreement whereunder Radiant Telecom would spin off most of its assets and operations into a new entity called Ntera, then vend Ntera into a small publicly traded company called World-Quest Networks, Inc. (Nasdaq: WQNI).

The deal had been announced just two and a half months earlier, on March 17, 2004. So far, I'd only glanced at the SEC filings, because nothing about this seemed anomalous. Engin Yesil had used the public equity markets before. I'd been assuming that buried some-where in the inner workings of the WQNI-Ntera merger would be a big finder's fee, or hidden options, or some other form of financial killing for Hirschfeld and Sensi.

But now I read the WQNI-Ntera merger filing carefully, and when I got to the bottom of the second page my blood ran cold. Upon consummation of the merger: Mr. Yesil would be the com-pany's largest shareholder, with approximately fifty-four percent of the outstanding capital stock; the company's president would be B. Michael Adler; and the chairman of the company's board of direc-tors would be *Robert A. Farmer.* Holy shit! Robert Farmer had for the past twenty years been the Democratic Party's most prolific fund-raiser. And Robert Farmer was now the campaign treasurer for the presumptive Democratic presidential candidate John Kerry.

I told you in the beginning, when it comes to covert political operations, I was trained by the master. It wasn't hard for me to see immediately what was going on here. It was either an enormous co-incidence that this merger had been orchestrated by a pair of rogue CIA agents and Republican covert operatives with long ties to the Bushes, or it was no coincidence at all.

I went online and saw that, even though the merger hadn't yet been legally consummated, the merging companies had already be-gun to consolidate their management and WQNI's website already listed Engin Yesil as its largest shareholder and Robert Farmer as its chairman. In other words, WQNI's website made it look as if the deal had already closed. So, what I was wondering next was when was the news going to break? Sometime soon, as a preemptive strike? Or would they wait until, say, October? Would there be trumped-up ar-rests of Engin Yesil and others to trigger the news stories, or would it simply be leaked to just the right reporters that Robert Farmer, John Kerry's campaign treasurer, was also the chairman of the board of a company controlled by an ex-convict Muslim Turk, which made its money supplying covert telecommunications services to Al-Qaeda operatives and laundering money for Al-Qaeda and a long list of drug barons? What would be the pullquote? And would they throw in right away an intimation that, although the investigation was not completed, investigators believed they may have spotted a trail of money—contributions—from Osama bin Laden to the Kerry campaign? Or would that be part of the follow-up leak?

The next thing I found on the Internet was a routine public record filing by John Kerry for President Inc. showing that, on the fifth of February 2004, just six weeks before the WQNI-Ntera merger was announced, Robert Sensi, lifelong Republican, longtime Republican fund-raiser and operative, had made a one-thousand-dollar contribution to the presidential campaign of John F. Kerry. *Shit!*

And there was something more. A shard of a memory that kept floating around the edges of my mind and then slipping away before I could get at it. Something I'd heard, not seen. It nagged at me until finally I got out my copy of Dave Kindred's tape of Richard Hirschfeld pretending to be Muhammad Ali. FAST FORWARD. STOP. PLAY. Try again. FAST FORWARD. STOP. PLAY. Try again. I'd listened to almost the entire tape when finally I found this, and it chilled me to the bone. REWIND. STOP. PLAY. . . .

KINDRED: What about the presidential thing? Are you gonna be involved in that too?

HIRSCHFELD (AS "ALI"): Yes, I am.

KINDRED: In what way?

HIRSCHFELD (AS "ALI"): Well, it's, it's, I told George Bush if he needed me I'll be there. I'm gonna help him.

All this time, I'd been running on adrenaline. Now I was running on adrenaline and fear. I knew a great secret; I was the only person in the world who knew it; and the person who stood to lose the most if the secret was revealed was the most powerful man in the world.

5. IN WHICH, POSSESSING A DARK AND DANGEROUS SECRET, I ATTEMPT TO SAVE THE WORLD

think I should point out to you that I'm not a Democrat or a Republican. And while I have been involved in covert political operations overseas, I've never been involved in any American domestic political operation, covert or overt. As of the fifth of June 2004, the day I discovered what I saw as Hirschfeld and Sensi's plot against John Kerry—and the first day of the week in which I learned what I'm made of—in the eight American presidential elections conducted since I'd reached voting age, I'd voted four times for Democrats, thrice for Republicans, and one year when the election rolled around I'd been so deep in darkest Africa that my absentee ballot never arrived. I have friends who are Democrats and friends who are Republicans. I voted for Ronald Reagan in 1984 and for George H. W. Bush in 1988. I did what I did in that June of 2004, and I am writing this book now, not out of any animosity toward the Republican Party.

On the morning of the day before the 2000 presidential election, I was one of the most sought-after of commodities, an undecided

Florida voter. By that evening, I'd decided to vote for Al Gore—and I did the next day, but with the feeling that I wouldn't be terribly upset if Bush won. I hadn't started out liking him at all, but during his second debate with Gore I'd seen a human and likable side of George W. Bush that I hadn't expected. Plus, he said he was a uniter, not a divider.

And he could've been. On the fourteenth of September 2001, the day he spoke, magnificently, at the National Prayer and Remembrance service at the National Cathedral in Washington, George W. Bush had almost every American squarely behind him.

But, in those first few hours after I connected the dots, while I pondered what I should do, what I couldn't stop returning to was how quickly Bush had squandered our national resolve. He fell under the spell of a cabal of neocon warmongers who'd never actually been to war themselves. He ignored the lessons of Mideast history, he got himself hooked on stovepiped intelligence, and then he launched a preemptive strike on Iraq that has been a FUBAR of biblical proportions.

Bush and his team sold us their plan for war with half-truths and hype, specious tales of African yellowcake and aluminum tubes, visions of Al-Qaeda mushroom clouds rising over our great cities. With weapons-grade sophistry, they divided America and rejected the sympathy and counsel of the world. Almost every foreign nation was behind us the day after the September 11 attacks—even the French, whose newspaper of record, *Le Monde*, proclaimed in a headline: "We are all Americans now."

But it seemed that was never enough for our defense secretary, Donald Rumsfeld, "Rummy" to those in the loop, and Deputy Defense Secretary Paul Wolfowitz, "Wolfie" to the anointed, or for the rest of the team. What we needed, what the whole world needed whether it liked it or not, was a preventive war, and history be damned. George Tenet and Condoleezza Rice, Dick Cheney and Richard Perle, Karl Rove and Scooter Libby, Rummy and Wolfie, all available hands and their minions, dug deep into the sacred texts and the intell looking for rationales to support what they wanted to do. Who among us who saw them will ever forget their magic lantern shows of charts and maps, satellite imagery, heat signatures and uranium, pratfall and misdirection, stage smiles? How could we know? How could any of us watching at home possibly know if what they were telling us was true?

In their search, they must've come across these words spoken by their own Republican general and president—wisdom they chose to ignore: "All of us have heard this term 'preventive war' since the earliest days of Hitler," President Dwight D. Eisenhower said in a press conference in 1953. "But a preventive war, to my mind, is an impossibility. I don't believe there is such a thing, and, frankly, I wouldn't even listen to anyone seriously that came in and talked about such a thing."

In 1917, just after Baghdad was occupied by the Anglo-Indian army, ostensibly to rescue the Iraqis from the clutches of the Ottoman Turks, but actually to secure the Iraqi oil fields, British lieutenant-general Sir Stanley Maude proclaimed to the Iraqi people: "Our armies do not come into your cities and lands as conquerors or enemies, but as liberators. You people of Baghdad are not to understand that it is the wish of the British Government to impose upon you alien institutions. It is the hope of the British Government that once again the people of Baghdad shall flourish, enjoying their wealth and substance under institutions which are in consonance with their sacred laws."

That sounded to me a lot like the rosy assurances our own leaders gave the Iraqis in 2003 not long after we flattened half of Baghdad and then drove our tanks into what was left of it. But history shows that eventually the British liberators were driven out of Iraq by pissed-off locals, the insurgency. Just as eventually British liberators were driven out of Palestine, by both Jews and Arabs. And just as Napoleon, the liberator of Egypt, had eventually been forced by the locals to abandon the Nile in humiliation. The track record of Western armies fighting local insurgencies in the Middle East is abysmal. If President Bush didn't know that, surely someone on his staff should have.

By early 1920, three years after Sir Stanley Maude's declaration of victory in Iraq, British occupation forces found themselves under attack by a ferocious Iraqi insurgency that had first sprung up in, of all places, Fallujah. For months, RAF biplanes rained bombs down on Fallujah and pockets of resistance inside Baghdad, while British troops fought their way house to house through the streets of Samarra. In August of that year, British generals announced that the insurgency was broken and would soon be wiped out.

But, in a dispatch from Baghdad for *The Times* of London, T. E. Lawrence, better known as Lawrence of Arabia, disagreed. "The people of England have been led in Mesopotamia into a trap from which it will be hard to escape with dignity and honour," he wrote. "Things have been far worse than we have been told. We are today not far from a disaster."

Lawrence had, while a British Army intelligence officer, taught Arabs the techniques of insurgency—materialize out of nowhere, strike, hide, melt away, lay low, start again—and then helped them use those techniques against the conventional army of the Ottoman Turks. He knew how difficult it would be to crush a rebellion of locals who knew the terrain, the language, the people, the sanctuaries, the culture of the battleground. "Analogy is fudge, anyhow,"

Lawrence wrote, "and to make war upon rebellion is messy and slow, like eating soup with a knife."

By that day in June of 2004, while I considered the implications of what I had just discovered, it had become the Bush team's party line that in Iraq they'd already won the war and would eventually win the peace. It sounded good. And no doubt that was why it had been so thoroughly embraced by so many. But what war, exactly, did we win? Our Coalition forces—as brave and honorable as they are—had defeated the uniformed Iraqi army. But the *uniformed* Iraqi army, it had turned out, wasn't the *entire* Iraqi army. There was also the ghostly-and-deadly-but-not-uniformed Iraqi army—the insurgency, or, as its members prefer to be called, the "mujahideen." And when they rose up against us they were armed and angry, just as we would be if we found Arab soldiers calling the shots in our cities and towns.

That Iraqi army has at times made the Coalition forces in Iraq look about as dexterous and in control of the battlefield as, some two hundred thirty years earlier, our Minutemen made the British Redcoats look when they tried to fight us on our home turf. It simply isn't true that in Iraq we won the war but lost the peace. This *is* the war. It's still being fought. We live now in an asymmetrical world, and this *is* the war.

But the war in Iraq is not the war on terror, in spite of intense efforts our administration has made to merge the two in the minds of the American people. We've spent hundreds of billions of dollars in Iraq in what's been billed as an offensive thrust in the war on terror, but our homeland security system is full of holes. The FBI's computers don't work. Thousands of illegals cross our borders daily. Our seaports are virtually unprotected. Our airports are protected with Band-Aids. Most of our security agencies still don't talk to each other, at least not candidly. They are underfunded and underled, and if you need to bring a suitcase-sized nuclear weapon into the United States and can't find any other way, there's always Richard Hirschfeld's sunset flight out of Tijuana. There are many talented and dedicated intelligence, counterintelligence, and security professionals on our side, but our government is almost as unprepared to handle terrorism on American soil now as it was on September 11, 2001.

Those were some of the things I was thinking while I wondered whether to do nothing, certainly the safest thing for me in the short term, or to do what I already knew was the right thing. I was also thinking about how, after the blitzkrieg arrival of our brave troops in Baghdad, George W. Bush explained the war to us in terms that made it sound a bit too much like an oil deal for my taste. And how he dressed himself up like a decorated-war-veteran fighter pilot, which he is not, posed before a MISSION ACCOMPLISHED sign, and told us that, now that we had won, our occupation and administration of Iraq would pay for themselves out of oil revenues. But, in the thirteen months that had passed since the day President Bush declared that the major combat was over, more than eight hundred more American troops had died in Iraq. And every day the situation on the ground was getting worse, not better.

I give the President the benefit of the doubt. He's got a job and pressures, responsibilities, no human should have to deal with. It can't be easy. That mask of decisiveness, that cocksure certainty he projects, must just be his style of leadership. Of course, he had night sweats, doubts, fears, uncertainty, as he weighed the options before he gave the invasion order, didn't he? I'm sure he believed he was doing the right thing in Iraq. But he fucked up, and he's never quite managed to admit that to us or apologize for it. And even if he were to apologize now, it's too late. As Harry Truman taught us, the buck stops at the president's desk.

I was thinking *that,* too.

And that the price of a barrel of light sweet crude was soaring to unheard-of heights, while the dollar was falling like an anvil dropped in a deep still lake. Our administration kept telling us that someday soon, when democracy bloomed in the Iraqi desert, we would be safer from terrorists at home. But this seemed to me to be another case of the administration playing three-card monte with facts. The fact is the vast majority of the Iraqi people are Shiite Muslims who, if given the chance, would turn Iraq into an Islamic state, not unlike Iran. Iran *is* a democracy—and the largest state sponsor and exporter of fundamentalist Islamic terrorism.

Meanwhile, in Iraq, the tales of African yellowcake turned out to be fictive; the "confirmed sightings of mobile biological warfare pro-ductions plants" were found to be sightings of trucks loaded with harmless devices for inflating weather balloons; and the weapons of mass destruction that posed "an imminent threat to America" had been a mirage.

Imagine, I thought, what will happen if George W. Bush and his advisors who got us to this place should win the 2004 presidential election and come to believe they've received a mandate from a grate-ful nation. What if Bush wins in November and, next year or the year after that, he and Cheney and Rumsfeld put their heads together and decide with all good intentions that it's time for a preemptive strike on Tehran? Or Pyongyang?

It seemed to me that our President was trying, but he just wasn't very good at the job. And that, for all our sakes, he needed to go home to the Prairie Chapel Ranch after just one term—to clear more brush, and make plans for what he'd do a few years later when he finally got what I suspected was still his dream job: Major League Baseball Commissioner.

But that was just my opinion, and Bush hadn't decided to quit and go home. He was standing for reelection, and our nation seemed so divided that it was going to be extremely close. Unless, for example, between that summer's night and the election, it could be made to look like John Kerry's campaign treasurer was also Osama bin Laden's U.S. campaign treasurer. And given the sublime talents of Richard Hirschfeld and Robert Sensi, that wasn't nearly as preposterous as it might sound.

What I realized then was I had already decided that, no matter how dangerous it might become, I had to warn John Kerry. But how? How the hell was I supposed to warn Kerry without far too many people learning my identity? Hirschfeld and Sensi were simply not like other men. I had little doubt what they, and whoever was protecting them in Washington, would want to do to me if they ever found out I was working overtime to sabotage their plan.

Another knock on my front door. And Guinness didn't move until we heard the knock. Someone had approached very quietly.

By the time I got to the door, Guinness had been there for fifteen seconds, thundering at whoever was on the other side.

It was a woman. She was in her thirties, short and slightly chubby, wearing khaki shorts and a sky-blue T-shirt. She wasn't a Jehovah's Witness, or from FedEx. I knew all that because I'd had a look at her through a side window before I went to the door. She was holding a wicker basket, beribboned and stuffed with colorful things. Maybe someone had sent me a gift. Or maybe she was from the Prize Patrol.

I opened the door and stepped outside to say hello. Guinness was greatly offended by this, left on the other side of the door as she was, yelping now.

The woman said she was from the A. C. Nielsen Company and the basket was for me, because this was my lucky day—my family had been chosen to become a Nielsen family.

With a bit of ceremony, she handed me the basket. Chocolates, two jars of jam, a bag of jelly beans, a foil pack of coffee beans, a box of breadsticks, another of vermicelli.

I did my best to say nice things about the basket—the way my mother taught me to when I was a kid and my aunt gave me something weird for Christmas. Then I set the basket down, because now the woman was pressing a big white, blue, and green brochure into my hands. The cover said: "Hook Up With/THE NIELSEN TV RATINGS SYSTEM/Help Us Measure Television Usage In Your Area."

What are the odds? I was thinking.

Inside the brochure was a picture of the back of a television set, with a little white box and some wires attached to it. Caption: "THE NIELSEN TV METER/The picture on the right shows what the Nielsen TV Meter looks like once it is connected to the back of a television set. TVs, VCRs and cable boxes are metered to obtain the channel being viewed. The meter connects to the television or VCR tuner and does not interfere with your TV or its reception. The meters are also connected to a small computer microprocessor where the viewing information is stored."

I remembered reading a magazine article once, something like twenty years back—an investigative report on the Nielsen TV ratings system, which is so important to television broadcasters and advertisers. It said the size of the statistical sample, the number of Nielsen families all across America, was much smaller than anyone would imagine. For example, the article said, the magazine's investigators had discovered there was just one Nielsen box in all of New Mexico.

"So how many Nielsen families are there in Florida?" I said.

The woman smiled apologetically. "We're not allowed to say."

"At least a thousand?"

"Oh sure," she said. "At least."

What are the odds, I was thinking, *that out of the seventeen million people in Florida, out of however many millions of households, mine would be one of, at most, a few thousand chosen to be openly hot-wired with sophisticated monitoring devices?*

I turned to the next page of the brochure, to a photo of a black box with toggle switches, several data ports, and a pair of phone jacks. "CONNECTING IT ALL TOGETHER/The Nielsen TV Home Unit."

On the other side of the door, Guinness began to bark at me more systematically, in the manner of Lassie trying to warn Timmy of something he was too human to see.

I said, "How does this black box work?"

"Well," she said, "first the little white boxes are attached to every television, cable box, VCR, and DVD player in your house. Then our technicians snake wires out of all those little white boxes. It's not obtrusive. We hide them very well. We pull up your carpets and bury the wires, then lay the carpets down again. Or we remove your baseboards, tack down the wires, and then replace the baseboards. All the hidden wires lead to this black box, and we can hide it almost anywhere—as long as it's near a phone line. We've got to connect it to your phone line."

"So, while you're gathering all this other intelligence on my family, do you tap our phones, too?" I said it with a big silly smile.

Still, it put her a little off balance. "Oh *no,*" she said. "But we do use your phone line, at no cost to you, and at a time that won't inconvenience you."

Then she told me how, all across America at night, every night,

Nielsen's little black boxes silently call Nielsen's home office, delivering data. And she said, your family has been very carefully selected, so, please, help us make television better for everyone; please, let us install the equipment in your house.

I said, maybe I will, I'll think about it, and for days after that, while I kept wrestling with how to deal with Hirschfeld and Sensi, and how to warn Kerry without losing my life for warning him, she kept calling me, e-mailing me, pushing me. Apparently, the A. C. Nielsen Company really wanted to get its equipment into my house sometime very soon.

E-mail traffic of June 8, 2004:

> **From:** [Her Name]
> **To:** L.J. Kolb
> **Sent:** Tuesday, June 08, 2004 12:29 PM
> **Subject:** installation appt.
>
> Dear Larry,
> . . . I've rescheduled your appointment for June 15 Tues, at 10 AM. Please let me know as soon as possible if this date will work for you.
>
> Thanks very much.
>
> Sincerely,
> [Her Name]
> Nielsen Media
> Membership
>
>> **From:** L.J. Kolb
>> **Sent:** Tuesday, June 08, 2004 12:38 PM

To: [Her Name]

Subject: Re: installation appt.

We'll be out of town then. Sorry. Gotta run to a meeting now. LJK

From: [Her Name]

To: L.J. Kolb

Sent: Tuesday, June 08, 2004 1:00 PM

Subject: RE: installation appt.

Larry,

Please pick a day and time I will make it work on this end, we would really like to get you up and running.

Thanks very much.

[Her Name]

Nielsen Media

Membership

But on the eighth of June 2004, I had a lot more than the A. C. Nielsen Company on my mind. Such as how to avoid ending the week dead, or otherwise unavailable.

I didn't know John Kerry. If I cold-called his Senate office or his campaign headquarters, I'd be passed up a chain of so many well-meaning innocents that, before I ever got a chance to speak to anyone who could possibly understand, I'd be blown. If I assumed Kerry's team didn't include at least one mole working for Bush, I would be as naive as one of the innocents who would unwittingly compromise me if I gave them the chance.

At first, I thought I should find a way to meet directly with Kerry. But something about that worried me, and I had enough to worry about. When you're as scared as I was that week, you go to bed scared, you wake up scared, and, in my case, among other prophylactic measures, you begin buying and using prepaid telephone calling cards and disposable cell phones for all your secure telecommunications needs. God owns the universe, but the devil rules the earth. There was no end to my insecurity that week, and it seemed to me that, even if I could get myself a meeting with Kerry, it would be very insecure.

I'd never been on the road with a presidential candidate, but I was familiar with what had to be one of the closest things to it. A typical day overseas with Muhammad Ali included an intimate breakfast with twenty of Muhammad's new best friends, lunch with a couple hundred more, dinner with a thousand, everybody jostling to get to him at once. And, between meals, huge crowds, lots of kissing of babies, speeches, traffic jams, local dignitaries at every stop waiting to get in a word with the man, and nothing ever quite going according to plan. On the road, the rules and the schedule changed by the minute.

So, even if I was promised, say, a ten-minute meeting with John Kerry and his campaign manager at 11:20 A.M. in a secure backroom of the Kerry for President district office in East Somewhere, Ohio— the meeting simply wouldn't happen on schedule. Kerry would be a little late or a lot late, and by the time someone remembered to bring him to me, or me to him, someone else would be pulling on him, saying, "Senator, we've got to go *now*. We've got twelve minutes to the photo op at the V. A. Hospital," and someone else would be saying to me, "We're running late, so come on with us, and you can talk to him on the bus, or later on the plane." But I did not want to be the new face on the bus or the plane, did not want to talk about anything in front of even the smallest of crowds.

I had an old friend, Bill Dewey, an American lawyer who lived in London, but still spent a lot of time in the States and seemed to know a lot of powerful Democrats. As important, he knew me well and trusted me. I called him, told him I couldn't say much on the phone, but I needed a very private meeting with Kerry and his campaign manager. Bill snapped to it. "Right," he said, "I'm way the hell out in Suffolk at the moment. But I'll be back in London tonight and, when I get there, let me ring a friend in Boston." The next day, he called and told me Kerry would be spending the following weekend in Nantucket. If I really needed to meet with Kerry alone, that might be the best time and place to do it, and it could probably be arranged.

That sounded good, and for a couple of days it was the working plan. But then Bill called back and said the Nantucket weekend had been put off for a couple of weeks—so I could wait until then or, if I gave him some time, he would think of another plan.

I felt like I was in a race against a ticking bomb. Sensi and Hirschfeld had enough connections inside the government that, I suspected, by now they knew "Marshall" had been identified as Hirschfeld. And that, I thought, would incline Hirschfeld to accelerate the plan to burn Kerry through Farmer. I wasn't sure that what I needed to talk to Kerry about could wait two weeks. My reaction to Bill's news was perhaps a bit too taut and uneasy. If we hadn't been good friends for twenty-five years, he would've cut me dead the next time I called him.

Begging helped, but took a while. In the end, after several calls, I got Bill back on board only by telling him as much of the story as I dared on the phone, and promising to send him a set of the documents. You will remember Dave Morrison, who drove me, at speed, from the Hollywood Hills to his house in Bel-Air on the night of the day this all began for me. It was Dave I turned to now.

Dave Morrison and his wife, Sarah-Jane Wilde, and their son, on his first covert op, transported the documents for me from America to London. There was nothing classified about the documents, or illegal about transporting them. I just didn't want anybody else reading them. Most of the material traveled at the bottom of a diaper bag. But the key, a two-page outline showing how to connect the dots, was folded twice and double-sealed inside a Ziploc bag and flew right inside the diapers the boy pharaoh wore. On arrival, the beautiful Sarah-Jane put on a miniskirt and fishnet stockings and a trench coat and went out into the rain and hand-delivered the documents to Bill Dewey, who sent me an e-mail message informing me I had a meeting the next day in New York with someone who could help me— someone who didn't even know my name, and would instruct his guards to require no identification from me. I would arrive at the appointed time and place, I would be six feet six inches tall, I would say I was Mr. Sanders. And I would be let in.

New York, on the ninth of June 2004. It was ninety-one in the shade, and humid, hotter than the horse piss I could smell wafting over from Central Park. I was wearing a sincere blue suit, underneath it my shirt was wet with sweat, and I was scared shitless. But determined. I hadn't slept well, but I had just enough Red Bull in me to keep me moving up the sidewalk on the west side of Fifth Avenue.

Even if I were a Republican, even if I were a pro-war neocon Bush Republican, I would've kept walking up that street to warn John Kerry. Because Hirschfeld's way lay madness. His scheme might work, but I understood Hirschfeld well enough to know it was his nature that eventually the whole thing would be exposed, even if he had to expose it himself. This would've been, if not his masterpiece, one of them, and he was too proud an artist to let it pass without receiving public adulation for it. Deep down, all Richie wanted was to be loved. Someday, the truth would out, and if, when it did, the charges against Kerry had stuck and Bush had won reelection, that could turn into another Watergate. We didn't need that.

Already, Americans were losing their First, Fourth, and Fifth Amendment rights. Our economy was stagnant, our armed forces were underarmored and overextended. Our emergency response agencies were ill-prepared for another attack on America. Meanwhile, half the Muslim world was armed and pissed and rising up against us. We couldn't stand another Watergate now.

No one seemed to be following me, but, with so many people around, you can never really be sure of that. There was a time when I walked this city so incessantly that I knew every crack in these sidewalks. When I was twenty-two I'd moved here, making New York my first home after college, my first home on my own. I'd come back to live here a few times since. New York still felt like home. Which is not to say that I felt safe just then. I kept walking.

Was I about to make a fool of myself? Could Hirschfeld *possibly* make such outrageous charges against Kerry and Farmer stick, at least until the election? Adolf Hitler posited the Big Lie Theory, but it was his propaganda minister Joseph Goebbels who perfected it. "Think of the press," Goebbels said, "as a great keyboard on which the government can play." And as to the efficacy of outrageous lies for demonizing enemies, the more outrageous the lie the better. Dr. Goebbels again: "If you tell a lie big enough and keep repeating it, people will eventually come to believe it."

If you doubt that, consider that George Bush carries two fillings in his teeth given to him by a National Guard dentist in Alabama in the course of his service to America during the Vietnam War. While John Kerry carries shrapnel in his thigh from his service in the hot zone during the same war. But now, just a few months before the election, it was Kerry, recipient of the Silver Star, and the Bronze Star, and three Purple Hearts in Vietnam, who was on the defensive about his war record. All week I'd been thinking, *If Karl Rove learns about the harmonic convergence of Robert Farmer, WQNI, and Al-Qaeda's telecommunications and money-transfer company of choice before I warn Kerry, it will not end well.*

I'd been living on adrenaline and fear, but I was also driven to save the world. That was what the stakes felt like to me. I turned east on Sixty-fourth, then north on Madison for a few blocks, then east again. It was so fucking hot. I passed the address and doubled back. No one seemed to be following me.

It was time. I rang the bell, said my fake name into the intercom, and was buzzed in. I offered the security man no ID. He let me pass. There was no turning back now.

Another man in a suit walked with me up a staircase and passed me off to a pleasant and very efficient-looking woman, who showed me into another room and said to sit down, he would be with me shortly, and I did, and then he was, and that was how I came to find myself in a townhouse in New York—sitting at a round table beneath a particularly lovely Childe Hassam canvas—sipping tea and telling my story to a certain gray eminence of the Democratic Party who was in a position both to understand the covert world *and* to talk down to John Kerry.

———

He was an attorney. When he sat down across from me, I asked if I could retain him, if our conversation could be privileged and confidential.

He said, "Yes, that's fine."

I said, "Well, Counselor, that's good, because I don't want anyone to know my name in connection with this. But I think you should know I have a background in intelligence, in particular in covert political operations overseas, and I believe I've uncovered a plot to scuttle John Kerry's presidential campaign by linking him to Al-Qaeda."

That was enough to get his attention, and I'd planned it that way. From the moment I'd learned whom I'd be meeting, I'd decided to deliver my message in inverted-pyramid style. I figured someone like him, with so many demands on his time, would give me fifteen minutes at the most; more like three or four if I didn't grab his interest quickly.

After the sound-bite version, I gave him the three-minute version, and still he didn't ask me to leave. So then I told him the whole story, starting way back in the White House in 1985, and as I spoke, he interrupted occasionally, asked questions, took notes. I found I was no longer tired. I was curiously calm and had what felt like total recall. My briefcase was stuffed with documents, but I didn't refer to them once. I was spouting names, dates, places, linkages, spelling names for him when he asked.

Forty minutes passed before anyone interrupted us, and then it was only the steward asking if we wanted more tea. He was Filipino and wearing a white jacket—just like the stewards in the White House mess. A complex, three-way discussion ensued, about beverages, beverage temperatures, the humidity outside, caffeine. Before it was over, we'd both switched to Diet Cokes. I went back to telling the story.

An hour later, I'd brought the timeline up to the present and he was still rapt, but now he glanced at his watch and said, "I had no idea of the time. Unfortunately, I've got to chair a meeting across town in twenty minutes."

I nodded, and was just starting to thank him for his hospitality when he interrupted. There was a gleam in his eyes now. "Wow!" he said. "I knew there had to be people like you still around. I just haven't met one in a while."

What could I say to that? I just smiled back at him.

"Before I go, a couple questions," he said. "Do you think the Bush campaign knows about this?"

"I don't know," I said, "but I hope not. Part of me says Hirschfeld can't be running free in America without somebody in Washington watching his back. Another part of me says never underestimate either Hirschfeld or the incompetence of certain federal agencies."

"Would you meet with Kerry and Farmer to explain this to them?"

"If I have to," I said. "But I'm wary of my name surfacing. As far as I know, you don't even know my real name, do you?"

"I don't." He was getting up from the table now. "You're just a friend of our friend."

I picked up my briefcase. "For now I'd like to keep it that way."

"That's all right. We can do it like that," he said. Then he added: "And I'd like it if you'd leave my name out of this, too." Which was how he became, for our purposes, the Gray Eminence.

He crossed the room and shook my hand, and said, "I'll be in touch, and thank you very, very much," and then he was gone.

———

Outside, after a few minutes of window-shopping on Madison Avenue, my shirt was stuck to my back and I headed to my hotel to change. I would've had me followed. I would've had anyone who walked in and told me a story as incendiary as the one I'd just told put under surveillance at once—to see if he was consorting with the enemy. And while I was having me followed, I also would've verified every detail I'd said was public record, and tried to get as much of a handle as possible on everything else I'd alleged. All that following and fact-checking, though, would have to be done very quietly.

I ditched my suit and put on a linen shirt and a billowy linen jacket, then headed out for lunch with my friend Daniel Raymont. The taxi driver I flagged down about went apoplectic after I climbed into his cab and told him we were going to Brooklyn. It was too late now to claim he was off duty. He spanked the steering wheel, then turned around and glared at me. "Do you have directions? How am I supposed to find my way around in *Brooklyn*?"

"Relax," I said. "It's only Peter Luger. I can find it. It's right on the other side of the Williamsburg Bridge."

He calmed down. "Why didn't you say Peter Luger's?"

He calmed down even more when I asked where he was from and he said Lima, Peru, and I spent the next few minutes charming him with my arcane knowledge of Lima neighborhoods. Some people, you've just got to find their soft spots if you're going to have even a halfway pleasant conversation with them. No one seemed to follow us when we got off the bridge and wound our way to the restaurant.

Inside, it was sometime between lunchtime and dinnertime. But people were still waiting for tables. After I'd gotten enough of the air-conditioning to tide me over, I went out to the sidewalk to wait for Daniel.

Across the street was a beautiful Old World building. "The Williamsburgh Savings Bank" was chiseled into the front of it. But it was owned and occupied now by the Hongkong and Shanghai Banking Corporation Limited, with its omnipresent red-and-white logo. Shimmering in the sunlight way off to my left were the gray towers of the Williamsburg Bridge. I was looking that way when she came around the corner of Driggs and Broadway and walked right past me.

Beauty in a minor key. All nuance and mystery. Light brown hair; most of it was pulled off her neck and pinned up because of the terrible heat. She was maybe five eight or nine, including her platform sandals; the cork was worn slightly on the insides of the heels. I watched her moving away from me up Broadway toward the Marcy Avenue Station. It used to be you had to go to India to see so much skin on a woman's midriff on a city street. Not anymore. Fully five inches above her belt, there were lovely dimples on her pelvic crests and a nice little mole on the back of her right hip. There was something special about the way she walked, something feminine but determined, as if she knew she had secret reserves of strength.

Daniel arrived from somewhere, walked right past her. He was wearing cowboy boots and jeans and a bright red cowboy shirt. He stopped in front of me, shook my hand, and said, "Whassup, bwana?"

Daniel had a reservation, and a thick German accent when he informed the hostess he was the Herr Doktor Raymont on her list. She took us straight to a table. By the time we made it there, he was thanking her profusely, in Cockney.

The decor was Tudor–German-beer-hall fusion. White plaster walls and dark beams, wainscoted, with two-foot-tall beer steins displayed all over the place. Daniel, who's an actor, ordered in his natural voice. Then, when our waiter had headed off to the kitchen, Daniel addressed me in the tones of a Deep South redneck. "Now, Mr. Kolb. I should warn you it's the tradition here that the service is pleasantly surly. Fuck you, but with a smile. It's part of the act. So don't be surprised if when he comes back here that old boy slams our plates down on the table and walks off."

Soon enough, the waiter slammed plates down in front of us and Daniel worked his way through a whole lot of accents while we ate the best steaks in New York, and I checked the faces of everyone who came in and out of the room.

Afterward we walked to the Marcy Avenue Station and clanged our way up the metal stairs to the elevated railroad tracks. While we waited for a train to Manhattan, two guys who'd been in the restaurant a couple of tables away from us came trotting up the stairs. Look—I told myself—probably a quarter of the people who eat at Peter Luger head back into the city by train from this station. It doesn't mean anything.

Late the next morning, I was in Tribeca and walking up West Broadway—just a few blocks north of Ground Zero—when I picked up a voicemail message from the Gray Eminence. He'd called the number I'd given him for my new, prepaid, disposable cell phone. He said he was in Washington, which didn't surprise me; everyone in his world was convening in Washington that day to attend the funeral of Ronald Reagan the following morning. What he needed now, he said, was a full set of the documents and a memorandum, not longer than two pages, covering everything I'd told him when we met.

I kept walking. Up West Broadway, then through three blocks of the chaos and tight squeezes of Canal Street, made to order for forcing watchers into the open, then around a corner and up Mercer, and around another corner onto Broome—and no one seemed to be following me. Not Democrats, or Republicans, or Hirschfeld or any of his friends. Not even the A. C. Nielsen Company. I seemed to be clear.

I spent a couple of hours up in my friend John Alexander's loft on Broadway—shooting the shit with John and our friend Van Schley, watching John paint, watching John boil us some shrimp, eating shrimp—and when I left, though I actually needed to go uptown, I walked downtown first. I did this only partly because I wanted to take one more shot at flushing out watchers—I'd pretty much given up on that—and mostly because I wanted to know what the hell they sold in a store named Yellow Rat Bastard. It was just down the block from the entrance to John's building, and it turned out to be a purveyor of the latest in urban streetwear.

At Broadway and Grand, I hung a left, then seemed to change my mind, turned, and went back around the corner and onto Broadway. Nobody froze. Nobody looked away or changed direction. Nobody cared. I turned around again and headed east on Grand. Two pages or less. How was I going to manage that? Maybe if I squeezed the margins and used small type. It was Miles who taught me that the shorter you have to make the text, the longer it takes to write it.

Sometime years earlier, I'd read an article by someone, maybe it was Norman Mailer, who offered a theory that every living thing is at every moment either strengthening or dissipating, and that when it is not acting bravely it begins to dissipate at a disproportionate rate. The thought had stuck with me, and perhaps it explained why I'd felt so dissipated for so long. After ten years on the beach hiding from agents of the Indian government, you wouldn't feel brave either. But now I was beginning to feel myself strengthening. I was afraid, but going ahead anyway, and that felt good.

I crossed Crosby Street, against the light, weaving through slow-moving traffic, and walked past Edison ParkFast: "We accept Master-Card, Visa, Discover, American Express, Diners Club, and License."

If you really wanted to connect the dots all the way back, there was no reason to stop at Bush introducing us to Sensi in 1985, or even at Casey and the October Surprise in 1980. It wasn't unreasonable to draw a line all the way back to Watergate itself. You wouldn't find Karl Rove's name in *All the President's Men,* but search the record carefully enough and you would find a 1973 *Washington Post* story about Rove's role in the 1972 presidential election. The Watergate investigations exposed a broad pattern of political espionage and sabotage conducted by Republican operatives against Democrats. The Republican operatives called their sabotage operations ratfucking, and the chief ratfucker was one Donald Segretti. During the 1972 campaign, young Karl Rove was a protégé and disciple of the chief ratfucker himself.

Rove had been ratfucking for Republicans ever since. His specialty was demonizing Democrats, and he was at his most effective in neck-and-neck races. Now that he was George W. Bush's chief political strategist and covert political operative—or "Turd Blossom" as the President preferred to call him—would Rove balk if Hirschfeld or an intermediary approached him with a scheme to link Kerry with Al-Qaeda? Read Rove's record, and you decide.

I wondered if I should try to fit *that* into the two-page memorandum. Probably not, I thought, but I would throw the *Post* story into the stack of documents. And while I was at it, I'd better make a set of documents for Engin Yesil; the Turk's life was on the line every bit as much as Kerry's candidacy. Somewhere behind me, a light changed, engines rumbled, cars and trucks pulled out. From somewhere else, a siren started up and faded quickly away. I crossed Centre Street and, as I did, beheld a magnificent building that, in this city of architectural wonders, I'd somehow never noticed before.

It was a big, white stone Edwardian baroque building with a dome on top, and it seemed to take up the entire block. When I got to the sidewalk on the other side of the street, I found the cornerstone. It was worn smooth in places and chipped in others. To read it, I had to back up a bit—that problem with my eyes I mentioned earlier. And when I backed up, I turned around to make sure I didn't bump into anyone. That, I realize now, was the only reason I saw the girl. She was stuck, couldn't keep standing there now that I'd seen her, so she walked past me.

After I read the cornerstone—POLICE / DEPARTMENT / THE / CITY OF NEW YORK / ~ MCMV—I fell into pace behind the girl, and my God she was beautiful!

She was in a hurry to get somewhere. She had short hair, so blonde it was almost white, in a pageboy cut, and she was wearing low-slung army-green fatigue pants. There was a lot of tan skin showing between the top of her pants and the bottom of her little yellow tank top. I was close enough to see tiny beads of sweat on the small of her back and nestling in the dimples in her pelvic crests. On her feet were gold lamé flats that were quite wonderful because the toes were pointy and twisted up toward the sky, in the style preferred by genies who reside in lamps. The heels were worn slightly on the insides. There was a little mole on the back of her lovely right hip, and it was only when I noticed it that I finally realized she was the same girl who'd walked past me the day before in Brooklyn.

She had the same determined walk. It was her, no doubt about it, and still I didn't get it. For the longest, stupidest moment, I saw it as just a miraculous coincidence and was thankful to get another look at her. Midblock, there were two stone lions guarding massive wrought-iron doors. It was such a beautiful building.

But her hair was different, and I realized now she was wearing a wig. Finally, I twigged to what was happening to me. My heart sped up but I slowed down and she kept going.

At the next corner, Broome Street, she turned right and, half a minute later, so did I. But the girl was gone. I turned around and headed back down Centre Street. Between the two lions were six steps leading up to the wrought-iron doors. I walked up the steps and a security man opened a door just enough for me to see his face and a chandelier sparkling behind him. "What is this building now?" I said. "Does it still belong to the police?"

"It's a private residence," he said, in tones that meant *Go away and never come back.* He shut the door.

It was hotter than hell, and humid. Except for horns blaring and petrocarbons on the breeze, the ambiance was swamplike. I strolled back up to the corner of Broome and Centre and turned right again, and there she was, just around the corner, trying to look lost. She turned away from me too quickly, or did I just imagine that? A block east was Mulberry Street, bare white lightbulbs festooned above the street, the entrance to Little Italy. I almost went that direction, but then turned around, crossed Centre, and hurried one block to Lafayette. I led, she followed, and so we danced through the streets. But I never made eye contact, and there were so many people with us on the sidewalks that maybe she thought I didn't see her.

When I got to Lafayette, I turned left, walked south twenty yards, then turned round and went back to the southeast corner of Broome and Lafayette. And there she was, about to turn the corner. Stuck again. She did her best to look lost. As if she didn't know whether to go south now, toward the sign that said "A. Trenkmann/Estate, Inc./Real Estate/established 1917," or just which way to turn.

The corner was messy and teeming. I stood on the curb with a bunch of people waiting to cross Broome. When the light changed to WALK, everyone moved but me. I just stood there, looking up at the second floor of the building across the street from me. "Sandra Cameron Dance Center," it said in the window. "Waltz. Tango. Hustle." On the south face of that same building hung seven air conditioners. I looked east, then west. And then I turned around, and she was almost right behind me. She turned, too, when she saw me, and now she finally seemed to find the place she'd been looking for all this time. It was the shop on this very corner: Double G Graphic Inc. And that was surprising, because Double G Graphic Inc. was inhabited solely by Asian ladies and gentlemen and its business was printing menus for Chinese and Japanese restaurants. Lost no more, she stepped confidently toward the glass door of Double G Graphic Inc., and what I did next was, in the ways of the secret world, very bad etiquette.

I wish I could tell you what I felt then was courage. But the truth is I felt like crying. Confronted—in the form of the girl in the gold lamé genie shoes—by unshakable evidence that I was under surveillance, for a moment I felt about as dissipated as I ever had in my life. *How could I let myself get back into this?* was the thought that came to me in that moment. I'd done a favor for a friend in the government, better than the government's own intelligence agencies had managed to do it—and wasn't that intoxicating! Now I was dodging through traffic and backtracking around lower Manhattan like a rat in a maze.

Then I remembered my training—London, Miles in the background, his man Tex speaking to me: *"Don't ever get cute. Don't make eye contact with a watcher. Don't play cat and mouse with watchers. Don't send a bottle of wine to their table across the room. Remain oblivious."* But that was so many years ago, and I'd been out of it for so long. When I no longer felt like crying, what I felt was fury. I hustled over to the door of Double G Graphic Inc. and held it open for the girl.

"That was stupid," Tex whispered in my ear, and the girl turned and drifted away, east toward Mulberry Street. She drew a phone to her mouth, and I imagined her announcing to someone that she was blown and I was an asshole. I found myself a taxi, got in, asked Mohamed Iqbal to take me to 600 Third Avenue. Then I sat back and contemplated how the central equation of my life had changed over the past twenty-four hours. I'd done what I felt I had to do. And my life was rich now with possibilities, though not all of them were good. Circumstances that had not yet transpired would determine whether the next January would find me in Washington at an inauguration or somewhere just outside Bumfuck, Egypt, in a safe house. Before I got out of the cab, I turned on my new, and disposable, cell phone and stuffed it between the cushion and the backrest of the passenger seat. Let them follow that for a while.

6. MENDING WALL

Back at home in Florida, three days later, I wrote the memo and got it to the man in New York. After that, all I could do was wait. All this time, I'd been ahead of the information curve. Now it was ahead of me, and I felt powerless.

Two days passed before the Gray Eminence left a voicemail message for me, no name, no number, just his voice and a request that I call him.

When I did, he said, "Well, Kerry's people have been warned of your suspicions."

"And?" I said.

"And it's the considered opinion of the top people in Kerry's team that you can't prove it."

"Prove what?"

"Farmer's got a title," he said, down a crystal-clear line from New York, "but he's not even really all that important to the Kerry campaign. He was given the title because he's been helpful to the party for so long, but this year he's not even all that involved. So even if Farmer's company is merging with a company that can be linked to Al-Qaeda, which is a stretch on its own, there's no way to prove Kerry's in on it."

"And do you agree with that?" I said.

"Not entirely. So what I called to ask is do you have anything more, any new information I can pass on."

"They're all lawyers, or most of them are, aren't they?"

"Yes."

"Well, actually, I don't have any new information," I said. "But I'd appreciate it if you'd pass on to them that I said they should pull their heads out of their asses for a few minutes and stop thinking like lawyers. Of course it can't be proved that Kerry and Farmer are tied to Al-Qaeda money. There's no evidence which would convict them in a criminal court. But that's irrelevant. Because the objective isn't to put Kerry or Farmer in jail; it's to smear them. All that matters here is appearances. That nonsense about Farmer not really being very involved in Kerry's campaign, only having a title—try explaining that fine point to voters if suddenly it comes out that Farmer is now the chairman of a company controlled by an ex-convict Muslim Turk with ties, however nebulous, to Al-Qaeda. Give me a break!

"One thing I *can* prove is this merger with John Kerry's campaign treasurer was orchestrated by a pair of longtime Republican covert operatives. Do they think that's a coincidence?"

He started to say something, but I kept talking. "Ask them," I said, "if they remember all the hullabaloo about Pete Townshend being a pederast, downloading child pornography, et cetera, et cetera, even while he protested he was innocent. Ask them if they remember seeing the TV footage, the front-page photos, the detailed newspaper accounts of his arrest. They'll remember that—because the media went balls to the wall with it. Then ask them if they remember seeing the little newspaper story about the charges being dropped, the police announcing that, after a thorough investigation, they realized Mr. Townshend was innocent. That story, of course, was only two or three paragraphs long, stuffed somewhere in the middle of the paper. And that story came out maybe a year after Townshend's arrest. A story about Kerry and Farmer and Al-Qaeda wouldn't have to last long. Just until the election."

"Point taken," said the Gray Eminence. "And I will pass it along to them."

"Let me ask you this," I said. "Has Kerry himself been told about this?"

"Everyone on the Kerry team, at the highest level, knows." He said it in a way which made plain it was the only answer I was going to get. At first I thought he might not know, but then I realized that was absurd. His answer meant *You're not cleared to know that.* Maybe his answer also meant *Read between the lines.*

"What about Farmer?" I said.

"Yes, Farmer has been told."

"And?"

"And Farmer is shocked."

"They all should be shocked," I said.

"I'm going to give them your message," said the Gray Eminence. "And I'm going to tell them I'm a good judge of people and it's clear to me you are who you say you are. You do understand intelligence, you have been around the covert world—I can tell—you know of what you speak. They should take this more seriously, I believe. That's what I'll tell them, and that's about all I can do."

After that he said good-bye, and about all I could do was wait. Again. And watch for a black Mercedes coming up my street. Those were long days of heat waves rising off my neighbors' rooftops, white skies with a silver sun. And dread. If I'd had something more to do, I would've been fine. But sitting and waiting, not knowing what was happening, ate at me. If Hirschfeld or Sensi came, before evil could start I would slip out my back door and through the thicket of saw palmettos and Spanish bayonets in the twenty-acre wood. It wasn't much of a plan, but it was the only one I had. I'd learnt the way long ago. No one else would be able to find it. Not in a hurry. Tex again, while training me in London: *"Life is all about escape routes. Don't forget that. Ever."*

But they never came. Hirschfeld and Sensi were already in hiding. As to who in the hierarchy of the FBI or elsewhere in our national security apparatus was willing to forgive Hirschfeld his trespasses, and tip him off that the Miami office of the FBI was about to arrest him, your guess is as good as mine. Someone did.

"Marshall" and Sensi were invited to lunch by an old friend—who was in league with the FBI. They accepted, and a date and time and place were agreed. When the date came, FBI Special Agents hid inside and outside the restaurant, which was somewhere in Miami, ready to pounce when Hirschfeld and Sensi arrived. But Hirschfeld and Sensi did not arrive.

Does that sound a little sketchy to you? It did to me, but it was all I was told. I never managed to learn further details.

At first I thought it might have been some animal logic, an innate sense of danger that told them not to show up at the restaurant. But then someone else told me this: On the day before the lunch appointment, Hirschfeld drove up to Radiant's offices in the black Mercedes—like he'd done a hundred times before. He got out of the car and was walking through the parking lot toward the building when his cell phone rang. He answered cheerfully, spoke for a few seconds, grew agitated. He hurried back into the car, took a quick look over his shoulder, then drove away, and was never seen at the Turk's offices again.

Who saw that and when, exactly, did it happen? It was the day before the lunch that wasn't. Other than that, I didn't know.

It seemed that, all that week, everything I heard was stale and vague. I was out of the loop.

Days after it had happened, Gary Messina told me the FBI had found the place Hirschfeld and Sensi had been living. In a luxury high-rise condominium building called The Pinnacle, on the beach in Sunny Isles, Florida, a Miami suburb just north of Bal Harbour. They'd shared the place with a fellow going by the name of David Phipps. *The third man,* who the hell was he? Phipps said he was an Englishman, and the managing director of Growth Enterprise Fund, S.A. And what was that? Why, of course, Hirschfeld and Phipps claimed, Growth Enterprise Fund S.A., headquartered in the United Kingdom, was "the CIA's secret pension fund, with assets in excess of twenty billion dollars." By the time the FBI got to The Pinnacle, Hirschfeld and Sensi and Phipps had melted into air, into thin air, and left not a rack behind.

Not knowing even who all the players were anymore, let alone who was doing what to whom, was decidedly bad for my appetite. The only good thing about being out of the loop, I thought, was maybe Hirschfeld didn't know who had fingered him. Maybe I would never be found out. Gary Messina promised me he'd made sure no government records on the identification of "Marshall" contained any reference to me. And I believe him. It wasn't Gary who blew my cover.

One night a friend from Washington called and told me Hirschfeld had been making phone calls to the United States but masking where they originated. And that the government believed Hirschfeld had slipped away to Cuba. Sensi—my friend informed me—had been sighted in Boston and Dubai. Maybe also in Mexico. But that was all my friend would say.

"It's all smoke," Gary said when I called him the next morning to ask if he had any details. "For all we know, they're probably staying in a hotel suite in Washington. Or maybe in the Lincoln Bedroom. Or Dick Cheney's bunker."

"Anyway," Gary went on, "here's one fact you can take to the bank: Sensi was in Washington earlier this week, seeing a psychiatrist. Socially, not professionally. Sensi's lost a lot of weight, I mean like maybe even thirty pounds, and he told the shrink he'd never really liked Marshall much."

"How do you know that?" I asked.

"For now," Gary told me, "you're going to have to take my word for it."

I did. Hirschfeld and Sensi were still at it. And at least one of them was somewhere in the United States. I couldn't shake the feeling something bad was going to happen.

The next time the Gray Eminence called, there was a new urgency in his voice. "The Kerry team gets it now," he said. "They're on the case. And Farmer has retained counsel to help him through this."

It had been less than a week since we'd talked last, but a lot had been happening. How much of that was due to Kerry? I wondered. Had the FBI given Hirschfeld a pass until Kerry demanded action? Maybe. I didn't know. And I was pretty sure no one was going to tell me.

"The attorney representing Farmer is a great guy," the Gray Eminence continued. "His name is Greg Craig. Do you know who he is?"

"Former White House Counsel?"

"Yes. That's him."

Greg Craig was White House Counsel for a time during the
Clinton administration. That was about all I could remember. But
while the Gray Eminence and I spoke, I Googled Craig and learned
more: Gregory B. Craig, currently a partner in the law firm Williams
& Connolly, Washington, D.C.; educated at Harvard College, Cam-
bridge University, and Yale Law School. Since Yale Law, a friend of
Bill Clinton and Hillary Rodham; White House Counsel, 1998–1999;
quarterbacked Clinton's impeachment defense team and presented
Clinton's defense to the Senate. Former senior advisor to Madeleine
Albright and Ted Kennedy. In private practice, Craig's clients had included Alexander Solzhenitsyn, Juan Miguel Gonzalez, the father of
Elian Gonzalez, and, during Watergate, *The Washington Post* and various of its reporters.

"He's a great friend of mine," the Gray Eminence was saying,
"has been for years. And he's just a terrific lawyer. I trust him, and you
should, too. I say that because of what I'm going to ask you to do
next. I know you want to stay anonymous, use me as a buffer. But I
don't know the facts half as well as you do. And Greg would like to
hear the background, from you. If you'll do it, you don't have to tell
him your name. Use my name and he'll take your call. It would be
very helpful."

"Who would I be doing this for?" I said. "Just Farmer? Or Farmer
and Kerry?"

"At the moment," he said, "all their interests and fates are pretty
much intertwined, don't you think?"

Apparently, I'd asked another question to which I wasn't cleared for anything more than a Delphic answer.

"And you want me to do this?" I said.

"Yes, please," said the Gray Eminence.

"Okay. I'll do it," I said, and then I took down Greg Craig's number and called him.

Greg Craig was affable as hell, and we talked for maybe twenty minutes. He thanked me profusely, twice, first for what I'd done, and later for the information I was giving him, while he slowly, cordially, sucked that information out of me. And after that, every time I called him looking for a bit of reciprocity, for information on what was going on, he stonewalled me.

"To be frank," Craig said—during my second phone call to him, just a couple of days after my first phone call to him—"your question troubles me, because I'm not quite sure what your continuing interest in this matter is. Why do you want to know?"

"Well, *gee*," I said, "Sensi and Hirschfeld are still on the loose. I'm the one that provided the background on the both of them and identified Hirschfeld. I presume you've been in touch with the FBI about this, and that you know more than I do about what's going on. I live in Florida. If they're still here, or if they're armed and dangerous and on the run, or if they happen to know who Homeland Security got its information from, I sure as hell would like to know about it—because I'm too young to die."

When Bob Chastain left for Vienna in December 1989, he told friends he was going to meet with Richard Hirschfeld and Mohamed Al-Fassi to close a deal. Instead, Chastain was found dead in a hotel room, a pill bottle next to his bed. Viennese authorities ruled he had died "by his own hand," from an overdose of barbiturates. Chastain's body was placed in a steel coffin, which was welded shut, and flown to the United States. It wasn't opened before the burial, but Chastain's ex-wife, his children, his mother, and several reporters saw his face through a window built into the coffin. There was no question it was Chastain. But when the FBI applied for a court order to exhume the body four and a half years later, they said they believed Chastain was still alive and the body inside the coffin wasn't his. Chastain's ex-wife said, "That's ridiculous. They were looking for foul play. They were looking to involve Richard Hirschfeld." Hirschfeld had, after all, collected nearly five million dollars from an insurance policy on his ex-partner's life.

Maybe the FBI did find evidence of foul play. Maybe they did involve Hirschfeld. I didn't know. Other than confirming that the man in the steel coffin was Chastain, the FBI never made known the results of their investigation. That was perhaps because, by the time the investigation was completed, Hirschfeld had fled the country.

Greg Craig wasn't moved by my concerns. He said he didn't see how he could help me.

So I called the Gray Eminence next, and after he'd heard my complaint, he paused long enough to make sure I was listening very carefully when he finally spoke. "I think you've done a terrific job," he said. "It's amazing, really, how you put all this together. But now you're the messenger, and as you know from reading *Oedipus*, sometimes the messenger gets killed."

Those were his exact words. I wrote them down because they pissed me off so much. I growled something back at him, can't remember exactly what it was. He said, "Look, just take care of yourself. And I'll try to warn you if I hear of anything that's imminent. Greg's a good guy. I'll follow up on this."

I calmed down and thanked him and I even believed him, but in the end it would be the Gray Eminence and Greg Craig together who blew my cover.

Meanwhile, the Nielsen lady kept calling me, the Jehovah's Witnesses never came back, America was still in schism, the insurgency was ratcheting up the chaos in Iraq, polls said Kerry had the slightest of leads over Bush, and I decided to take a new, proactive stance and do whatever I had to to get back in front of the information curve. I called lawyers, lots of lawyers, all friends of mine, and all of whom represented me in various capacities. I told each of them what I'd discovered and what I'd been up to, and that if an elephant happened to run over me anytime soon, or I was found in a hotel room in Vienna with a bottle of pills by my side, or if John Ashcroft locked me up and refused me access even to attorneys, I wanted all of Christendom to know the background. Otherwise, our conversations were to remain privileged.

Dan Schwartz, once the general counsel of the world's largest spy agency, the NSA, had assisted me in removing classified information from *Overworld*. Dan left the NSA and is in private practice now; but once you've been initiated into the secret society of America's intelligence services, you are never entirely out. Dan had friends in all sorts of interesting places. Early in July, I went to Washington and met with Dan in his offices, just three blocks from the White House.

Many times since then I have thought about that meeting, and how things might've gone for me if I hadn't had the inspiration I had toward the end of our conversation. I told Dan the story. I gave him a set of the documents. I asked him to tell every newspaper reporter on earth about it if anything happened to me. Then I remembered something Vince Messina had told me by phone earlier in the day. Engin Yesil needed an attorney.

I'd warned Yesil by sending a set of documents on Hirschfeld and Sensi to him in care of Vince, who agreed not to reveal my name to his client. Farmer had also warned Yesil. And therein lay a problem, one of many Yesil faced at the moment. The merger between WQNI and Ntera couldn't just be called off without explanation. The deal had been announced. WQNI was publicly traded, so the SEC was involved and full disclosure was required by law. What the press releases about the deal hadn't made clear, however, was that the CIA, FBI, DEA, IRS, and pretty much the whole Department of Homeland Security were also involved. It was a mess. Extricating Yesil from it was going to require someone who not only had the talents of a corporate attorney but also knew the back channels and players of the Washington intelligence community.

Dan Schwartz has a neat gray beard and the subtle, inscrutable intellect of a Graham Greene double agent. His face tells you nothing, until he wants it to. He is calm, until he needs to be something other than calm. And he was sitting right across the boardroom table from me. All of a sudden, Dan Schwartz looked like just the man— for Engin Yesil and for me.

"Dan," I said, "I think I have a client for you. Engin Yesil, the Turk, who you will remember is the most recent victim of Messrs. Hirschfeld and Sensi, needs a Washington attorney in the worst way. I think I could arrange for him to retain you. If I did that, I would only ask this: If ever you learn I may be in jeopardy—for example, if you find out Hirschfeld and Sensi know I identified Hirschfeld for the Feds—you'll warn me right away."

Dan smiled a sad smile and spoke in cautionary tones. "I would entertain representing him," he said. "But *he* would be my client, not you.

Whatever information I obtained representing him would be privileged. So I couldn't warn you of anything without his permission."

"I understand that," I said. "And all I ask is, if you find out I have a problem, right away you will tell him you happen to know who warned him and that you'd like his permission to warn me."

"I can do that. I'll agree to that," Dan said.

So that same afternoon—just four months away now from the presidential election Engin Yesil had been saved from inadvertently playing a large role in—I arranged, through Vince Messina, for Engin Yesil, who didn't even know my name, to retain Dan Schwartz to represent him in his dealings with Robert Farmer, Richard Hirschfeld, Robert Sensi, various of their affiliated companies, and the gaggle of government agencies breathing down their necks. And it was a few weeks after that that Dan Schwartz informed me I'd been blown.

Miles would've told me it was my fault more than anyone else's, and he would've been right.

One of the first things he taught me was: *Trust no one.*

Just because the Gray Eminence had agreed to treat our relationship as privileged didn't mean I should trust him to keep his word. Leaving behind even one biographical trace of myself to be tweezed out of the two-page memo the Gray Eminence requested of me was colossally stupid.

True, I addressed it to him specifically in his capacity as an attorney, my attorney, I marked it PRIVILEGED AND CONFIDENTIAL at the top of both pages, and, in my opening paragraph, I thanked him for allowing me to retain him in order to warn Kerry "in a manner so secure that my identity will not be exposed to those who would wish to harm me in connection herewith." The Gray Eminence had to have understood I didn't want anyone else to see the memorandum.

"Larry," Dan Schwartz said, "I'm calling to tell you that yesterday Greg Craig circulated to the other parties in the WQNI-Ntera transaction a memorandum which seems to be written by the person who, in consultation with the Department of Homeland Security, identified 'Mr. Marshall' as 'Mr. Hirschfeld.'"

"Oh, shit," I said. "Does it have my name on it? Because I never put my name on any memorandum relating to this."

"Your name's not on it."

"How many pages is it?"

"Two."

"Who's it addressed to?"

"There's no addressee."

"Does it say 'Privileged and Confidential' at the top?"

"Not at the top of the first page. But it does at the top of the second page."

"Son of a bitch!" I said. "I never would've believed it. He redacted his own identity and 'Privileged and Confidential' off the top of the document. Then he sent it to his buddy Greg Craig!"

"That's what I was thinking."

"So he protected himself, but not me."

"It seems so," Dan said. "Your name's not on it, but it might as well be."

"How so?"

"Well," Dan said, "in the second paragraph, it says, 'In early 1985, when the Reagan White House secretly asked my friend Muhammad Ali to use his credibility in the Muslim world to engage in a covert dialogue with the Ayatollah Khomeini to try to procure release of hostages in Beirut, Vice President Bush gave me the business card of Robert M. Sensi.' I've read your book, and as soon as it comes out, anyone who reads it and reads this memo is going to know who wrote it. And Sensi and Hirschfeld won't even need to read your book to know who wrote this memo.

"In the third paragraph, you say, 'In 1985, I went to Beirut with Mr. Ali, and others, including Messrs. Sensi and Hirschfeld.' And in the fifth paragraph, you say, 'In 1986, I was in Cairo with Mr. Ali, Mr. Hirschfeld, and others, when I took a call from Ferdinand Marcos.'" Dan paused. Then he seemed to be speaking both for himself and for Miles when he added, "You didn't really need to write it in the *first* person."

I stopped to think.

"I did it that way," I finally said, "because I wanted to remind him I knew this story firsthand, that it wasn't something I'd fabricated, or heard from someone else. I did it that way to convey credibility. Shit! So what did Craig say about how he got it?"

"He didn't say how he got it, only that he had received it, and it's material so he had to give it to the other parties."

"Parties? Isn't your client the only other party? Who else did Craig give it to?"

"No," Dan said. "WQNI has separate counsel. Greg Craig is representing Bob Farmer personally. That's how seriously Farmer and the Democrats are taking this."

"And as I understand it," I said, "now that my own lawyer has breached privilege, it's no longer a protected document. It *is* material. Craig *did* have to give it up. Now third parties have it and, as far as the law is concerned, they could print it in a newspaper if they wanted to."

"That's true," Dan said. "But they won't."

"Why?"

"It gets better."

"Go on."

"The WQNI attorneys Craig gave the memo to are from Baker Botts."

Baker Botts was the venerable Houston law firm of one James A. Baker, III, Secretary of State to the first President Bush, senior counselor to the Carlyle Group, and engineer of the second President Bush's dodgy recount victory in Florida. "I'm totally fucked," I said, "aren't I?"

"Well," Dan said, "Jim Baker's not involved in this personally. But partners of his are. Normally, they wouldn't talk with Baker about a transaction like this. But they're free to. In the normal course of business, they're probably not used to running across M&A documents that read like spy novels and suggest a pair of rogue CIA agents and Republican operatives with long ties to the family of the sitting president of the United States are currently consorting with the Russian mafia *and* running a covert op against the Democratic candidate for president."

Dan took a breath, or paused for effect, or both. "I don't know if Baker's seen this," he said. "But I think you've got to assume he has."

"Which means," I said, "I've got to assume the White House has also seen it."

"I would," Dan said.

"Which also means," I said, "I've got to assume Sensi and Hirschfeld have seen it, too."

Dan said, "I would think you've got to, to be safe. Wouldn't you?"

I let out a long, deep breath, then thanked Dan for warning me, and soon enough after that got off the phone and went into hiding, from my own stupidity, from big-time Democrats who didn't seem to care if the messenger got killed, from Sensi and Hirschfeld, and God knew how many other Republican operatives.

On a street corner in Washington, Gary Messina slid up beside me in a pale Mercedes. He'd already unlocked the front door. I slipped into the front seat and we were off in seconds. Gary's in his early fifties, I think, but looks younger than his age. It must be the Messina genes. He was wearing a beautiful lightweight blue suit and a white dress shirt, no tie. "I hope you don't mind that I came casual," he said.

"Not a problem," I said, and I pulled off my own tie, rolled it up, and stuffed it into a pocket of my suit jacket.

There are two schools of thought about talking in cars. Miles taught me to think of every car I'm ever in as a rolling recording studio. "In a car," he said, "never say anything you don't want everyone to hear." On the other hand, a car can be very effective as a rolling safe house. Think of how long the D.C. snipers evaded one of the most extensive manhunts in history, just by staying in their car. CIA officers routinely debrief agents in cars.

Shake off any watchers. Pick up your man, or woman, at a pre-arranged location, or, if still under surveillance when you reach that location, at a prearranged fallback. Drive around while debriefing and instructing and paying your source. Then drop off the source someplace busy and crowded and drive away. It happens every day and every night, in major capitals and backwater satrapies the world over.

If Gary's car were wired for sound, that would suit me just fine. I hoped someone big and bad was listening to us. But I also hoped audio surveillance was the last thing on Gary's mind. "Now that we're alone," I said, "please be so kind as to tell me what the fuck's really going on."

Gary filled me in while we took the scenic route to Union Station.

Inside, we found a white-tablecloth restaurant and had dinner, and after that he walked with me to the tracks. There didn't seem to be a whole lot of post–September 11 security around the station or the trains or the cargo handlers or the passengers. In fact, there seemed to be none at all. "I'm sure," I said, "that the crack Homeland Security counterterrorism forces deployed here in case Al-Qaeda rolls into our capital with a trainload of nuclear weapons are all wide awake and watching all of this, and hidden just out of sight."

"Yeah, right," Gary said.

On a platform between two trains, we sat on a golf cart the Red Caps used for moving luggage. We talked some more, and it wasn't until they called my train that I remembered the book. I opened my briefcase and pulled out galleys of *Overworld* bound inside a thick paper facsimile of the dustjacket design. I was still trying to get used to a painting of my eyes staring out from just beneath the title. "These are uncorrected proofs," I said. "The book won't actually come out until sometime in the fall. Anyway, I hope you'll enjoy reading this."

I gave Gary the book and his face lit up. "Thanks so much," he said. "Would you please sign it to me?"

It was the first book I ever inscribed, and doing it felt oddly pretentious. I handed it back to him and said there was one more thing I needed. I asked him to speak with the man I'd be meeting the next day, to confirm to him the story I was telling was true. Gary said, yes, fine, he would do it, and I could give the man Gary's home phone number. Then he shook my hand and we said good-bye, and I hopped a night train to New York.

Between the depots and the city lights along the way, I stared out my window into the great American blackness and all I saw reflecting back at me was a king-hell of a fever dream—featuring fear, evil, the unknown. Who was behind this? I didn't know. Were Hirschfeld or Sensi after me? I didn't know. Were any of the President's men aware of this? I didn't know. But I had to assume the worst. Hirschfeld and Sensi acting on their own, to curry favor from Bush and Rove after the fact, that was scary enough. Especially if they already knew what I'd done. Hirschfeld and Sensi working in concert with Rove, that was terrifying.

I'd been led to believe Sensi and Hirschfeld had conned Paul Bremer, head of the Coalition Provisional Authority, into granting them the mobile satellite telephone franchise for Iraq. But Bremer was Bush's man, and all the juiciest Iraq reconstruction contracts appeared to be passed out to administration cronies. Would as debauched a pair of crooks as Sensi and Hirschfeld have gotten the satphone deal if they weren't on the White House friends and family plan? That seemed unlikely now.

In a book I'd been reading, *Bush's Brain,* James Moore and Wayne Slater said it was Karl Rove's M.O. to use layers of operatives to separate himself from the character assassinations, targeted disenfranchisements, and other black ops conducted at his behest. He was often seen suspiciously at the periphery of shocking events that turned elections. But nothing ever linked Rove directly to those events. By the time anyone figured out what had happened, the evidence was gone. These two sentences from the book kept repeating themselves in my head: "It became his motif. There is no crime, just a victim."

Things I'd learned from Gary on the way to Union Station were bothering me. Item: For the first three weeks after I'd identified "Marshall" as Hirschfeld, the FBI had been unable to find, or had claimed it was unable to find, the two outstanding federal warrants for Hirschfeld's arrest. Item: In addition to the late lamented Robert Chastain, it had emerged that there was another convenient dead body in Hirschfeld's past. Gary dropped that bomb on me but didn't say more. Item: There was now a paper trail suggesting Engin Yesil was to have been next. Gary didn't know all the details. Maybe that made it even more alarming for me. Portents were everywhere. A storm was coming. The only good sign was that in the past few days I'd been skimming and re-skimming *Oedipus Rex,* and I could not find a messenger getting killed.

From Washington to Baghdad on the Hudson in a little more than three hours. When you're on the run, Tex taught me, vary your normal patterns. If you're used to flying first class, fly coach. If you're used to taking limos, take a bus. If you're used to staying in grand hotels, stay in dumps. After midnight, I checked in to one of the cheapest hotels in Manhattan. Four and a half hours later, I forced myself awake, dressed, stumbled to the Korean deli on the corner, chugged down two Red Bulls, sipped a third, ate a chocolate croissant, and caught the Hampton Jitney. In the Hamptons, they gentrify things. Jitney means bus. Three hours after I got on, I got off the bus in Amagansett.

Down Main Street a few hundred yards from the bus stop was a beat-up old barn my friend John Alexander had kindly invited me to visit for the day. John is a painter of some renown. His canvases hang in important collections all over the world, and in major museums. Even the Metropolitan Museum of Art in New York has one of John's paintings. He's got a big loft in Soho in the city—I had just left there on the day after my meeting with the Gray Eminence when I found myself dancing through the streets with the girl in the genie shoes—but nowadays John seems to spend three or four months of every year in Amagansett.

The Hamptons have gentrified even his painting. John has always painted, among other recurring subjects, birds and swamps and seascapes. But now they look real. They used to look like birds and swamps and seascapes on acid.

This barn was John's studio. Paul McCartney had been known to hang out here, painting with John or just watching him paint. But today John had set up a rickety folding card table in the middle of the room and he'd moved his easel and lights closer to the wall. And today, unlike most days, the barn door was closed while John worked. Because today John had enticed his friend Steve Kroft, *60 Minutes* reporter, into the barn, and while John worked on a lovely portrait of an angry sea, Steve and I sat across the card table from each other while I told him what I'd put together and what I'd done about it and that ever since then I'd been running scared.

It turned out that Steve had known Miles Copeland, had made the pilgrimage, as I had so many times, to Miles's ivied cottage in the tiny village of Aston Rowant in Oxfordshire. So Steve knew what Miles was capable of, and by extension perhaps he knew a bit about me.

Steve had arrived professing to have just thirty minutes for our meeting. But thirty minutes into my tale he pulled out his cell phone and called someone and said he was going to be half an hour late. Thirty minutes after that, he called again. This time he paced out the back door while he spoke to someone, and when he came back he said, "Okay, I've bought us two more hours."

I kept talking while Steve made notes on a green legal pad and John painted and occasionally interjected comments like "These people are fiends!" and "It's despicable people like this who are fucking up this whole beautiful country!" and "God damn, Larry boy! How do you remember all these names and dates and spellings and addresses and phone numbers without even looking at notes?"

It was nearly three hours after he'd bought us two more hours that Steve finally left. He'd given me his home and cell phone numbers, and his e-mail address. He left with Gary's home number, and all my phone numbers, and bound galleys of *Overworld*. I'd told him the story of Sensi and Hirschfeld and George H. W. Bush begins there.

Back in the city that evening, I called Gary and several other people and said I'd met with a reporter from *60 Minutes* and I was fairly certain that, if I got blown away, the whole ugly story would come out. I used my regular cell phone, billed in my own name, and I assumed someone was listening, or that someone I talked to would tell others, especially since I asked them not to. Soon, the right people would know my demise would no longer be in the best interests of anyone. For the first time in a while, I felt almost safe. I took a train to Florida.

A few weeks later, on Friday, the thirteenth of August 2004, Hurricane Charley made landfall as a Category Four on the Gulf Coast down near Sanibel Island. It chewed its way diagonally across Florida, sucking up swamps and sand, and had weakened to Category One by the time it got here. It didn't do much damage to our property, other than splitting trees and knocking down limbs and plastering our walls and windows with something gray, gritty, and stinking. Three weeks later, to the night, Frances, Category Three, hit about thirty miles south of us and inched its way up the Atlantic coast. Winds howled all night, while Guinness shook, Kim cringed, sang, and passed around crackers and fresh batteries, and our son sat right beside her and tried to appear unfazed. It started raining inside and Kim said we'd lost our roof. I ran around the house investigating. No we haven't, I said. Don't worry. It's just the skylights. They'd flown away. Branches and shingles began dropping into our living room, our bathrooms, our bathtubs. Everything's okay, I said. Just stay away from the skylights. Then about three quarters of our roof peeled off and all we could do was sit in a mostly dry corner in the hot wet night listening to water cascading down our stairs. Kim took up smoking again that night, after years of abstinence. Guinness shat in the corners. I forgot all about Sensi and Hirschfeld. In the morning the storm was still roaring, the house was stretching and rattling, we could see now that the rain was not so much falling as flying, sideways, and, twenty nights later, when Jeanne arrived, another Category Three, it sheared off most of the rest of our roof and deposited our pool house into our pool.

Debris. Heat. Sweat. Blue skies and broiling sun. Drinking hot Cokes, hot water, hot Red Bull. No roof. No electricity. No telephone. No Internet. Waiting in soup lines, and bread lines. Gas lines. Ice lines, when the FEMA trucks finally arrived. Eating MREs and Slim Jims. Eating basically anything we could get. Dragging branches and fronds and trees out of our backyard to the street in front of our house. Filling wheelbarrows with rubble and piling it on the street in front of our house. Mountains of rubble and trees on the street in front of our house, and lining the streets, all the streets, for miles around. Martial law. National guardsmen out in force on the streets, just like Iraq. Live electrical cables sizzling in puddles by the sides of the roads. Traffic lights in pieces all over the intersections. Crawling all over the top of our house, unfurling tarps, nailing down tarps. Waiting for the next one to hit. Hammering plywood sheets over windows. Removing plywood sheets from windows. Sleeping outside in the rubble at night, on lawn chairs, because it wasn't quite as hot outside as inside. Listening to television on battery-powered radio. County officials issuing edicts. Governor Bush sounding quite competent and telling jokes. And the next morning, every morning, more cutting and dragging, staggering, storm after storm, it's all blurred now in my memory.

At some point, exactly when I'm not sure, I remembered Richard Hirschfeld and Robert Sensi, and by then I was so miserable I started to feel maybe I wasn't safe after all. Spending hours at a time on top of my house, silhouetted against the sky—there couldn't be a much better place to catch me in crosshairs. But all I could do was keep hammering, and watching for the black Mercedes that never came.

Meanwhile, the world was spinning out its destiny without me. President Bush dropped in, not forty miles from my rubble field, rolled up his sleeves, and passed out bags of ice to carefully vetted, searched, and stage-managed hurricane victims. I heard it on TV.

Hurricane Victim Number One said, "Thank you, sir."

The President of the United States said, "It's my honor."

Hurricane Victim Number Two said, "Thanks."

The President said, "It's an honor."

The local news reporter gushed about the President and then, re-membering that most of us were only listening, added this telling detail: He'd rolled up his sleeves to help. Florida was a battleground state and Bush and Kerry were still dead even.

I was living in a rubble field, totally fucked and useless. Even when our street got power back, we couldn't turn ours on because our walls and wires and conduits were wet. Inside my office, which was hot as hell, but intact, I jerry-rigged a laptop computer to grab Wi-Fi from my neighbor's network. I could communicate with the world by e-mail. Later my cell phone started working, too. Then something wonderful happened. I only wished I'd been there to see it.

———

"Where?" Gary Messina said. "Where? Are you kidding me?"

I'd just told Gary where Hirschfeld had been all this time. He hadn't fled to Cuba after I identified him. On the very day he was last seen outside Ntera's Miami offices—the day it seemed someone called him on his cell phone and warned him off—Richard Hirschfeld had simply, calmly, moved into a mansion on the water in Fort Lauderdale. He'd bought the place about a month earlier and hadn't planned to move in yet. But these were difficult times.

"And he bought the house in *what* name?" Gary said.

I'd already told him, but Gary couldn't believe it. "He bought it in the name of Global Telesat Property Corp," I said. GlobalNet and Global Telesat were two of the names of the companies Hirschfeld and Sensi had used to run their satellite telephone business, the one that had extensive contacts with the federal government.

"Global Telesat Property Corp. is a Florida corporation, formed last May," I said. "And get this: The articles of incorporation list Bob Sensi as the incorporator and president. The articles also include the address of the house. It's listed as the corporation's principal place of business."

To Gary, who knew more about computers and databases than I ever would, I didn't need to add that all of this information was available online, for free, and accessible in seconds.

"Jesus Christ!" Gary said. "And it took them *how long* to find Hirschfeld?"

At just before 3:30 in the afternoon on the first of October 2004—just a month and a day to the election now—FBI Special Agent Paul Russell slipped through a back door into Hirschfeld's house. *This place is big enough to play football in,* Russell thought.

Hirschfeld's Andalusian redoubt—eight thousand four hundred square feet of living space, with cathedral ceilings, a four-car garage, guesthouse connected by vaulted loggia to the main house, fountains, wine cellar, an elevator to the third-floor deck—had cost him four million eight hundred thousand dollars six months earlier. The house was on the New River, in Colee Hammock, one of Fort Lauderdale's most exclusive neighborhoods.

A tactical squad of FBI special agents, traveling in four unmarked Crown Victorias, had timed their arrival on the street side of the house to coincide, to the second, with the arrival of Russell and his squad, by speedboat, on Hirschfeld's dock. Russell entered the house first— wearing Kevlar body armor, POLICE in huge yellow letters across his chest, and bug-eyed combat goggles. He was carrying a big black gun and must've been a frightening thing to behold when Mrs. Richard Hirschfeld, Loretta, came down the hallway expecting to find that a door blown open by the wind was the reason the alarm had gone off.

Loretta turned around and tried to run. But by then there were more men inside her house. One of them stopped her and sat her down on the staircase.

"Is there anyone else here with you?" Russell asked her.

"My husband," she said. She pointed down the hall.

Russell crept down the hall to the office where, when Loretta left him, Hirschfeld had been sitting at his computer, checking his e-mail—rickyricardo999@aol.com. But Hirschfeld wasn't there. Russell found him in a big walk-in closet where files and office supplies were stored.

Russell said, "Richard Marshall Hirschfeld."

Russell grabbed Hirschfeld, told him he was under arrest, flashed him his badge, told him to keep his hands in sight, and started to cuff him.

While Russell closed a handcuff around one of Hirschfeld's wrists, Hirschfeld put his other hand in his pants pocket.

At that point, Russell stopped calling Hirschfeld by his name. "Listen, little fucker," Russell said, grabbing Hirschfeld by the neck and squeezing. "That was against my direct orders! If you do that again, you're gonna get shot."

Russell let go of Hirschfeld's neck and told Hirschfeld to give him his hand.

Hirschfeld stuck it back in his pocket.

Russell knocked Hirschfeld down and pinned him to the floor.

Russell hooked Hirschfeld up, then searched his pockets for a weapon. All he found on him, in the pocket Hirschfeld had risked his life to reach into, were a roll of bills and a telephone calling card.

Hirschfeld's new home was the Miami Federal Detention Center, and when I heard about it, only about an hour after they got him there, I called Gary Messina, Dave Kindred, Dan Schwartz, Dave Morrison, Greg Craig, John Alexander, Steve Kroft, and, when I finally got through to him, Vince Messina. For a man living in a rubble field, I was quite a proud and happy man. "Look what we've done," I said to Vince. "Look at what you and I have done."

A few days later, Gary called and told me Sensi was telling friends, "Richard's problem is being taken care of, in Washington. He'll be let out of jail soon."

"Not until after the election, he won't," I said.

Letting a convicted felon who was now accused of suborning the blinding of a federal judge, who'd just spent eight years on the lam from the Feds, and who happened to have direct ties to the Bushes, out of jail now would've been almost as stupid as I had been when I included clues to my identity in my memo to the Gray Eminence. And it might've been just enough to get the story of Richard Hirschfeld, Bob Sensi, Al-Qaeda, Bob Farmer, and the Bushes onto *60 Minutes* before the election.

After meeting with me, Steve Kroft had spoken by phone for more than an hour with Gary Messina. Gary had agreed to let Steve interview him on camera. Then Steve had told John Alexander he was going to Washington to see Gary and to investigate. I don't know if Steve eventually would've reported the story, but I thought so—until Rathergate. While I was busy fighting hurricanes, Dan Rather had served up a *60 Minutes Wednesday* segment on George Bush's service in the Texas Air National Guard during the Vietnam War. The very next morning, Bush loyalists had begun disputing the authenticity of documents central to the story. Several experts said they were forgeries. CBS News seemed to have wronged the President of the United States. Two weeks after Rather's segment aired, CBS announced it could no longer vouch for the authenticity of the documents and Rather personally apologized on *The CBS Evening News.* From then on, I'd been relatively certain *60 Minutes* wasn't going to report anything ambiguously unfavorable to Bush, not until after the election. Let Hirschfeld out now, though, as Sensi was telling people was about to happen, and all that could change.

Hirschfeld sat in federal jail in Miami while John Kerry swept George Bush in the presidential debates. Even the majority of the Republicans polled after the debates admitted Kerry kicked Bush's ass in the first debate and, though Bush did better in the second and third, that Kerry won those, too. Cheney got caught telling baldfaced lies in his vice-presidential debate with Kerry's running mate, John Edwards. Cheney said Edwards showed up so infrequently to do his job in the Senate that Cheney had never even met Edwards until the night of the debate. Cheney also said he'd never claimed there was a connection between Iraq and 9/11. Within an hour, the networks were airing footage of previous meetings between Cheney and Edwards, and of Cheney—in the course of selling the war—pronouncing gravely on Saddam's role in the 9/11 attacks. But none of that mattered. Bush and Cheney said, over and over, "We live in a dangerous world," then they beat the war drums, and even the fact that the war wasn't going well, by any reasonable standard, didn't matter either.

Only half of the American people seemed to see what I saw. George and Rummy's Excellent Adventure in Iraq had turned into a horror show. So much glory, and so much oil, had looked to be there for the taking at the start of it all. Wolfie had predicted American troops would be greeted in Iraq with flowers and sweets. But it had turned out Iraqis preferred the RPG and the IED over rose petals when it came to welcoming Americans to their country. With rocket-propelled grenades, improvised explosive devices, and every other weapon they could get their hands on, Iraqi insurgents were slowly bleeding the neocon dream to death.

Meanwhile, inside the George Bush Center for Intelligence—which is the official name of the complex in Langley, Virginia, commonly known as CIA headquarters—even though a purge was under way, a whole lot of career Mideast specialists were still royally torqued and would still not shut up or spout the party line. We knew better than this nonsense, we knew this would be a disaster, we said not to do it—they said—but no one listened to us, and we're not going to take the rap for it now. But maybe they were. Tenet was out. Good Republican Goss was in, and blood was washing down the halls.

Powell was out, too. He hadn't resigned yet, but everyone knew he was going to. He'd never been quite one of them, having actually seen war before they started all of this. Now everyone knew he was pissed off at Rummy and Condi and Bush for making him deliver a speech full of lies at the United Nations to make the case for invading Iraq.

Even the first President Bush was out. When Bob Woodward asked our current president if he'd sought the advice of his father before deciding whether to launch the war in Iraq, George W. Bush had informed Woodward, "There is a higher father that I appeal to." That was symptomatic of what I'd been hearing from a friend who had sometimes walked the marbled halls of the Carlyle Group with the first President Bush. My friend said there was a lot of snickering inside the Carlyle Group these days because everyone there above a certain rank knew that privately George H. W. Bush had counseled, then almost begged, George W. Bush not to invade Iraq. Finally, my research on Oedipus was coming in handy.

And yet George W. Bush and Dick Cheney and Karl Rove knew better than John Kerry and John Edwards and all the rest of us what America wanted just then. That was for someone strong to tell us we are living in a dangerous world, and then to beat the war drums some more, and bang on Bibles, and tell us if we didn't elect them what was coming next was called the Apocalypse.

On November 2, 2004, America voted and Bush won. The next day, coming to grips with that, I was afraid. Not long after Kerry finally called Bush and conceded he'd lost Ohio, and thus the election, I called Steve Kroft and asked whether it was true that for most of the previous day exit polling had shown Kerry was winning.

"Yes," Steve said. "Yesterday afternoon we all thought Kerry was going to be president. Pennsylvania broke for Kerry. Florida broke for Bush. It became clear Ohio was it. And all the exit polls coming out of Ohio showed Kerry beating Bush there, pretty solidly. The Democrats I talked to were really happy. The Republicans were grim."

"So what the hell happened?" I said. "And what about these stories about the Republicans rigging the computers? Do you think they stole Ohio?"

"No," Steve said. "What happened is the Republicans knew they had a big problem and from then on they outworked the Democrats in Ohio. They beat them with logistics. They got out the vote. Their lawyers went to court and got key polling stations kept open. In some precincts in western Ohio, after nine o'clock last night, Republicans were still standing in line to vote."

When all the Ohio votes had been cast and counted and recounted, out of nearly five and half million votes for president, Bush beat Kerry by about a hundred thirty-five thousand votes.

"So, four more years," I said.

"And how does that make you feel?" Steve asked.

Over the summer, I'd taken a stance—and a risk. But I'd always believed somehow Kerry would win and after that I would be safe. I was living in a Winnebago parked in my driveway, calling Steve from the faux-wood dinette table just behind the driver's seat, and feeling about as powerless as I'd ever felt.

"Vulnerable," I said. "It makes me feel very vulnerable."

A month after the election, I flew to New York to meet with my editor to talk about a book I'd started to write. Over lunch at Blue Ribbon Sushi, in Soho, he polished off a Honoo Platter while I explained to him all I'd discovered recently about how difficult it is writing in a rented motor home that is also occupied by one's wife, one's son, one's dog, one's remaining worldly possessions. He said keep trying and I said I would, and that was that. I hadn't come to New York for what happened next, and I'd almost rather not mention it. Like so much of the rest of the true story of my life, with all its fateful coincidences and synchronicity, it's preposterous. But it's relevant, it happened, and should you doubt it, I can only invite you to verify it for yourself.

It may, I grant you, take some effort to find video of the sidewalk on the west side of Park Avenue, just above Sixty-first Street, at 8:58 P.M. on the second of December 2004. But in a city as heavily laden with CCTV surveillance cams as New York is today, there's bound to be extant at least one recorded view of what happened. Let Dashiell Hammett be your guide: There always is—there must be—a trail of some sort. Find the recording. The rest of the verifying shouldn't be as hard as finding the video. Write John Kerry's office, ask someone there to search through his calendar, and I'm confident they'll confirm to you Senator Kerry was in New York on the date in question, and that at about 9:00 P.M. he left The Regency Hotel. Ring the Regency, speak to the bellmen, the doormen, the security staff, and no doubt at least one of them will remember that, yes, at about 9:00 P.M., Senator Kerry passed through the lobby and stepped out the front door onto Park Avenue to get into a waiting automobile. You'll also want to get my cell phone records, plus whatever tracking information my cell carrier can provide you, and you'll want to talk to my banker. But while you're on the line with the Regency's security staff, that might be a good place to start looking for the video. If they don't have it, you'll have to move on to police cams, or security cams from other buildings, or traffic cams. Don't give up. There are so many cameras watching us today. Eventually, you'll find it. And when you do, watch it unfold—another little piece of this story.

That's me, the tall fellow in a leather jacket and a watch cap, walking south on the sidewalk on the west side of Park Avenue. The time is actually 8:58 P.M. I know because I'm supposed to meet a friend at the front door of the building on the southwest corner of Park and Sixty-first at 9:00. I've just checked my watch and noted that, for once, I'm going to be on time. It may look like I'm talking to myself, but I'm talking into the microphone dangling from the earpiece connected to the cell phone in my pocket. I'm leaving a voicemail message for my banker.

In front of the Regency, above its main doors, a flat, wide, black metal awning is cantilevered over the sidewalk. I'm not staying in the Regency now, but I've stayed here so many times recently that I just about can't walk past these glass doors without thinking I'm meant to walk through them. I'm looking into the lobby as I start to pass under the awning. And just then John Kerry steps out of one of the doors, almost as if to greet me. He isn't there for me, of course, and in fact, by the time it registers on me who he is, an elderly couple on their way into the hotel has seen him and spoken to him in kindly tones and he's turned away from me to speak with them and shake their hands. I don't know how many hundreds of thousands of hands he's shaken in the past year, but right now I'd bet he's wishing he shook about a hundred forty thousand more of them in Ohio.

I've stopped walking. "There's John Kerry," I say. "I'm sorry. I'll call you back." I hang up the phone, and stuff it and the earpiece and the cord into my pocket.

There's no doorman out here bowing or scraping, and that seems odd. Once the elderly couple goes inside, it's just John Kerry, two younger guys in suits—who'd walked out just behind him, aides, I thought—and me. Kerry steps over to the right rear door of a big, boxy SUV that looks orangeish in the yellowy light but is probably actually red. His back is to me. Over next to the hotel wall, the aides, or whoever they are, are patting their pockets and earnestly discussing something I can't make out. From here, it looks like a pantomime— "*I thought you had the keys.*" "*No, I'm sure you had the keys.*"—and Kerry doesn't seem to be bothered by the wait.

There's a part of me that remembers dates, times, facts, sees linkages, connections, patterns others might miss. It isn't lost on me that exactly one month ago, to this very hour, the votes were being counted, and about now the results, which had looked so promising for Kerry all day, were starting to turn against him. Longfellow said, "The holiest of all holidays are those kept by ourselves in silence and apart, the secret anniversaries of the heart." For a moment, I'm wondering if Kerry is remembering one month ago right now.

"Senator," I say.

He turns around to face me, says "Hello," smiles a toothpaste ad smile. He's wearing one of the medium blue suits I saw him wearing so often on television during the campaign. He's quite tall, but not as tall as me.

"I'm really sorry things didn't work out better for you last month," I tell him.

"Well, thank you," he says. "Thank you very much."

Part of me wants to tell him I risked my life for him last summer— wants to mention the Gray Eminence, Greg Craig, Bob Farmer, Al-Qaeda, the warning—but this isn't the place for that, and besides, at the moment I look more like a cat burglar than the dignified citizen spy I'd like him to see me as while I discuss with him what I'd discovered and what I'd done.

"I'd hoped to meet you in the White House," I say, "instead of here."

"Well, thank you," he says again, and reaches out to shake my hand.

My first impression, while we're holding on to each other, is *My*

God! He's light as a bird. But, of course, I don't say that. I don't say anything, in fact, because just then a realization is coursing through me. What I'm thinking is: *It's best that Bush won. Because no one can clean up the terrible mess Bush has made in Iraq. Whoever tries is going to fail, and that honor deserves to go to Bush.*

"Better luck next time," I say. He nods, smiles, and I smile, nod, and start walking again, down Park Avenue. When I get to the other side of Sixty-first, I can hardly believe what's just happened. I turn around to make sure I didn't dream it. Kerry is getting into the SUV now. One of the aides is closing the door. The brake lights go on.

7. THE FATAL SHORE

But what of Hirschfeld, last seen disappearing into federal custody in Miami? And what of Sensi and, for that matter, Phipps, and the special branch of the CIA, and all the human wreckage they'd left behind?

Within days of his arrest, Hirschfeld had mustered, briefed, paid, and deployed three separate teams of lawyers to fight for him on three separate fronts. One unit would remain in Florida to deal with federal authorities there. Another was dispatched to Virginia, under cover of negotiating a plea bargain Hirschfeld knew he would never actually agree to, with the real objective of blocking, or at least delaying, his extradition to Norfolk. The third team went to Washington, to whip up support for him in Congress and the Department of Defense.

For Hirschfeld, who wore the mask of respectability so well, and could sell fried snowballs to the great chefs of Europe, rallying reputable, effective attorneys to his side had been no problem. His three teams of advocates were eminent men and women. But Hirschfeld, who made plans within plans within plans, and imparted them strictly on a need-to-know basis, hadn't told them everything. And once he'd sent them off to play their roles, he launched a propaganda offensive to soften up the battlefield for the final push, to the White House itself.

His arrest had made headlines all across the country. Now he meant to keep the story alive, and expand upon it, to his benefit. Through leaks passed on to the media by members of his family and other visitors, and through at least one epic letter he wrote and mailed from jail to a reporter, Hirschfeld, the general in his labyrinth, told a long, sad story of injustice suffered at the hands of wicked federal prosecutors, and of his own pluck and hope and patriotism in the face of it all. It was a beautiful story—containing many truths, and at least as many half-truths.

When I wasn't busy clearing rubble, or tearing down walls, or ceilings, or decked out in a hazmat suit and gas mask, fighting back the mold colonies that were taking over what used to be my home, I sat in my sweltering office and did my best to sort out the bullshit from the truth. With facts I found scattered among Hirschfeld's lies, plus information I got from new sources he would never have wanted me to find, I pieced together a picture of his years on the lam. And what he was really running from.

It was the middle of November 1996. Hirschfeld went to Washington to visit his old friend Senator Orrin Hatch. Hirschfeld had received a subpoena ordering him to appear at a hearing in federal court in Norfolk on the twenty-first of November. Though the charges were still sealed, Hirschfeld knew he'd been indicted for his utterly creative Habitat for Humanity prison furlough scam. And he knew that at the hearing he would likely be ordered back to prison.

Hirschfeld asked Hatch for help. Hatch declined, told Hirschfeld he was disappointed in him, didn't believe in him anymore.

Hirschfeld told Hatch he was a political hack who wouldn't help a true friend, just because it was no longer politically expedient.

Hirschfeld went home to Virginia and said good-bye to his wife and kids—sent them off to Marco Island, in Florida, where the family spent Thanksgiving every year. He told them, "I'll see you there tomorrow."

Instead, he packed his Rolls-Royce full of legal briefs and bespoke suits, photo albums, corporate seals, and other goods and chattels, and shipped it to Cadiz. Then he went to Virginia Beach to see his mother and father and sister. He didn't say good-bye, didn't tell them he was about to flee the country, just dropped in to visit. "That was the most devastating experience I can recall," Hirschfeld said in a thirty-one-page, single-spaced, handwritten letter he sent from jail in Miami to Bill Burke, a reporter in Virginia, "especially since my dad was pretty far along with his Alzheimer's affliction and I had no idea if I would ever see him again."

From his parents' home, Hirschfeld went straight to the airport in Norfolk. He caught a flight to New York and then a flight to Madrid. When he didn't show up at the hearing back in Virginia on the twenty-first, the presiding judge issued a bench warrant for Richard Marshall Hirschfeld. But the FBI had no clue where he was. And it's unlikely they would've found him any time soon had he not, just two weeks after the hearing, walked into the Madrid office of the Associated Press and introduced himself, then announced he was wanted in the United States and that he had applied to the Spanish Interior Ministry for political asylum.

"I've done nothing criminal," Hirschfeld said, and as I worked at my desk all those years later, reading the quote in an old newspaper clipping, I could almost hear the martyrdom in his voice, the air of injured piety he was so good at summoning. So many people found it difficult to disbelieve anything Hirschfeld told them. I think that was because, with his infinite capacity for self-deception, he believed it all himself. "I've done nothing criminal," he repeated loftily on that long-ago day in Madrid. "I have internal Justice Department documents which show I'm the victim of a vendetta by federal prosecutors in the United States. For years now, they've been conspiring against me for political reasons of their own."

All Richie was looking for was love and respect. But when American papers ran the AP story about his application for political asylum in Spain, U.S. authorities asked the Spanish government to arrest him. Eventually, the Spanish National Police found Hirschfeld's Rolls-Royce about as far away from Madrid as it could be and still be in Spain. The car was parked outside a beachfront apartment building in Playa de las Americas, in Tenerife, off the coast of Africa, in the Canary Islands. On the twenty-ninth of January 1997, they arrested Hirschfeld inside his apartment there. He spent the next four months in jails in Tenerife and Madrid, briefing and debriefing his attorneys, attending hearings, charming nearly everyone he met, fighting extradition, petitioning for bail. Finally, he was granted bail. He put up thirty-five thousand dollars, was told not to leave the country, and walked out of jail.

For the next few months, he drove around Spain in his car, homesick, listening to Elvis Presley on the stereo. Eventually, a Spanish judge decreed that, under the doctrine of duality of law, Hirschfeld couldn't be extradited for the charges then pending against him. Federal prosecutors in Virginia reacted to that news by indicting Hirschfeld again. They had plenty of charges to choose from. Perhaps the one they selected was calculated to win them the most sympathy from whatever Spanish judge would be reviewing their next extradition request. This time, they indicted Hirschfeld for plotting to blind United States District Judge J. Calvitt Clarke, Jr.

Upon receiving notice of the new indictment, a Spanish judge summarily ordered Hirschfeld arrested and extradited. But for Hirschfeld, who had the terrible gift of inspiring loyalty from men and women he barely knew, there was a call in the night, a warning, and our boy tiptoed to the nearest international airport half a day before the authorities got round to looking for him. But where to go next?

Cuba was to Americans a forbidden land, and it had no extradition treaty with the United States. Havana, a city of perpetual shortages, was just the sort of place a hunter-gatherer and fixer like Hirschfeld could thrive. The crumbling architectural glories. The proud people carrying on gamely in the face of suffering brought on them by the unjust American government. Hirschfeld bought himself a one-way ticket to Havana.

When his flight landed at José Marti airport, Cuban police officers boarded the plane, told everyone else to sit tight, and told Hirschfeld to come with them. He thought he was about to be arrested. Instead, he was put into a limousine and whisked away like a VIP.

Hirschfeld was driven to the residence of Juan Vega Vega, law professor and Fidel Castro's personal attorney. Hirschfeld later claimed that, at their first meeting, Vega told him he'd read the American charges against him and found them absurd. But I find that unlikely. Less than twenty-four hours had passed since Hirschfeld decided to fly to Cuba. I doubt any Cuban law professors would've been familiarizing themselves with the niceties of Hirschfeld's legal situation before they knew he was coming to see them. Nonetheless, Vega and Hirschfeld hit it off.

Hirschfeld began lunching every Friday with Vega. After a while, it became lunch every Friday with Vega *and* other members of Castro's inner circle. Soon, Richard M. Hirschfeld, Esq., formerly of Norfolk and Charlottesville, had a grand apartment in Havana, with a Cadillac parked outside, and a condo on Varadero Beach, and a hundred-fifteen-foot yacht at Marina Hemingway, and, of course, by then he was on backslapping terms with Fidel Castro.

So claimed Hirschfeld from the jail cell in Miami in which he saw out 2004. It was just the sort of thing Hirschfeld, with his tropism for the famous and powerful, would boast about whether it was true or not. Especially while he was busy writing and propagating his own myth so prolifically that my Hirschfeld file had now swelled to three accordion files, each one five inches thick. But I checked it out, I talked to people who spent time with Hirschfeld in Cuba—and by all accounts, including those of honest people with absolutely nothing redeeming to say of Hirschfeld, it was true.

He first met Castro at a wedding at which Castro was best man. "I'd spent the better part of a day trying to have my suit drycleaned," Hirschfeld wrote, "only to see Fidel show up in his trademark Army fatigues and black boots. Fidel is always full of surprises. I decided to dress down for our second encounter, only to have him appear dressed to the nines in a Hugo Boss suit."

Cuba is a police state. But whenever Cuban police challenged Hirschfeld, he fished into his pocket like the magician he was and presented them a card. A Cuban source who saw this card told me, "It said, in rough translation, 'Do not fuck with the bearer of this document, or you will answer to me,' and it was signed by Raúl." Raúl was Cuba's First Vice President, General Raúl Castro. Fidel's brother. With that, Hirschfeld would be invited to have a wonderful day and sent happily on his way, in his bright blue Cadillac, or his cherry red Mustang convertible, or on foot, in a snappy linen suit, carrying his tan leather briefcase, off to perpetrate whatever the hell he was perpetrating down there.

He became a regular at La Floridita, Hemingway's haunt, where my mother once ate. Effortlessly, he wormed his way into Havana society. When Dale Cooter, an attorney from Washington, went to Havana to visit Hirschfeld, Cooter said he was struck by how much access to the Cuban power elite Hirschfeld had gained in so little time on the island. One day, while Cooter and Hirschfeld were meeting to discuss Hirschfeld's legal problems in the U.S., Hirschfeld excused himself and disappeared into another room for a business meeting with Cuba's Minister of the Interior. Another time, Hirschfeld introduced Cooter to the Speaker of the National Assembly, who then proceeded to drive Hirschfeld and Cooter around in the Cadillac. "I never really understood why the Dennis Hastert of Cuba was our driver for the evening," Cooter said later.

While living in Cuba, Hirschfeld traveled abroad quite often. And that might have presented problems for a lesser man. There were American and Spanish arrest warrants and Interpol red notices for Richard M. Hirschfeld duly entered in the computer systems of immigration officials all over the world. Hirschfeld was subject to arrest at nearly any international airport or border crossing. And he likely would've been arrested had he traveled under his American passport. Instead, he used travel documents kindly provided him by the Cuban government. I don't know what name he traveled under. The real question, though, wasn't what pseudonym the Cuban government anointed Hirschfeld with, but why they did it at all. Why all the favors? I asked myself that question at least a dozen times, and each time I got a different answer.

Sitting at my desk, windows wide open, listening to the twenty-acre wood in the night, I wondered if Hirschfeld was doing little favors for Cuban intelligence in return for their help. Perhaps. Or did he simply pay them for protection? Maybe. More likely, I thought, was that Hirschfeld, the confidence man, had inspired in someone very powerful in Cuba rock-solid confidence in Hirschfeld's sure ability to bring them whatever it was they wished for most. I suspected it did not end as well for the Cuban as it did for Hirschfeld. But I didn't know. Like so much of the rest of Hirschfeld's life, the more I learned about his Cuban period, the more of a mystery it became to me.

One thing I was fairly certain of was that Hirschfeld was not in Cuba for the CIA. His long transit through durance vile in the American and Spanish penal systems *was not* an elaborate exercise in building for Hirschfeld a cover that would bring him acceptance and credibility upon his arrival in Cuba. In fact, though it had never come out in the press or the courts, by the time he fled Virginia for Spain, Hirschfeld was on the run from the CIA.

Or so said a wild man named Nat Bynum—who, while reading *Overworld,* e-mailed me at the address linked to the promotional website listed on the dustjacket of my book. The book was out now, and I was receiving a steady stream of e-mail from readers. Most people finished the book before they wrote me, but Nat Bynum was still in the middle of Part I, which features my father the spymaster, and me, just a kid trying to make sense of the secret world, spying on my father and the spies who worked for him. That was what prompted Bynum to write me. He thought perhaps his late father had worked for the CIA as a pilot. His father had been a U.S. Air Force colonel, Bynum said, but after retiring from the Air Force he'd kept flying, all over Asia and the Middle East and Africa and Central America, still working for the government, he'd intimated to his son, but covertly now. Bynum asked if I had any suggestions concerning how he could find out if his father had worked for the CIA. At the bottom of his message was a postscript:

P.S. I almost forgot the most important thing. I used to work for Richard
Hirschfeld, the Virginia attorney and financier who was once Muhammad
Ali's lawyer. So you and me are almost kin! Hirschfeld used to work with
the CIA. Have no idea why you might care, and haven't read far enough to
see if you mention him. Later. Nat Bynum

It took an act of will for me to wait a day to respond. You never
want to seem too anxious. When I wrote back, I started by thanking
Bynum for reading my book, and asking him questions about his father, and suggesting a few ways he might be able to learn more about
what his father was up to after he left the Air Force. Eventually, I said
I had known Hirschfeld, years earlier, and that he is indeed mentioned in *Overworld,* and then, as casually as I could, I asked Bynum
when he had worked for Hirschfeld and what he'd done for him.

Some hours later, his response arrived in my Inbox. He told me
that, after the Air Force, his father had flown for CAT, Flying Tigers,
Southern Airways, Evergreen, Air America, and the United Nations.
He told me he'd once seen a photograph of his father "perched on the
tail of a plain-Jane cargo plane parked by a shot-up sign that said
'Welcome to Leopoldville, Belgian Congo.'" And he told me that, a
few years after his father died, President Ronald Reagan had sent
Bynum "a nifty certificate attesting to the old man's service to his
country."

Then he got to what I'd been waiting for:

I always thought Hirschfeld was pretty damn fascinating but nobody I
tried to tell about him ever did. Except you, apparently. Come to think of it,
maybe it actually wasn't they didn't think it was interesting. "What the
fuck have you been smoking, Nat? Pull on that bottle or pass it on" tended
to be the response I got to my Hirschfeld story. I guess they thought it was

bullshit. I'm just a schmuck from Missouri and no one I know could believe I was hooked up with a mover and shaker like Hirschfeld.

When I met Hirschfeld I was running hot here in St. Louis, had big bona fides as an investigative reporter. I was the muckraker in town. I'd busted open a city police pension fund scandal that landed a bunch of city officials in prison.

I was hired by Hirschfeld in January 1995 after I returned from seven months in Bosnia. I got hired because I had an interest in Bob Chastain's exhumation in Purdy, MO. Chastain was a goofy guy who committed suicide or was whacked in Vienna over a $5 million insurance policy. Chastain had worked with Hirschfeld and maybe the CIA and I had gone to Utah and interviewed Chastain's widow for a story I was peddling to a magazine, and somehow got hooked up with Hirschfeld as a result. At the time I was out of work and buddies with a lawyer named Bob Ramsey. Ramsey was working for a colleague of Hirschfeld.

Richard hired me to "prove" he was a real CIA agent who had worked for them clandestinely with Chastain. The Feds were on Richard like white on rice. And I mean all kinds of Feds. FBI, Postal Inspectors, IRS, SEC, CIA. And he knew it too. He'd been out of prison for a year and now the Feds were playing him and another guy off.

In the worst way, Richard wanted to prove what he'd done was done for the CIA. He paid really well—although slowly—paid me almost $20,000 in the course of about a year and a half. But he was always trying to screw me out of expenses and that sort of thing. Richard was working out of Norfolk and Ft. Lauderdale. Richmond too. He would pick me up in his yellow

Rolls-Royce at the general aviation terminals and squire me around and give me orders. He was big into showing how wealthy he was, and took on airs, like the Rolls-Royce, and spending $200 for lunch, and that sort of shit. His shirts cost more than my suits. He was always telling everyone he was Muhammad Ali's lawyer. He always told me who was calling him if it was some bigshot. He got a lot of calls like that. Especially from Orrin Hatch, and once from Bob Dole. Hatch and Richard seemed to be pretty tight. Ali never called though, or I would have heard about it the rest of the day.

The case had started here in St. Louis as a wire fraud investigation through the Postal Inspector's office. I had an in because I was the federal courts reporter for the old St. Louis Globe-Democrat before it folded and I knew a bunch of postal inspectors. That was another reason I got hired. The postal inspectors started it but after a while a bunch of other agencies got into the fray. Very convoluted mofopery, it was.

Richard had been running coke and marijuana out of Colombia to Panama. There he was exchanging the shit for arms, Soviet machineguns, rifles, and hand grenades, small arms Israel captured from the Egyptians and Syrians in '67 and '73. The Israelis picked them up off the battlefields, cleaned them up, put them into giant fucking warehouses, and now they were selling them off. After the exchange in Panama, the drugs went to the US and the bills of lading said the arms were going to Gen. Pinochet in Chile, but they weren't. A guy from Chile was shipping them straight from Panama to Iraq, to Saddam Hussein's army. And Richard and Chastain were right in the middle of it. Richard said he'd done it all for the CIA.

Only thing was the Feds were on him now. And Richard was desperate to prove he was a good American. Supposedly whoever got Richard and

Chastain into this convinced them they were CIA operatives and they were doing their patriotic duty. A guy named Bob Sensi was key to Richard's defense. I never met him but I tried to. Richard maintained to me and in affidavits before the federal court in Richmond that Sensi was his handler and that he was—for lack of a better term—a "freelancer" who Sensi used from time to time because of his wealth and unique position in Washington. There were charges about some scam involving Jimmy Carter's home building program Habitat for Humanity that pissed off a federal judge. I was at the pre-trial meeting where this guy named Joe Seriani and his wife made a deal with the Feds to testify against Richard for that, and formalized it in a document they signed. But that was nothing compared to all the shit that was about to go down, and Richard knew it. Everybody, even the CIA, was coming down on him at once. It was getting bad and that was the real reason he fled to the Canary Islands and sought political asylum in Spain.

I stopped reading and picked up a phone and called Gary Messina. He answered on the first ring.

"You're not going to believe *this*," I said.

"What?" Gary said. He knew it was me.

"According to one of my faithful readers, who says he used to work for Hirschfeld, the real reason Hirschfeld fled to Spain was he was about to go down for running coke out of Colombia to Panama, exchanging the drugs for arms, and shipping the arms to Saddam Hussein."

"No shit?"

"I don't know yet if it's true," I said. "But I've got a feeling. It sure explains a hell of a lot."

"I wouldn't put it past him," Gary said, "that's for sure."

By now I was wishing I hadn't called Gary yet. My eyes kept drifting back to my computer monitor, to the e-mail message. "I'll call you later, when I know more," I said, and then I hung up and continued reading.

I traveled the country and the world looking for links between Richard and Chastain and Seriani, who was very bright and very crazy and a glib liar, and a host of other weird people and the CIA, all the way from Virginia, West Virginia, Florida, to Panama and Chile. Richard said all these people were involved in the deal and knew it was a CIA Op.

There was a guy named Eugene Fischer involved. He was a marine architect who designed ships with secret holds and barges with double hulls to bring marijuana and cocaine into the US from Colombia. Fischer got caught when a double-hulled barge he designed was used to import marijuana into the Brooklyn Navy Yard and two guys died from methane gas inhalation when they cut it open to get the dope out. The barge was towed out to sea off Bayonne, NJ and sunk with the two bodies still on board. Their families took $100,000 to dummy up and then when the money ran out told the Feds.

Richard sent me to visit Fischer in Atlanta Penitentiary where he was/is doing life without parole for being a drug kingpin and then trying to escape via helicopter from the Miami Federal detention facility. His wife and sons and brother were hiding out in the Dominican Republic. When I got there Fischer had been in solitary for five years. I bought him a candy bar and he started crying . . . weird. Anyway, what he told me wasn't what Richard had anticipated. Fischer said Hirschfeld was a major drug dealer and he was prepared to testify as much. The Feds tried to compel me to testify what Fischer said but, technically, I was working for Ramsey, not Richard, and he was protected under attorney-client privilege. I couldn't testify, so they really got pissed and started screwing with me. Come to think about it, just about everything Richard sent me to do got people pissed at me. It was a very bizarre time, but interesting.

Richard sent me to West Virginia to find a mobster named Spadafora I think it was. I can't remember his name for sure but back in the Sixties he was a famous gangster. He was the cellmate of one of Richard's partners in Federal stir and was supposed to know about the cocaine deals and all that. When I found the guy he was semi-retired and ran a little Italian restaurant in the boonies of W Va. He had originally fronted money for a deal Richard was in. I got really fucked up with the Feds for that one. They picked me up and interrogated me about our conversations, etc.

After I got released I got picked up again in Richmond while waiting to appear in court there on an affidavit Richard had gotten me to sign about this prosecutor, a professional asshole, named Barger who was all over Richard. Barger had an FBI bean counter sidekick named Oberlander. The Feds said they were going to charge me. It was all bullshit intended to intimidate me—which it did.

Richard also sent me to Panama to look for a guy who was supposed to be the head of a shipping company called Pan Nordic while I pretended to be a writer for Nations magazine. It turned out the guy was a Panamanian Supreme Court Justice and I got arrested and literally thrown out of the country by no less than the Panama Chief of Police, personally. He said to me, "Nat, we could be friends, but too bad you are leaving Thursday." (It was Tuesday.) I said, "I'm not leaving Thursday," and he said, "Oh yes," and I was put into detention in my hotel room and escorted to an American Airlines flight bound for Houston.

I picked up the phone again. In my mind, Nat Bynum's credibility had just increased by about a thousand percent. I dialed Gary's number, got his voicemail.

After the tone, I said: "I'm still reading this. It's a roadmap of drug kingpins and mobsters and arms dealers and cutouts and Latin officials involved in high crimes committed by Richard M. Hirschfeld. I don't think this guy who says he worked for Hirschfeld is making it up. At first I thought maybe this was just a creative guy who pulled a lot of information about Hirschfeld out of newspapers and was getting his kicks making up a fantastical story to tell me. But there's so much detail, and he's just thrown out the name of a company in Panama, Pan Nordic, which I know Hirschfeld was involved in. The name of the company has never appeared in the papers, though. A few months ago, I found it, buried in the most obscure of public records. I'm telling you, Gary, this guy is for real. Stay tuned. I'll call you tomorrow."

I hung up and read on, and by the end of the next paragraph, chills were running down my spine.

I found nothing in Chile except great grapes, but right after I got back from there a self-described "Mossad agent" named Will Northrup showed up. Northrup was a very weird guy, who seemed to be interested in the same Chilean deal I was interested in and told me he was tracking this Israeli guy named Mordechai Golan who was selling hand grenades in Chile, Uruguay, and Paraguay. Golan was purportedly a former major in the Israeli army and a war hero. Before coming to the U.S. Golan had owned a Ford dealership in Brasilia and had traveled extensively through Central and South America. Northrup said Golan was Hirschfeld's conduit for the Israeli side of the drugs for arms deals. All this time that I'd been working for him Richard had been involved in an unrelated (although it was all sort of mixed together) scheme to take over Lens Express, this huge mail order contact lens company down in FL. Seriani claimed he'd founded the company or conceived it or something. I never was sure who really owned it, but Seriani hired lawyers to get it back for him. Seriani didn't have any money and Richard was paying the freight as Seriani's "silent" partner. That was another thing Richard had me doing—he paid me to go down to Ft. Lauderdale and stay at the Ft. Lauderdale Inn downtown and drive around with this Jewish PI who had been a Secret Service agent and was married to a French tennis pro who had big tits and looked kinda like Barbra Streisand. Can't remember her name but she had a red Jag convertible with heated seats and we drove around for days checking out cocaine dealers that Richard had identified and also tailing Mordechai's crazy son Yali Golan and his Turkish sidekick Elgin.

I stopped reading, clicked Reply, and typed a message asking Nat Bynum if he was sure Yali Golan's Turkish sidekick was named Elgin. Was that a typo, did he possibly mean Engin? Half an hour later, Bynum's reply hit my Inbox.

Re: Brain fart

Yes, Engin. Engin Yessel. How did you know? Seems like you might know more about all this than you're letting on. Yessel's old man had the monopoly on shoes for the Turkish army. Yali Golan was a dangerous SOB with good martial arts skills and a big bastard too. Richard had me dig up all the FBI reports and a whole lot more, actually everything available, on those two. They had been going to the U of FL before they got busted. After Hirschfeld fled to the Canary Islands Golan took control of Lens Express from Hirschfeld and Seriani or made them give up their claim or something. By the way, I am halfway through your book and sneaked a peek toward the end. I really like it. No shit Tonto. You are both a better story teller and even weirder than me, and I mean that with the greatest ADMIRATION. Reality is more fun than fiction and the world is a truly weird place.

Nat

I called Gary's voicemail again. "Holy shit!" I said. "This new source of mine is for real, and Hirschfeld has been targeting Engin Yesil since even before Hirschfeld fled the country for Spain and Cuba. Since way back in *1995*. Maybe even before that. I need to talk to Engin Yesil, right away."

The WQNI-Ntera merger had been called off. WQNI's announcement had cited delays in completing due diligence, with nary a mention of con men, rogue CIA operatives, or Republican plots to link John Kerry's campaign treasurer to Al-Qaeda. Dan Schwartz's job was done, and he was no longer representing Engin Yesil. So I called Vince Messina. He wasn't usually easy to reach by phone, but this time I got him right away. I summarized all Nat Bynum had told me, and Vince whistled in appreciation a few times while I did. Then I asked if he thought Engin Yesil would be willing to meet with me, and Vince said yes, but I'd have to wait a while, because Engin was out of the country.

While I waited, I learned more. I learned that in August 2000, while still living in Cuba, Hirschfeld entered the United States, flew to Philadelphia on a friend's private jet, and, with only a mustache and goatee as disguise, attended the Republican National Convention, which nominated George W. Bush as its presidential candidate. One morning during the convention, Hirschfeld spent an hour in the hotel room of his friend from Virginia, Edward Garcia, talking about politics, talking about old friends. And when the hour was up Hirschfeld said, I'll see you around, Eddie, I've got people to see. Then Hirschfeld shook Garcia's hand and was gone.

I learned that, after he attended the convention under the noses of multitudes of Secret Service and FBI special agents and God knows how many other federal law-enforcement officers, Hirschfeld returned to Cuba and lived there for most of the next year.

I learned that one day in San Clemente, California, in the late 1970s, our former first lady Patricia Nixon served Neapolitan ice cream to Hirschfeld's son and stepson in one room, while Richard Nixon and Richard Hirschfeld sat in another chatting at length about politics.

I learned that it was in 1988, during George H. W. Bush's successful presidential campaign, that Hirschfeld was first introduced to the candidate's son, George W. Bush. And that, according to Hirschfeld, in May of 1990, he and his son Todd and Muhammad Ali attended a Texas Rangers baseball game and had dinner with the team's owner, George W. Bush, and his wife, Laura, at Arlington Stadium in Texas.

I learned that every time I tried to shoot holes in Nat Bynum's story, I couldn't. The more I checked it out, the more it seemed to be true.

One day, I received a handwritten letter from Eugene A. Fischer, Inmate 32904-004, incarcerated now in the United States Penitentiary in Coleman, Florida. "I am ready to testify," he wrote, "and can coordinate the testimony of my mother, my brother, Laura Prewitt, Inocencio Jimenez, etc. concerning the fraud perpetrated on my mother Anneliese Fischer by a group of conspirators led by Richard Hirschfeld, Robert Sensi and Guillermo Olle. Willingly or unwillingly the attorney Steven Saltzburg and General Wayne Jackson were also involved (knowingly or unknowingly). They promoted their connection with Sen. Orin Hatch and Sensi's background with the CIA and their contacts within the Justice Department." The letter went on and on, but there was no explanation of the fraud Fischer claimed Hirschfeld and Sensi had committed. And there was no direct statement that Hirschfeld had trafficked in drugs. Convicted drug kingpin Eugene Fischer's charges were totally unsubstantiated, but he sure as hell seemed to know Hirschfeld and Sensi.

I e-mailed Nat Bynum:

Any idea of the identities of two characters named in letter from Eugene Fischer: Guillermo Olle and General Wayne Jackson?

Twenty-nine minutes later, I got this:

Yeah. Olle was a turd drug dealer involved with Fischer et al who I think flipped or else absconded and was later turned and General Wayne Jackson was the head of the Federal Parole Board and took a shine to Hirschfeld and Seriani.

That rang a bell, ever so faintly. But it wasn't until sometime later that night that I remembered something and bolted out of bed and went to my Sensi file and eventually found that, back in 1981, Sensi had written a Kuwait Airways check for the princely sum of one hundred twenty-five dollars to General Wayne Jackson, and that, during testimony in his embezzlement trial, Sensi had said he was a friend of Jackson but couldn't remember what the check was for.

It was more corroboration for Bynum's story, and Fischer's. I sent another message to Bynum:

Hi Nat, any idea what the hell Hirschfeld and Sensi were up to when they dangled their relationships with Gen. Jackson and Sen. Hatch and the Justice Department in front of Eugene Fischer and his mother?

The next morning, Bynum replied:

Sure. They stung Fischer's mother for money they said they needed to reduce his sentence to "time served." They took the dough but the sentence reduction never came through. Pissed Fischer off, I mean really pissed him off. Nat

That had happened way back in the early nineties. But it sounded to me like a variation on the games played on Engin Yesil, Boris Birshtein, and others in the new millennium.

There was a whole lot of prison time under the bridge since our golden boys had scammed Fischer's mother. Between Hirschfeld's release from federal custody and his hegira to Spain, Sensi had been away. So when *did* they reunite? Was it at the convention in Philadelphia? Did Sensi visit Hirschfeld in Cuba? Or did Hirschfeld, always the senior partner in this equation, wait until he'd relocated permanently to the United States before he called Sensi and said, "Let's fleece these fuckers."

I didn't know. Maybe I'd find the answers in Miami.

Vince told me to pick him up in front of his hotel in South Beach. I did, and it was good to see him, but I was edgy. During my drive down, it had occurred to me that Engin Yesil might not be as happy to see me as I'd imagined. I had blown up a merger that would've netted him a profit of about fifty million dollars.

After he got into the car, Vince said, "There's been a slight change in plans." That was all it took to double the intensity of whatever it was roiling inside me.

"You're the boss," I said, sounding dead calm. "Where to?"

Vince told me, vaguely, and we drove south between the sea and Art Deco buildings painted in the colors of Necco wafers, and then we turned west and went over the causeway toward downtown Miami and, while we did, Vince caught me up on Hirschfeld.

His new attorney, it seemed, was no less than C. Boyden Gray, who had been White House Counsel under the first President Bush. The pattern of highest-level Republicans aligning themselves with Hirschfeld was holding. Gray went to the White House to make Hirschfeld's legal case for clemency. But that was just stage one of the final push. Soon after sending Gray to the front door in his behalf, Hirschfeld had sent a confederate to the back door of the White House to initiate a covert campaign to blackmail the administration into setting him free.

"Over what?' I asked.

"All we know," Vince said, "is our good friend Richard says he's got something on the government and he expects to get a pardon or he will expose them, for whatever the hell it is. Sometimes we hear it's Iraq. Sometimes it's the election. Maybe it's both."

"But why?" I asked. "Why now? Why, if he thought he had Bush by the balls, did Hirschfeld wait until after the election to squeeze?"

Vince just didn't know. We talked about it for a couple of miles, and the only reasonable answer we came up with was Hirschfeld never could do anything straight. On one level, he couldn't even see the contradiction in working all the angles, legal and illegal, at once. On another, he was so used to controlling perceptions that he didn't think anyone would connect the overt and the covert things done on his account.

"Whatever's going on beneath the surface in Washington," Vince said, "Richard has entered a manic new phase. Inside prison he's just as relentless and energetic an asshole as he always was outside. For all we know, these days, when he's worn all the attorneys and prisoners and guards and rabbis and imams around him out, he spends his spare time tunneling. And lately he's turning into a chatterbox. He will not shut up."

That, I thought, had to mean Hirschfeld was getting desperate.

"Fuck him," I said. "So give me a hint. Where are we going?"

We were going to see Arik Meimoun.

After we'd found 100 North Biscayne Boulevard and a place to park, and showed picture IDs to a guard in the lobby of the New World Tower, which seemed to pay more attention to security than Amtrak did, we rode up to the twenty-fourth floor and stepped out of the elevator straight into the offices of Next Communication. Vince walked me past a boardroom and down a hall past a couple of closed doors to a large corner office. Inside it, he introduced me to a big, happy guy named Arik Meimoun.

Arik was wearing jeans, and he had a cell phone in his hand and another blinking on his desk. He looked like a taller, beefier version of Tom Cruise, in a role that called for a spiked-up flattop and youthful innocence. The first time I'd heard of Arik Meimoun was soon after I'd identified Richard Marshall as Richard Hirschfeld. Someone from Homeland Security had told me Arik was twenty-nine years old, and Israeli, and smart as hell, and that Arik and the computer geniuses he regularly imported into the United States were suspected of working for Mossad. That was about all I knew about him except that, on our way upstairs in the elevator, Vince had told me it was Arik who introduced Engin Yesil to Richard Hirschfeld.

"Sit down, please, please." Arik spoke in the sweet, dark rhythms of the Middle East. "Would you like some espresso? Cappuccino?"

Pretty much all at once, the cell phone still in Arik's hand and the cell phone on his desk and his desktop landline phone began ringing. He ignored them.

"I know what you like, Vince," Arik said. Then he looked to me. "How about you? Espresso? Cappuccino? Coke?"

I asked for espresso, and Arik raised his voice and called—just loud enough to be heard in the next room—toward the door we'd come in through for someone to bring us two double espressos and a cappuccino. Then the phones stopped ringing and Arik leaned back in the chair behind his desk, and smiled and said, "Well, Vince, what sort of interesting person did you bring to me today? Are we going to do some business?"

"Larry is the guy I told you about," Vince said. "Larry used to work in intelligence, and Larry wrote the book I told you you should read. It was Larry who identified Richard as Hirschfeld."

Arik turned to me, and now he was beaming. "No shit!" he said. "So you are the guy! My man! You saved my life, bro! Wow! Really nice to meet you." He paused for a moment. Then he said, "How did you know? How did you know his name is Hirschfeld?"

"I used to know him."

"Was *Ree-charred* really CIA?" It took me a moment to realize he was asking about Hirschfeld.

"Well, sort of. Maybe," I said.

"You spy guys are very vague. Clear as mud what you tell me. Was Richard CIA? Yes? No?"

"I'm really not sure," I said. "He probably was, long ago. But I'm pretty sure he wasn't working for the CIA recently, not when you met him."

Arik could say things without speaking. He widened his eyes and pursed his lips and nodded his head at me three times. Then he stopped dead still, and raised his eyebrows and turned his palms up and gently wobbled them in front of his chest. *Yes, yes, yes, I see, that makes sense, go on,* he was saying.

"How did you meet him?" I asked. "How and when and where did you first meet Richard?"

Before Arik could answer, a smiling girl slipped into the room with coffees. And before she finished handing out the paper cups, a slim young Israeli fellow in jeans and a T-shirt arrived. This, Arik informed me, was Effi Yeoshoua, attorney and in-house counsel for Next Communications. Effi was tan and his head was shaved and he was very polite. There were more handshakes and pleasantries, and inquiries about how Vince had been, then Effi sat down and Arik told Effi who I was and that I had once known Hirschfeld. Eventually, equilibrium returned to the room and Arik said, "I was just about to tell Mr. Larry how I met Richard." Then he gave Effi one of his meaningful looks, and this time what Arik meant was *Should I?*

Effi nodded.

"I got this call from a guy I know—James. Jaime, people call him." Arik pronounced "Jaime" in the Latin way—rhymes with "Fly Me." Arik went on. "Jaime said, 'Arik, I'm going to Cuba. It's legal. I have a special permit to deliver medicines there. It's a humanitarian mission. Why don't you come with me? I can add your name to the team.' So I said 'Okay' and Jaime sent me a certificate from the U.S. government. It had my name and said it was okay for me to go. So I went."

"When was that?" I asked.

"Sometime in spring, 2001," Arik said. "So we got to Havana and Jaime took me to the yacht club, the Club Nautico, and there I first saw Richard. He was busy when we got there. He was sitting talking with a woman everyone said is the sister of President Kennedy. Jean Kennedy Smith or something. And after she left, Jaime introduced me to Richard. Richard asked what I do. I said 'Telecommunications,' and he said that's very interesting and we should get together tonight and go to nightclub. He was a nice guy and friend of Jaime, so I said okay. That night we went to club."

"What club?"

"It was"—Arik stopped talking and blinked a few times, trying to remember—"the Commodore Club. I mean it was inside the Commodore Hotel. I don't know the club name. And Richard walked in with this guy with long hair. Introduced me to Alejandro. Said he is Alejandro Castro. Son of Fidel. Everyone in the club recognized him, or at least was looking at him, and all the chicks I asked said, 'Yes, yes, that is Alejandro Castro, the son of Fidel.' So, I was thinking, *Who the hell is this Richard?* Especially since he told me he loved the telecommunications sector and he could make my company a Fortune 500 company.

"Afterward, Richard took me to his apartment. Right on Fifth Avenue. Yes, in Havana they have a street with an American name: Fifth Avenue. It's a diplomat building—only ambassadors, other big diplomats, and VIPs. Upstairs, in Richard's apartment, in the living room he had a wall with, without exaggeration, one hundred pictures, all celebrities, with Richard. I mean Richard and John Wayne.

Richard and Muhammad Ali. Shimon Peres. Bibi Netanyahu. All of them hugging him, like they are best friends. So I am like, *Oh, my God! This is a no-joke person.* Already it was a little bit scary.

"Then Richard tells me he works for the CIA, and he has a boat. Looks like yacht, but it's full of electronic equipment, listening devices. Richard asks me if I want to go with him out on this boat. I am thinking, *Let's see. Nice Israeli boy from Beersheba. First trip ever to Cuba. Gets caught on CIA spy boat.* I say, 'No thank you, Richard.'"

One of Arik's cell phones interrupted us. I hesitate to say it rang. Actually, it began to sing, like a siren beckoning from the rocks. A girl's voice was calling "Arik, Arik, Arik . . ."

Arik smiled. "Sorry, bro. I have to take this one."

Effi said, "This is the special ring tone he has downloaded for this girl who calls him."

Arik was speaking guardedly into his cell phone and looking pleased.

Outside his windows, the view was fabulous. The Port of Miami, cruise ships, Biscayne Bay, Government Cut, South Beach, the ocean.

Arik said good-bye, shut off his cell phone, came back to our conversation.

Life is never easy. Everyone you meet is fighting a tough battle. But Arik Meimoun was trying to bear his with some grace. His story of what Hirschfeld had done to him was full of good-humored astonishment at just how trusting and fooled he had been, of wonder and regret, betrayal, fear, deliverance from evil—but not a note of anger. Very pleasantly, Arik told me how, after four or five days of hanging out and nightclubbing together in Havana with both the great CIA agent Richard Marshall *and* Fidel Castro's son, Arik had gotten so scared he'd fallen into the middle of something very dangerous that he left Cuba earlier than planned. Arik told me how, after that,

Richard had called him from time to time from Cuba and Mexico, and how, a couple of months after his visit to Cuba, Arik had received in the mail a very generous gift, a stock certificate in his name for ten percent of the shares of Cohiba Rum Distributors Ltd., which heretofore had been owned exclusively by Alejandro Castro and Richard Marshall.

Arik told me of Hirschfeld's arrival a few months later in Miami, wearing red hair and a wispy red beard and a funny hat. It was still 2001, and now it was sometime after the September 11 attacks. Other than that, Arik wasn't really sure of the date. Hirschfeld said he was still needed in Cuba and would spend time there, but he was also needed in the United States, to help fight the war against terrorists.

Arik told me Sensi arrived in town just a few weeks after Hirschfeld. Soon they were semipermanent fixtures in Arik's life, and his offices. Though, for every time he saw Sensi, Arik thought he must've seen Hirschfeld ten times. In the lexicon of con men, Sensi was the outsideman and Hirschfeld was the insideman. The outsideman is a role player, a reinforcer of perceptions, sometimes a catalyst. The insideman stays much closer to the target, slowly works on his mind.

A con is a dream, and Hirschfeld was such a sandman that soon Arik was entirely, incontrovertibly under his spell. It started with immigration problems. "Until then, bro, I did not even know I had immigration 'problems,'" Arik told me. "I thought I only had immigration 'issues.' I had a temporary green card, and my permanent green card application was being processed. But Richard informed me I had problems, big fucking trouble with the INS. But I shouldn't worry. He and Sensi would fix it."

And fix it they did. One day Hirschfeld arrived in Arik's offices with a general, a four-star general in a U.S. Army uniform. Hirschfeld said the general would take care of Arik's immigration problems. Arik said, "Thank you, sir." Then Hirschfeld asked, "Is there anyone else in your office with immigration problems? We might as well help them, too." The general smiled and nodded. Arik said, "Three or four." Hirschfeld said, "Give us their names, too." Arik gave the names to the general.

"Was it a real general?" I asked.

"I thought so. Now that you ask, I am not so sure."

"And did the people on this list get taken care of?"

"No!" Arik said. "What the fuck are you talking about! They got in trouble. Big trouble." He laughed. Then laughed again. "But at first we didn't know that. We thought: *No more immigration problems.* We were sure of it. I mean, a few weeks after the general visited, Richard and Sensi took me to meetings in Washington. We even met in buildings of the federal government with big officials. Richard and Sensi were carrying around gold CIA badges. Of course, we didn't have any more immigration problems. That was clear. Everything was fixed."

Arik laughed again.

"I tell you what, bro, Richard was so fucking brilliant to tell me he was CIA. I mean, think about it. When someone is CIA, any little thing which usually would make you suspicious, it doesn't make you suspicious. You think, *Of course there are inconsistencies. He can't tell me all the truth, can he? He is CIA.* That's what you think. And you don't ask CIA a lot of questions either, do you?

"For example," Arik said, "once I flew with Richard to Mexico. We came out of the airport and were driving to a hotel. We heard a gunshot. Then more gunshots. We were driving fast, ducking, and we heard a bullet hit the car. When we got to the hotel, there was a bullet hole in the side of the car. Now that I think about it, this is a very bad example, bro. Any time a bullet hits a car you are in, it is a big thing. Not little. Of course, I said, 'Richard, what the fuck was that all about?' And Richard said, 'I honestly don't know.' But my point is after that I didn't ask any more questions. I just told myself this is CIA business, not mine, and I don't want to know. But Richard, and Sensi, who met us in Mexico, made some calls about the bullet, the gunshots. I heard that much. And the next day I left. So many things around Richard were so mysterious."

Arik had big ambitions and his new friend Richard was just the man to help him achieve them, and to see him through anything.

"The main appeal was Richard is absolutely the number-one best fucking lawyer I've ever met," Arik said. "He was going to negotiations with me and making brilliant suggestions. He really understood everything I needed. And after the negotiation, Richard would go to a computer, start typing, like a madman, and thirty minutes later he gave you a brilliant forty-page contract. All straight out of his head!"

Soon Hirschfeld was Arik's go-to guy whenever there was a problem to be solved. Such as a certain problem in Las Vegas. Arik started to tell me about it, but stopped himself. "It's better if Effi tells you. He was here. With Richard."

Effi reached out from his chair and tapped my arm. "There is this company we do business with," he said. "A phone company. It owed us one hundred twenty thousand dollars. In fact, we had a judgment against them. But we couldn't collect. Arik was going to Vegas to a big telecom trade show. On the day before he would leave for the show, we heard that this company that owes the money was going to be there. We talked about whether we might be able to collect the debt right there in Vegas, and decided it wouldn't be possible on such short notice. Arik was exasperated. He said, 'They are going to be there.

And I want my money. What can I do?' And Richard overheard this. Richard gave us the name of an attorney in Vegas and said to wire him a ten-thousand-dollar retainer right away.

"And what Richard did next was he called this attorney. Just a young guy, he sounded like. I was listening on the speakerphone. Richard told the guy to prepare an order granting us the right to seize this company's booth at the trade show. And to have it ready to be signed by a judge the first thing the next morning. The attorney said there was no way a judge would sign such an order, not the next morning, and not without hearing the other side of the story first. And I agreed with him. But Richard just *screamed* at this attorney— this is something lawyers don't do—but Richard screamed at him: *'You just make sure the fucking document is right and I'll take care of the judge!'*

"So the next morning," Effi said, "Richard called the attorney and told him which judge to take the order to and to get his ass over to see him right away. The attorney did what Richard told him, and the judge signed the order immediately. This is unheard of. But then, not only had Richard arranged for the judge to sign the order, as soon as Arik arrived in Vegas the judge also sent a sheriff's deputy to go with Arik to the show to seize the booth."

"No shit?" I said to Arik.

"That's right, bro," Arik said. "The sheriff went with me. We told the guys I owned their booth now. And pretty soon the president of their company walks over with me to the tellers' window in the casino of the Bellagio. He asks them, 'How much credit do I have?' They check and tell him 'one hundred thousand.' So he signs a paper, a marker, for it, and they give him the cash. He hands me the cash and I tell him he can have his booth back now. So I call Richard and tell him, and he is very proud of himself. He says, 'You see! I am *still* the best damn lawyer I know!'"

"And that," Vince said, "is further evidence of what I've been saying all along. Yes, Richard is smooth, and slippery, and he fooled a lot of people. But he didn't just con everyone. No judge signed that order because he thought Richard was working for the CIA. Richard has real people, powerful people, in Washington, and apparently also in Nevada, who know who he is and have been helping him."

"There's no doubt about that," Arik said.

"That's right," Effi said. "It has to be that."

"But, at least on that one occasion," I said, "Hirschfeld actually helped you. He got you a hundred thousand dollars."

"Well, yes and no," Arik said.

"Oh? Tell me."

"I flew home with the money in a plastic shopping bag. And Richard said he needed to see me right away. On my way home from the airport, I met him at Einstein Bagels in North Miami. He had a story about how he needed the cash and he would give it back in a few days. Richard took the sack, bro. And I never saw the money again."

"But that," Effi said, "was just a small piece of what he got."

"That's right," Arik said. "He washbrained me. He . . ."

Effi interrupted, in a fascinating sentence that began in Hebrew and ended in English. Arik corrected himself. "Richard brainwashed me. He always had an explanation and I always believed him. That was just a little bit of the money. He scalped me for two years, bro. He got almost nine hundred thousand dollars in cash. Plus he cost me another fifteen million. I had a contract to sell Next to Phone One for fifteen million dollars and Richard fucked that deal up. Because he wanted to buy the company himself, for a lot less. But I still own the company, bro. And I am alive. I have no doubt Richard had some kind of key-man insurance on me. But now I am sitting here. And Richard is sitting in jail, thanks to you."

It was a little astonishing to realize all the damage Hirschfeld had inflicted on Arik was collateral. Bilking him out of nearly a million dollars had been merely a sideshow. There was no way to interpret the evidence to indicate anything other than that Hirschfeld's main objective in befriending Arik was to gain access to Engin Yesil. But apparently Hirschfeld never could pass up a chance to steal.

Arik had reached the point in his narrative I'd been waiting for. I'd wanted his story to wind down on its own. Before he answered my next questions, I wanted his mind unburdened of everything he thought it important to tell me. It was good we'd finally come to this point, because Vince caught my eye now and made a gesture of tapping his watch.

I stood up and walked over to the window. From up here, the ships in the port looked like toys. "Why did you introduce Richard to Engin Yesil?" I asked. "Did Richard ask you to?"

"No, it wasn't that," Arik said. "What happened is I found out Engin had immigration problems, too. And since Engin was my friend and Richard, I believed, had done such a good job fixing my immigration problems, I thought Richard could help Engin, too."

"Did Engin Yesil tell you he had an immigration problem?"

"No," Arik said. "Engin didn't tell me. Somehow I just found out. I don't remember how exactly. But it must've come somehow, not directly but indirectly, from Richard."

"Are you still friends with Jaime?" I said. "Would you mind giving me his number?"

"I wouldn't mind," Arik said. "But it's not possible. Jaime died."

"When?" I said. "How?"

"I think it was a few years ago, not so long after I met him. Engin told me he called to invite Jaime to his wedding. But whoever answered said Jaime was dead. Later, Engin told me Jaime drank himself to death. He was found inside his house with lots of whiskey bottles around him."

Vince started moaning. Finally he spoke: "Oh Jesus!"

Afterward, in the car crossing the causeway, I asked him if, at that moment in Arik's office, he'd been thinking of the same thing I had. "Yes, I expect so," Vince said. "I was thinking of Richard's acolytes Bob Chastain and Jaime, both found conveniently dead next to bottles. Jesus!"

8. BYZANTIUM

Engin Yesil had a very nice house. At least, it seemed so from the other side of the massive coquina and wrought-iron gates out front. The name of the house, according to the weathered bronze plates on the pillars on either side of the gates, was Villa Luna. Vince was standing in front of one of those pillars now, hard at work pushing and re-pushing the intercom button. No one seemed to be home. It was evening, nearly dark. The house, as seen through the scrolled ironwork of the gates and a riot of ferns and tropical tree branches, was about seventy yards back, glowing in a soft yellowy light. Eventually, Vince came back to the car and sat down beside me.

"It may be," he said, "that Engin has decided not to see you. It occurred to me, while we were with Arik, that Engin may be mad at you for spoiling his merger."

Thanks, Vince, I thought. *That's just the reassurance I need right now.* I said: "Why don't you try calling him?"

Vince pulled a phone out of somewhere, dialed it, spoke to someone for a minute or two, then hung up. He got out of the car, went back to the pillar, and pressed a code into the keypad next to the intercom button. The gates slowly parted and swung open. When he got back into the car, he said, "Engin says he's on his way, he's running about twenty minutes late, and we should go on inside and make ourselves at home."

There was a circular drive in front of the house, and on it were parked a Rolls-Royce, a stretched Mercedes limousine, a Mercedes sedan, and three Porsches, all of them black and gleaming. The house was Italianate and rococo, a three-story twenties mansion of stucco and stone. The front door was beautiful dark wood, with six little windows in it. One floor up, directly above the door, was a wrought-iron-and-stone balcony that looked quite suitable for Juliet Capulet.

The door was unlocked. Vince hunted around for a light switch, then showed me the way to the living room. We sat down to wait. This gave me plenty of extra time to wonder whether Engin Yesil, who seemed to have the resources necessary to get what he wanted, wanted to kill me for blowing up his deal. I let my eyes wander around the room. First I looked at Vince, who was sitting on the other end of the long white sofa I was on. He seemed to be asleep, or meditating. Anyway, his eyes were closed. On the low table in front of us were photographs in silver frames, a silver bowl filled with fresh-cut flowers, and a jewel-encrusted silver peacock. The top of the table was almost as broad as it was long. On three sides it was surrounded by sofas and chairs, and the fourth side faced an elaborately carved stone fireplace. There was a tray ceiling with intricate dentil plaster-work. There was coquina molding around the doors and windows.

"Vince," I said.

He opened his eyes.

"Do you think this room is bugged?" I asked.

"By whom?"

"I don't know. You tell me."

"By Engin, no," Vince said. "By the Feds, maybe."

"Well, actually," I said, "I don't care if the Feds hear this: Henry Hyde. And Jim Sensenbrenner. Jerris Leonard, too."

"What?"

"I didn't want to say it in front of Arik and Effi, because I just met them. But, from the inquiries I've made, there's evidence that the Washington power figures who were actively helping Hirschfeld and Sensi included Congressman Henry Hyde, Congressman Jim Sensenbrenner, and George Bush Senior's old attorney Jerris Leonard.

"I hear," I continued, "that during his last couple of years here in the States, Hirschfeld liked to make a show of telling people, 'I've got Henry Hyde in my pocket. Henry will do anything I ask him to do.' Whereupon Hirschfeld would pull out a cell phone, dial a number, wait, then say, 'Henry! Hi, it's Richard. I want to introduce you to my friend Joe.' Or 'Bill.' Or 'Sergei.' Whoever. Then Hirschfeld would hand the phone to whoever it was and tell them to 'Say hello to Henry Hyde.' Of course, when you're on the phone, you can't see who you're actually talking with. And Hirschfeld does have a history of fraud by telephone. There's no guarantee it really was Henry Hyde on the other end of the connection. *But*—my source, who I don't want to mention in case we're being listened to, says it really was Hyde, Hirschfeld really does know him, and Hyde did occasionally do things, or ask others to do things, for Hirschfeld."

Vince was sitting up a little straighter now, listening, nodding.

I kept talking. "*Still*—that doesn't mean Hyde was doing anything wrong. It's entirely possible Hyde thought Richard was 'Richard Marshall,' businessman and Republican financier, had no idea he was really Richard Hirschfeld, con man and Republican fugitive. My source has no information, either way, on that."

Vince said, "And the others?"

"It's pretty much the same story with Sensenbrenner," I said. "My source says Hirschfeld knew him and dealt with him, and that Sensenbrenner from time to time did favors for Hirschfeld. But, again, it may be Sensenbrenner thought he was dealing with 'Richard Marshall' and had no idea he was cooperating with a criminal. There's no evidence Sensenbrenner intentionally did anything wrong.

"Here's where it gets very curious, though," I said. "Jerris Leonard. As you probably remember—if you read through the documents I sent you last summer—back in the eighties, Jerris Leonard knew Hirschfeld and Sensi very well. Knew them as a team. He went together with them to a congressional hearing. And he represented each of them in separate matters. Even in those separate matters, Sensi and Hirschfeld were each cooperating with the other. And my source is quite certain that, during the past two years, Sensi has been in meetings in Jerris Leonard's office in Washington, during which Richard called in to talk to both Sensi and Jerris Leonard. On those calls, both Sensi and Leonard referred to him only as 'Richard'—no last name used. It's possible, I suppose, that Jerris Leonard doesn't remember Hirschfeld's voice. And that Jerris Leonard didn't put two and two together and suspect or know the 'Richard' Sensi was now in league with was Sensi's old friend and partner Richard Hirschfeld. It's possible Jerris Leonard thought Sensi's new partner was Richard Marshall, not Richard Hirschfeld."

"Do you think so?" Vince said. "Do you really think that's possible?"

"It's possible," I said. "Theoretically."

"But do you think Leonard really didn't know who 'Richard' was?"

I told Vince my opinion on that. Vince told me his.

After that, we both went silent for a minute or two. Eventually, I said, "There's more."

"Oh Jesus!"

"The links between Hyde and Sensenbrenner are obvious," I said. "As I'm sure you know, they're both biggies on the House Judiciary Committee. They're both Republicans, of course. And everyone knows Hyde and Sensenbrenner worked together very closely to impeach Clinton. Well, Sensenbrenner's from Wisconsin. As is Jerris Leonard. Leonard came to Washington in the late sixties. A Nixon appointee. Assistant Attorney General for Civil Rights. During Watergate, Leonard left the government and went into private practice. His first clients of note were George Bush, Senior, and the Republican National Committee. Bush was the RNC Chairman at the time, and Leonard has reportedly said his job was insulating Bush and the RNC from Watergate. You probably already know all that, Vince. But perhaps you don't know that, before he came to Washington, Leonard was a Wisconsin state senator. In fact, he was Republican majority leader in the Wisconsin senate. And guess who was one of State Senator Jerris Leonard's key aides? Don't answer. That was a rhetorical question. You guessed it—Jim Sensenbrenner. Since Sensenbrenner was seventeen years old, Leonard has been his mentor."

I couldn't tell what Vince was thinking. He didn't say a word. He had, however, picked up a throw pillow and was hugging it to his chest.

"From what I'm told," I said, "Henry Hyde, Jim Sensenbrenner, and Jerris Leonard are asshole buddies. They work together. And now, in addition to being an attorney for clients like George Bush Senior, Richard Hirschfeld, and Bob Sensi, among others, Leonard's a big-time lobbyist and political fixer for all sorts of powerful interests."

"Jesus!" Vince said. "How high up do you think this goes?"

"We've got Hyde, Sensenbrenner, Leonard," I said, "and now you tell me C. Boyden Gray's joined in. It's already pretty high, don't you think? It's already one degree of separation from as high as you can get."

I hadn't heard a door open, or close, but now I heard footsteps on the keystone floor of the entry hall.

He didn't look like a man from the mysterious East, from Istanbul, a/k/a Constantinople, once the capital of the world. Nor, for that matter, did he look like a businessman-tycoon. He didn't look like a niche-marketing genius, or a great lover suspected by the FBI of having anatomical advantages. He didn't even look forty-two years old. He looked younger than that. And he was hip. Wearing black stovepipe pants, a silk shirt, and lace-up, square-toed, brown alligator shoes. He resembled a slim young Al Pacino, hurrying into the living room with a frown on his face. As soon as he saw us, his face brightened. "Vince!" he said. "I'm so sorry I'm late. The traffic! So much traffic."

Then he turned to me and smiled, shook my hand. "I'm Engin Yesil," he said in a quiet voice. He had brown eyes, dark brown hair, a long, handsome face. "I'm happy to meet you. Very happy. I believe you saved my life."

How do you respond to that? I smiled a shy smile. I shrugged. "I'm Larry Kolb. It's nice to meet you, too."

Engin was standing in front of the sofa facing the one Vince and I'd been sitting on. As he sat, he pointed me to the armchair nearest to him. "Sit here," he said. "So we can talk easier." He'd lived in the States so long that he sounded almost American, with only traces of an accent. "So here you are!" he said. Then he laughed, a bit uncomfortably, and I realized he might be as nervous as I was. This wasn't at all what I'd expected. "I finally get to thank you," he said. "There is no question in my mind—you saved my life."

I met his eyes for a moment. "I only did what I thought was right. Richard had to be stopped. That's all."

That said, I found myself looking down at my hands. There was nothing intimidating or threatening about Engin Yesil. I'd already figured out he wasn't there to decide whether to have me killed. At the moment, there was an emotion in me I didn't quite understand. It had something to do with two different people, within a couple of hours, thanking me for saving their lives.

More than thirty years ago, when I was in college, and a lifeguard, I'd drowned. My lungs filled with water. My heart stopped. And I was saved—by a student who'd learnt mouth-to-mouth resuscitation and heart massage in a scuba class. Months of recuperation later, when I went back to school, I made a point of finding the guy and thanking him for saving my life. I was a shy kid and the words hadn't come easily. But I had said them. And meant them. I had a feeling then that I'd been saved for a purpose, that there was something on this earth I was meant to do.

Eleven years later, in Birmingham, England, in a crazy crowd of a few thousand people trying to follow Muhammad Ali through a tight passage between two walls, I'd saved the life of a little girl who had gotten separated from her mother, had fallen, and was being trampled by the oblivious crowd. Afterward, police had brought her mother to me and she had thanked me. Ever since then, a part of me had felt that maybe my purpose was served. That there was no more reason for me to be here.

"Well, thank you again," Engin said.

We needed to change the subject.

"So Richard's been inside this house?" I asked.

"A hundred times he's been in this house. He sat in the same chair you're sitting in. And on this couch. And that couch, right where Vince is sitting. But he's not here anymore. Thanks to you."

"*And* Vince," I said. "None of this would've happened if Vince hadn't been looking out for you." Vince was sitting very quietly, a primatologist in a rainforest, watching Engin and me.

"Yes," Engin said. "And Vince."

I looked at Vince long enough to see him smile. Then I caught myself looking down again, at my fingers. I made myself look up. "Did you ever speak with Richard after you learned his real name?"

Engin grinned. "Right after I found out, I called him and said, 'Richard?' He said, 'Hi, Engin! How are you?' I said, 'Richard *Hirschfeld*.' He didn't say a word. Silence. Then I said, 'Richard, *you motherfucker!*' And he hung up."

"Good riddance," Vince said.

Whatever I'd been feeling, it had passed. "I asked to meet you," I said, "because I wanted to tell you I've discovered Hirschfeld was targeting you way back in 1995, maybe even before that. He's been after you ever since then."

Engin nodded. "I know."

So much for my big surprise.

"I'm very sorry," Engin said. "I knew Vince was coming over for a little while this evening. But until this afternoon, I didn't know you were coming, too. Now I've gotten here late, and I have people coming over soon. So, while we have this time, let me quickly tell you what I know of how all this adds up."

"Yes, please."

"As you probably noticed out in front of the house," Engin began, "I love cars. When I was a kid, I had posters of cars all over the walls in my room. When I came here to go to college, there were currency-transfer restrictions in Turkey. It was easier for my father to send my living expenses in one lump instead of sending a little bit every month. Do you know what I'm saying?"

"Yes."

"He sent me thirty-five thousand dollars. I didn't need all that right away. So I set aside twenty thousand dollars. It became my working capital. I found a car, a 1981 Porsche 928, in wrecked condition in New York. I bought it at an insurance auction for eleven thousand dollars. Towed it back to Gainesville on a U-Haul behind my girlfriend's Camaro, spent seven thousand dollars fixing it. I did all the work myself. Then I traded it for a new 1984 Corvette. And I turned around and sold the 'Vette for twenty-four thousand dollars. This netted me six thousand dollars, the first money I ever made. My first deal! After that, I was always buying high-end wrecked cars, fixing them, and selling them. That was my first business. It was so successful that I never needed any more outside capital. Everything grew from that. Do you know what I'm saying?"

"Yes. Wow! A very nice return on twenty thousand dollars."

Engin smiled.

"As you've also heard," he said, "I went away to prison. What you probably heard was I went away for distributing cocaine. Which isn't exactly true. Actually, it was *conspiracy* to distribute cocaine. I never actually saw the cocaine. I wasn't a drug dealer."

"I've seen the papers," Vince said. "That's true. The charge was 'aiding and abetting' distribution."

Engin said, "Back in the eighties, I met a guy in Daytona Beach who *was* a drug dealer. He said to me, 'I'll give you fifty thousand dollars if you introduce me to someone in Miami who is a big supplier.' Being the little entrepreneur that I was, and not understanding the conspiracy laws, I stupidly agreed. I was a cool kid. I liked the night life. I knew a lot of people, including drug smugglers. Miami was the capital of drug smuggling in the eighties, so it wasn't difficult for me to make a quick fifty thousand. I introduced them and bought myself a Lamborghini with the money.

"Some years later, these guys got busted and they turned me in to lower their sentences. Five years after I introduced them, I got indicted for conspiracy. By then, I had a business called Lens Express. The prosecution tried to confiscate the business, claiming I had used that fifty thousand dollars to start it. I proved I had used the money for a car instead. So I made a fifty-thousand-dollar restitution to the government and the forfeiture action was lifted from my business. Big difference. We'll come back to Lens Express. You will see—I mentioned it for a reason.

"Anyway, I made a youthful mistake and paid the consequences. I served twenty months. It was a humbling experience, and it was difficult. But, now I look back and say, hey, I paid my dues, I didn't get away with anything. So, my conscience is clear. Do you know what I'm saying?"

"Yes. Where were you in prison, by the way?"

"Mostly Eglin. When I got out, there were more consequences: The INS was trying to deport me. For eight years, I fought it. That's how I met Richard. And Sensi."

"How?"

"Well, Arik—who called me and told me he met you today and you are all right, not to worry—introduced me to Richard here in Miami. A few days after that, I went to Washington with Richard. In Washington, Richard introduced me to Sensi. Sensi showed me his CIA badge, and we went to a restaurant."

"Which restaurant?"

Engin stopped to think. "I don't know," he said eventually. "It was a steak restaurant is all I remember. Richard said, 'Engin, there is no justice. There is *just us*. We can solve your immigration problem. But to do that we need two hundred thirty thousand dollars and thirty percent of your telecommunications company.'"

"He just flat-out said that?" I asked. "No mating dance? No patriotic pitch about how the CIA needed special funding off the books?"

"No," Engin said. "But to be clear: Richard said he was an attorney who sometimes did secret work for the CIA, and sometimes did legal work for the CIA. He said he also did legal work for other clients, privately. Richard said he could fix my immigration problem in exchange for legal fees of two hundred thirty thousand dollars and thirty percent of my telecommunications company."

"They're pricks," Vince said. "They're just cold-blooded pieces of shit."

And on that note, Engin's guests started arriving.

The first one walked right into the living room. Engin got up, said hello, slapped him on the back, then, in what I thought was Turkish, sent him off to another room. When the next guest showed up, a few minutes later, Engin went through the same thing, then took off in search of his staff—none of whom Vince and I had seen since our arrival.

Soon there was a Brazilian woman standing in the entry hall to direct traffic, and Engin was back on the sofa telling his story. "I had lived here since I was seventeen years old. I could go back to Turkey and live like a king. But I love America. The style of business. The opportunities. Here I had my telecommunications business and other businesses I've started. And most important, by now I had a son, who lives in North Miami with his mother. I love my son. No price was too high. I told Richard, 'Okay, that's fine, I'll do it.'"

What happened next was a stroke of luck for Hirschfeld and Sensi, who'd never made a habit of actually delivering what they'd promised. The Supreme Court ruled in Engin's favor, and the INS dropped its deportation order against Engin and gave him back his green card. This was due entirely to Vince Messina. He'd found a major flaw in the government's argument and written a brief. The INS had quickly capitulated. Hirschfeld and Sensi, though, had portrayed it slightly differently: "There is no justice. There is *just us,*" they reminded Engin. Then Richard took Engin's money, and an option on his shares, and suggested he shouldn't even bother paying Vince's bill for legal services.

Delivered from deportation, Engin slipped into a dreamworld where his perceptions were climate-controlled, force-fed, and manipulated for maximum effect. "When I look back now," he said, "I can't believe how stupid I was!"

Engin told me about his meeting with a U.S. Army general, in a hotel room in Miami Lakes. Apparently, the general played a recurring role in Hirschfeld's repertory company. In this scene, he was there not to offer assistance with immigration issues but to enlist Engin's help in the war on terror.

Engin told me about the day Hirschfeld showed him five passports—each in a different name, each issued by a different country, each bearing Hirschfeld's photograph. Engin said, "Are these real?" Hirschfeld said, "Yes. Would you like me to get you some?" Engin said, "No, thank you."

Engin told me about the five cell phones Hirschfeld carried. Each with a different ring tone. Each answered by Hirschfeld with a different identity. CIA, all the way, thought Engin.

Engin told me how, one day in Istanbul, Hirschfeld had shown up on his doorstep. Hirschfeld said he was on his way to Baghdad to see Paul Bremer but had decided to stop by and say hello to Engin first.

Guests kept arriving. The other side of Villa Luna was getting clamorous. Engin picked up his pace. Once he got going, his memory was a remarkable, whirling thing, full of precise details, names, dates, sums—together with jump cuts, vast gaps, and storylines that seemed to just peter out until he raced on to the next subplot. Still, I could tell what I was hearing was an extraordinary mind, and I had no doubt he would tie it all together in the end.

Engin told me how Hirschfeld and Sensi isolated him. How they drove a wedge between Engin and Arik. And another between Engin and Vince. Then they told Engin he was in big fucking trouble with the FBI, the IRS, the DEA, the DIA, the BCIS. And that much was true. But what Engin didn't know was he was a priority target of a multitude of federal agencies precisely because Richard "Marshall" had told them Engin was aiding and abetting terrorism.

One day, Engin got a call from his pilot. DEA agents had just interviewed him about Engin's travel patterns. They seemed particularly interested in Engin's baggage and whether he'd ever come home with more luggage than he'd left with. Engin grounded his plane, then sold it. "I decided, forget the plane, I can fly commercial. Do you know what I'm saying?"

Next Hirschfeld told Engin the DEA and the IRS suspected Engin was laundering drug money. Engin hired Kroll Associates, a huge private intelligence and investigatory firm that is America's preeminent expert on money laundering. Even the federal government often hires Kroll to investigate money laundering. Kroll performed a comprehensive forensic audit on Engin and his companies, then gave him a clean bill of health—and an invoice for three hundred seventy-five thousand dollars in fees. But the pressure from the government only increased.

"By now, I was going out of my mind worrying about all this," Engin said. "I finally realized just how extensive these investigations were when I got a call from Turkey. From a former employee of mine. His name is Korhan Aydin. I have a business in New York that does proprietary trading of stocks and foreign currencies. We're not brokers. It's all my own money. You need very smart guys working for you to make a business like this succeed. I used to try hiring American MBAs, but there was so much competition for them, it was hard getting good ones. So I started hiring the very brightest Turkish MBAs, from the most prestigious Turkish universities. Right after they graduated, I would get them visas and they would come to the United States and work for me.

"Suddenly, there were problems getting the visas. I realize now it was because Hirschfeld and Sensi told the government I was using this business as a front to smuggle in terrorists. Korhan, who used to be my employee and was trying to get a visa to come back to America, called me. As is his right, he had requested a copy of his INS transcript. When he received it, he found the INS had made a mistake. They'd included with his transcript something else from his file: a copy of a report from an office inside the U.S. Embassy in Athens to an office inside the U.S. Consulate in Istanbul.

"He said, 'Engin, it's frightening. These guys know every place I took a crap in my entire life! They investigated every personal detail about me. They talked to my old friends and everybody else I ever met. They talked to every one of my professors, showed them my picture to see if they remembered me, and to see if I really got an A in such and such a class and a B in another class. This is not normal procedure for a visa application, Engin.

"'And it gets worse. They interviewed me and asked me about other Turkish guys who went to America to work for you. They asked if I knew them, what they looked like, if they really worked in your offices, what their jobs were. They asked me about thirty names, Engin! This investigation covers thirty of us. All of us Turkish MBAs who went to New York or Miami in the last three years to work for you.'"

I've never actually been in a bar in Istanbul. But to my ears, the other side of Engin's house was now sounding a lot like a bar in Istanbul. A bar in Istanbul with a big soccer match on the television. Faint sounds of clinking glasses and ice cubes kept wafting into the living room, with occasional explosions of cheering and groaning, followed by excited voices in a stew of English and what I assumed was Turkish.

Engin excused himself, said he would go and ask his friends to give us a few more minutes. When he got back, he told us how, now that they'd created a huge problem for him, Hirschfeld and Sensi offered to solve it. There's no justice. There's *just us*. It would cost him, of course. But by then, money was the least of Engin's worries. He had done nothing wrong and he hadn't been formally charged with anything—but there were U.S. government agencies that, forget prison, seemed to want to lock him up in a cage in Guantánamo.

Hirschfeld collected more cash from him and got him to sign away more options and things. Then Hirschfeld and Sensi introduced him to Bill McCollum.

"I'm sorry," I said, trying not to sound excited. "Would you repeat that."

He did.

"Do you know who Bill McCollum is?" I said to Vince.

Of course he knew—at least, that McCollum was a former U.S. congressman. But Vince was good at playing dumb. And he knew I was trying to tell him something.

"I don't know the names of every congressman from every state,"

I said to Vince. "Since you're not from Florida, I should tell you that for something like twenty years Bill McCollum was the U.S. congressman from up around Orlando. He's an arch-Republican and was big on the House Intelligence and Judiciary Committees. If you'll think back—along with Henry Hyde and Jim Sensenbrenner, Bill McCollum was one of the House Managers, the prosecutors, in the Clinton impeachment trial. Now he's out of Congress and doing some sort of Florida homeland security consulting for Jeb Bush. Do you remember him now?"

"Yes," Vince said. "Jesus! *That* Bill McCollum."

Engin went on.

Hirschfeld wrote a letter to the assistant director of the FBI, John Collingwood. He wrote it on the letterhead of Engin's company, Radiant Telecom, and Engin signed it. The letter was to be personally delivered to Collingwood by Bill McCollum. In the letter, Engin explained Radiant's capabilities and offered to do anything possible, in the U.S. or abroad, to assist the United States government in infiltrating or eavesdropping on terrorist groups. And he offered logs, traffic analyses, and other transactional data for all of the millions of calls placed through his equipment. Engin had now granted Hirschfeld and Sensi access to everything they needed to take credit for an intelligence score.

"Did you ever hear back from McCollum?" I asked.

"No," Engin said. "Not after the letter. But I've been wondering about this: Yes, Richard and Bob are con men, and good at it. Maybe McCollum didn't know that. I didn't. They fooled me. But they could not have fooled everyone. They were in Washington, dealing with the FBI, DEA, CIA. These cannot all be stupid people. And they are very good at finding things out. I think someone in Washington, someone very big, had to be protecting them. Do you know what I'm saying?"

"Yes. I think you're right."

"But who?"

"I don't know," I said. "Not yet. But I'm working on it."

"I read in a memo," Engin said, "that Muhammad Ali and Hirsch-feld first met Sensi through Bush. Bush Senior. Right?"

"Yes."

"That was the memo that killed my WQNI deal," Engin said. "You wrote it?"

"Yes."

He was looking right into my eyes, and he still didn't look like he wanted to end my life.

"Come with me," he said. "Vince, you too."

Engin led us out through a mahogany-and-glass rear door, then across coquina flagstones and under two orderly rows of royal palms to the edge of his lawn—which was guarded by a pair of winged lions, gargoyles, carved of stone. At first I thought we were out there because he was concerned about eavesdropping devices in his living room.

We stood together between the winged lions and Engin went on with his story. "After you warned John Kerry, Bob Farmer warned me. And you were absolutely right, Larry. Farmer said Kerry's people had investigated and found Richard was trying to set Kerry up, and to set me up. In exchange for a pardon, Richard was going to plant the story of Bob Farmer, John Kerry's campaign treasurer, now working in partnership with an ex-convict Muslim Turk drug dealer, et cetera, et cetera, who supplies terrorists their telecommunications needs." Engin paused for a moment, remembering. "They also looked at the checks for Kerry which Sensi and Richard and his son had given me to give to Farmer. Every one of them was a subtle violation of the campaign finance laws. It was clear. You were right. But at the time, I didn't know you existed. I thought Kerry's people had figured this out for themselves. Until I saw the memo, weeks later, I didn't know you had warned them."

"I didn't either," Vince said. "Larry did that on his own."

"So I was in my office," Engin said, "and an FBI man walked in. He showed me his badge. Then he showed me a photograph of Richard. He said, 'Is this the man who told you he is Richard Marshall?' I said, 'Yes,' and he said, 'Thank you,' and took off right away."

From where we were standing, it was about twenty steps across the lawn to the seawall and Biscayne Bay. Engin's house is on the southeastern side of Star Island. Across the black water, maybe eight hundred yards away, South Beach was glowing in the night. Five hundred thousand lights were twinkling over there.

When you wake up from the dream, you see everything differently. Now that he knew he'd spent the last couple of years amongst thieves and con men, Engin reevaluated all his dealings with Sensi and Hirschfeld. Mostly Hirschfeld. Sensi hadn't been around nearly as much as his partner. For Hirschfeld, the insideman, who became Engin's closest friend and legal advisor, Engin had signed pretty much anything Hirschfeld advised him to sign. There was a part of him, though, that hadn't fallen totally under Hirschfeld's spell. Engin had kept copies of everything he signed. He went back through the documents now and found his death warrant.

It was hidden inside an option agreement between Engin, personally, and David Phipps's company Growth Enterprise Fund, S.A., which Engin had believed was a secret pension fund for highest-level CIA executives. The agreement gave Phipps's company an option to acquire from Engin twenty percent of the shares of the company created by the merger of Ntera and WQNI. In exchange for these shares,

Engin was to receive sixteen million dollars' worth of shares of Global-Net, a public company controlled by Phipps.

But read the agreement very carefully, as Engin now did for the first time, and you would see that Phipps's company's rights to acquire Engin's shares were virtually perpetual, could be exercised at any time after the merger. But Engin's right to receive sixteen million dollars' worth of stock for his shares was personal to him, would expire upon his death, was not transferable to his estate or assignable to anyone or any entity. Engin had never seen any provision like that. Nor had his attorneys. The bottom line, they said, was that, if Engin were dead, Phipps's company could take Engin's shares for nothing. And, by the way, Phipps's company was actually owned and controlled not by Phipps but by Hirschfeld. On top of that, Engin said, Hirschfeld had taken out about twenty million dollars in key-man life insurance on Engin.

Engin grabbed one of my arms now, and one of Vince's. "Look over there," he said, talking fast and letting go of our arms and pointing now toward South Beach, "at that big building on the water with the pinkish glow. Now look just to the left of it, at the lower building also on the water. Do you see it?"

"Yes," we said.

"The day after I found out what the agreement meant, we discovered Richard had rented an office there, in that building, right across the water from my house, perfect for watching me all day long with a telescope, perfect for focusing listening devices on my house, perfect for a sniper with a rifle." For just a moment, Engin grabbed our arms again. "I was going to be whacked!"

He paused. Calmed down.

"So, again, I must thank you."

"Jesus!" Vince said, looking back over the water.

Engin said, "Let's go inside. I have to get going. But first there's one more thing I want to tell you."

Once we got inside, though, Engin's guests spotted him, and he was in demand. He ended up walking with us through the house out to the front doorstep, where we kept talking.

"This motherfucker Richard is so relentless," Engin said. "When I found out his real name, I got a pile of documents about him. I got some of them online, and some of them Vince sent me."

"Larry sent me those," Vince said. "For you."

"So, hour after hour, into the night, I was reading through these documents," Engin said, "learning what a criminal Richard Marshall Hirschfeld is. I read one page. 'Oh, my God!' I read another page. 'Oh, my God!' I read another page. 'Oh, my God!' It just kept getting worse and worse. All these things Richard had done! Every page was something more. He's been very busy doing bad things. Do you know what I'm saying?"

"Yes."

"So then I read this newspaper story about Richard trying to con his way out of prison, with the fake letter from Habitat for Humanity. And when I saw who wrote the letter for Richard, the hair stood up on my arm. Joseph Seriani!"

Engin paused for breath, but not for long. "When I went away, I went with my friend Yali. He was in it with me. I mean, in the deal, and in prison. We were sentenced together. Yali was my roommate in college in 1983. In 1984, Yali graduated and moved to Miami. He met Seriani and started working for him. Seriani was the visionary behind selling contact lenses in the mail. But he was a bad businessman and failed twice trying to make his idea work.

"I came down to Miami late in 1985, or maybe early '86. By the time I got here, Yali and Seriani were not on speaking terms. Yali was unemployed and trying to sell insurance for a living. He kept telling me about the mail-order lens business. He said, 'Engin, it's a great business. It would work, but Joe Seriani is a crook.' By the time Seriani came to Florida, he'd already been run out of Ohio and West Virginia, barred from practicing optometry there. Seriani was receiving orders, from thousands of customers, charging their credit cards, keeping the money, and not shipping the lenses. There were mail-fraud cases against him, and eventually he was convicted."

Vince cleared his throat. We were standing between two black wrought-iron lampposts that framed the front door. The lamps were on and the lenses of Vince's glasses were reflecting the lights. There was now a fourth black Porsche parked in Villa Luna's circular driveway.

"Seriani's company USA Lens was dead," Engin said, "and Seriani was in trouble. Meanwhile, Yali kept saying we should get in this business. When I was in college, I had accidentally thrown my girlfriend's lenses into a lake. It cost me three hundred fifty dollars to replace them. So it made sense to me immediately when Yali talked about selling contact lenses at a discount. Yali kept talking about it, and finally I said, 'Okay, let's do it.'

"We formed Lens Express in Fort Lauderdale on July 16, 1986. For the first three months, we used Yali's apartment as our office and warehouse. Then we moved into a small office on Commercial Boulevard. We worked hard. We executed. Ideas don't mean anything unless they are executed. Seriani is a perfect example of this. It requires hard work and brains to actually build a company that can service millions of consumers, shipping eighty thousand lenses a day. That's what we did.

"Then, right in the middle of it, Yali and I had to go away. While we were in prison, we were served papers. A complaint. Joe Seriani was suing us for treble damages under the RICO statute. When I read it, it was so well written that I nearly believed it myself. It said we were using Lens Express to launder our tens of millions of dollars in cocaine profits. It said we started the business by stealing Joe's customer lists and some of his inventory. It said we had falsely imprisoned Joe and threatened him and his family. None of it was true. Other than the fifty thousand dollars I told you about, we didn't have any cocaine profits. We didn't want Joe's customer lists—they were angry-customer lists. We advertised on TV and in *Cosmopolitan, Vogue, Mademoiselle, Glamour.* This was how we got our customers. After I read it, I said, 'Yali, did you falsely imprison Joe, or threaten him or his family?' Yali said, 'No.' I said, 'I didn't either. But you should read this. It's such a great story that you'll almost believe we did it.'"

Vince looked up at me and nodded. "I've read it," he said. "It's quite a masterpiece."

"The first lawsuit was dismissed, for technical reasons," Engin said. "But Seriani kept amending the complaint and re-filing. I don't know how many times, but it was a lot. This was still going on long after Yali and I got out. Seriani kept suing us. I thought this was one relentless guy.

"Over and over he sued us, but the case never got to trial stage. Finally, we received a new complaint. We had had this employee named Phyllis. She had worked for Seriani, and later she worked for us. In a deposition, she had backed up the government's story, the truth, which had sent Seriani to prison. She testified that Seriani was cheating customers, et cetera. But Phyllis got AIDS, and she died. After that, and after Joe Seriani went away to prison for mail fraud, and even after Yali and I sold Lens Express, we received another complaint. It came with an affidavit from *a priest!* Vince could explain this better than me. But one of the exceptions to the hearsay rule is a deathbed confession."

"Exactly," Vince said. "Ordinarily, hearsay is not admissible as evidence. But one of the exceptions to that is when the hearsay is a deathbed confession. In fact, under the law, deathbed confessions carry a lot of weight. There's a presumption that they tend to be true, because in their dying moments people unburden their consciences by telling the truth."

"Yes, that's it," Engin said. "So Seriani's lawsuit came with an affidavit from a priest who said that, on her deathbed, Phyllis confessed to him that Yali had forced her to testify falsely for the government so that Seriani would go to jail and it would be easier for us to steal his business. She said Yali threatened to kill her if she didn't go along with it. It was totally false. But that's how relentless Seriani was. At least, I thought so. But then, when I saw Seriani's name in the newspaper story about Richard, suddenly I knew that all along it was Richard behind these lawsuits, Richard writing this amazing story, Richard never giving up, Richard cooking up this deathbed confession.

"Then I finally understood that, although I only met him about three years ago, Richard had been after me since 1986, and he had come from Cuba just to get me. He came to get revenge from me and take money from me. He came to take advantage of the government's suspicion of Muslims after 9/11, which made me an easy target. Richard came here to use me every way he could, including getting a pardon for himself. Do you know what I'm saying?"

"Yes."

"I picked up the phone," Engin said, "and called Arik. I told him who Richard really is. Then I said, 'Arik, listen, I'm sorry we fought. That was all Richard's doing, you know. And I tell you this, man, we're both lucky to be alive.'"

"That you are," I said. "Do you remember the name of the priest?"

"No," Engin said. "I've forgotten." After he'd thanked me again and invited me to "come back whenever you like," and after we'd all shaken hands and said good-bye, and Vince and I had gotten into my car and left Star Island, over the little bridge to the causeway, and turned toward South Beach, Vince started laughing his head off.

"What?" I said. "What?"

Vince snorted, and laughed some more. "Jesus!" he said. Then he sputtered a while.

It was beginning to rain. I switched on the wipers. *"What?"*

Finally, Vince gathered himself and spoke. "I was just thinking," he said. "I wonder if it was Father Sensi."

It is recorded that, in that December of 2004, over cocktails at a Christmas party, C. Boyden Gray told White House Counsel Alberto Gonzales he was seeking a presidential pardon for Hirschfeld. And that Gray drafted, and personally delivered to Gonzales at the White House later that month, a forty-one-page clemency petition positing that Hirschfeld had been the victim of selective prosecution, a politically motivated vendetta against an innocent man who had done great things for his country.

It is also recorded that Jerris Leonard asked Senator John Warner to sponsor a pardon for Hirschfeld, and that Warner said no dice. Pat Robertson also declined to ask the President to let Hirschfeld go. Orrin Hatch was out of the question. No one even bothered to ask him to help Hirschfeld anymore. But Jerris Leonard kept working the food chain, looking for someone with clout to lend a hand to "a brilliant man and a fine lawyer" and "a real patriot for his country."

Leonard's précis on the Hirschfeld case went beyond vague pronouncements of Hirschfeld's tireless patriotism. According to a classified Department of Defense report cited, but not read, by Leonard,

Hirschfeld had played a key role in capturing Saddam Hussein. How? Telephonically, of course.

The DOD report, which must have been all the more alluring to Leonard because he didn't have the security clearance required to actually read it, said Hirschfeld's satellite phone company had supplied the Defense Intelligence Agency a revolutionary new surveillance device that could be used to monitor movements of friendly or hostile forces or individuals. The device was said to be "copperplated" and "about the size of a cigarette pack," small and light enough to be concealed within a handheld satphone.

According to Leonard, DOD officials confirmed to him that Hirschfeld's contributions to national security had been "so important" that they were willing to lobby for a pardon for Hirschfeld. Thomas E. Mooney, Sr., staff director and general counsel for the House International Relations Committee, acknowledged he'd been briefed on the DOD report, and went on to say that Hirschfeld's purported role in locating Saddam was "fascinating, like something out of a spy novel." Mooney also said his boss, Henry Hyde, the committee's chairman, might have "written a letter to the Justice Department asking for a review" of Hirschfeld's case.

We're lucky to know that much. So much of what happens in the backrooms of the powerful, in Washington and around the world, is never even hinted at. Sometimes, as in this case, we get a few clues, trace evidence of what really happened versus what we were told happened, or what we were never told about at all. Think of what we do know about the attempt to free Hirschfeld as outward signs that something much bigger happened. What exactly, we can't know.

As to whether Henry Hyde, himself, was briefed on the DOD report, or whether Jim Sensenbrenner or Bill McCollum was also involved in the campaign to spring Hirschfeld, there is no known record. A published account says that at that Christmas party, Gonzales told Gray he would telephone him to discuss Hirschfeld's clemency petition. But there is no available evidence as to whether Gonzales did call Gray about the matter, or whether Karl Rove or President Bush was informed of the situation.

The few published references to the secret war over the fate of Richard Hirschfeld, as incomplete as they are, do provide us one more tantalizing clue as to who was involved and what was really going on. One newspaper account says the DOD report central to Hirschfeld's clemency campaign was written by two "covert government operatives for the Defense Department" and that the co-author of the report had "close ties" to a "former CIA operative, who now works as a consultant for the Defense Intelligence Agency."

There are many former CIA operatives, and certainly more than a few of them consult now for the DIA. But I suspect I know the name of the former CIA operative who seems to have co-authored the classified report oft cited by Jerris Leonard. And I believe Richard Hirschfeld played an important role in the capture of Saddam Hussein about as much as I believe Saddam Hussein bought mountains of yellowcake uranium from Niger.

These things I know firsthand:

In the afternoon of the tenth of January 2005, I called Steve Kroft. I called him because I had just read a news story that said the independent panel report on Rathergate commissioned by CBS had been released earlier that day, and that insiders said there was an almost palpable feeling of relief inside the offices of *60 Minutes*. It seemed to me like a good time to call.

When I did, Steve asked me where things stood, and I told him

Hirschfeld was still in federal lockup in Miami, threatening to blow the whistle on the White House for something, while mysterious forces in Washington campaigned for his release. Meanwhile, I said, federal prosecutors in Virginia were still trying to extradite Hirschfeld, a Virginia attorney hired by Hirschfeld was attempting to restart stalled plea-bargain negotiations, and the last thing I'd heard was that Hirschfeld had been manically calling friends, announcing he was "calling from the Graybar Hilton," and telling them he was confident everything would work out and he would be home soon.

Steve said, "Why don't you call down there, talk to your old buddy Hirschfeld, and ask if he'll give me an interview for *60 Minutes*."

"Okay," I said. "That sounds like fun. I will. And I'll call you back tomorrow."

The next afternoon, with my heart pounding, I reached Steve on his cell phone.

"I just made that call to Miami," I said, "and there's going to be a problem arranging the interview."

"What did he say?" Steve said.

"I didn't talk to him. Hirschfeld's dead. He died this morning."

"*What!* In *federal custody*? Has there been an autopsy?"

"I don't know. I was told he killed himself. The details I got are sketchy. But I was also told it's going to break on the wires sometime soon. Maybe there'll be more information then."

After that, Steve asked me to keep him apprised as I learned more, and I said I would. I don't remember if I told Steve what I was feeling just then. But I do remember that, after Steve, I called Vince Messina, Gary Messina, Dave Kindred, John Alexander, Dave Morrison, and Bob Marx, one by one, and after announcing Hirschfeld was dead, I told each of them the pride I'd been feeling since Hirschfeld's arrest had vanished and what I felt now was a terrible sense of guilt.

If I was partly responsible for Hirschfeld's arrest, I was also at least partly responsible for his death. That calculus had been gnawing at me since I heard the news.

It only got worse when one of Hirschfeld's sons contacted me. A couple of weeks after Hirschfeld's death, I opened the webmail site readers could use to send me e-mail, and in the Inbox was a message "From: Kevin Hirschfeld/Subject: Richard Hirschfeld." I didn't want to click it open. I was afraid not to.

By then, I knew the official version of Hirschfeld's death: On the eleventh of January 2005, Richard M. Hirschfeld, Inmate Number 24226-083, hanged himself in the laundry room of the Miami Federal Detention Center. When found, he was alive but unconscious. Paramedics were called. He was rushed to Jackson Memorial Hospital in Miami. There he was pronounced dead at 9:42 A.M.

Newspaper reports said prison telephone transcripts revealed Hirschfeld called his wife Loretta a few minutes before he took his life, asking her to forgive him and not hate him.

"How could I hate you?" Loretta replied, according to the newspaper stories.

"For giving up," Hirschfeld answered, according to the same stories.

Certain newspapers reported he then carried his laundry bag into the prisoners' laundry room, removed the cord from the bag, fashioned a noose, and hanged himself from an overhead pipe. But *The Washington Post* reported Hirschfeld hanged himself with plastic wrap. And another account said he wrapped cellophane from his breakfast tray around his face and then hanged himself with a rope.

By the time I received the e-mail message, I also knew rumors were swirling in the intelligence and homeland security communities that the official version of Hirschfeld's death was a cover-up. Some said Hirschfeld had been whacked. Others—sane, experienced intelligence professionals I spoke with—theorized that he wasn't even dead. They suggested he could've been spirited out of the jail by operatives posing as paramedics, then put on a plane bound for Israel or some other far-flung destination while, back in Miami, he was declared dead and a body was substituted for his. "Why wasn't there an autopsy?" was one of the questions I heard more than once. Another was "Did you know the body was cremated, and that cremation is against Jewish law?"

So when I received the e-mail message "From: Kevin Hirschfeld/ Subject: Richard Hirschfeld," the first thing I felt was fear. It was a fear, I realized immediately, not unlike the fear Dave Kindred had told me he'd felt when, long after he'd thought he'd heard the last of Richard, he'd received an e-mail message from Cuba asking for information about Hirschfeld. A part of me wondered, *What if it's not really Kevin Hirschfeld, but Richard Hirschfeld writing me?*

I clicked the message open.

Mr. Kolb, I recently lost my father to suicide. He was an intriguing individual, and a loving father. From your book I believe you may know more of his life than I actually did. You only made reference to him in Overworld once, but it sounds as if your lives may have been much more entwined. If you could possibly enlighten me I would be very grateful.

Thank you,
Kevin Hirschfeld,
SON OF THE LATE RICHARD HIRSCHFELD

Reading it, I started feeling guilty all over again. Despite all the rumors, and notwithstanding the moment of fear I'd felt before I opened Kevin Hirschfeld's message, I had come to the conviction that Hirschfeld was dead. Now I felt myself falling through a trapdoor back into the first few days and weeks after my own mysterious father's sudden death. I would never have another chance to talk to him, to ask him questions, to learn more about who he really was. Kevin Hirschfeld, I thought, was feeling the same things I'd felt once.

I could've told him his father was a world-class shit, a crook and a con man who'd left human wreckage everywhere he passed. I could've said that, as far as I could tell, there was no arc to his father's integrity, no defining moment before which he was good and after which he was bad—he was born bad. I could've told him a friend of mine had once tracked down his father's first babysitter, who'd said, "From the time he could talk, Richie would rather lie to you for a dime than tell you the truth for a dollar." I could've told him that, if ever in the future he heard tales of his father's clever adventures and was tempted to feel pride or admiration, he should remember the toll his father had taken: real people, ripped off, stung, cheated, robbed blind, their businesses and reputations ruined by a man they'd trusted—for his father was a visionary who destroyed as he created. And maybe Kevin Hirschfeld was looking for the truth. But if I was remembering accurately my own feelings in the first weeks after my father's death, what I most needed then was consolation, not truth.

I read Kevin Hirschfeld's message again and again. *Overworld* was about my life in intelligence, and reading *Overworld* gave him the impression his father's life and mine might be intertwined. If he wasn't subtly telling me he knew I'd brought about his father's capture, and thus his father's death—Kevin Hirschfeld was asking me if his father was really a CIA agent, a good man who'd done bad things for a good cause.

So in my reply, I told Kevin Hirschfeld how lost I'd felt when my father died. I said I did know more about Kevin's father than I'd let on in my book, and would be glad try to answer any questions he wanted to send me. It wasn't until our second round of messages that I told Kevin I knew Bob Sensi had recruited his father for the CIA, then used him in various covert capacities, about which I couldn't say more because of the federal laws that prohibit disclosing intelligence sources and methods.

That was true enough, if grossly incomplete, and right away it brightened Kevin Hirschfeld's tone. We chatted occasionally by e-mail over the next several days, but he never again seemed as alone or as anxious to know what I knew. Once I'd soothed his soul, I did what I was trained to do. I extracted as much intelligence about Richard Hirschfeld as I could get out of Kevin Hirschfeld—and that made me feel even guiltier.

9. APPOINTMENT IN SAMARRA

Vince and I were back in South Beach now, seated across from each other at another table, this one in a fine Italian clip joint on Lincoln Road. Across the room from us, on the other side of the windows, it was pouring down rain and, a first for me in Miami, it was cold out there. Vince was polishing off a plate of linguine with clam sauce. He seemed to be enjoying it, and that was what mattered, I supposed. I tried not to see an augury in the fact that it was the same dish he'd eaten during our lunch at The Palm—but I do notice these things.

Anyway, this was dinner in Miami, not lunch on the other side of the country. What could go wrong? Vince was drinking red wine, I was drinking Red Bull, and we'd spoken about pretty much everything there was to speak about except the one topic we knew we'd get to eventually: Hirschfeld, Sensi, and their labyrinth of backers, bosses, confederates, victims. Vince was such a wonderful talker. He'd just told me of his recent travels in Libya. Then he'd moved on to Kuwait. Now, while I poured him some more Barbaresco, he crossed the border into Iraq.

It sounded as if he'd had quite a time there. He told me of the harrowing run from Baghdad International Airport, through badlands where anything can happen, the checkpoints, the barbed wire, the hellscape, past the burnt-out, tangled wreckage of a city, into the administrative heart of the occupation—the fortified and barricaded American ghetto called the Green Zone.

Nothing was going right in Iraq from an American perspective, unless you were a war profiteer. We talked about that for a while, and just when it seemed we were about to leave Iraq and spend the rest of our evening discussing Richard M. Hirschfeld and company, Vince smiled and got a faraway look in his eyes.

"One morning in Baghdad," he said, "a rich businessman sent his servant to the soukh to buy household supplies. After a while, the servant came back, trembling, afraid. He said, 'Master, just now in the soukh, a woman bumped me, and when I turned and looked at her she made a threatening gesture. Please, master, lend me your horse and I will ride away from the city.'

"I wish you could've seen this horse, Larry," Vince went on. "He was a big white Arabian stallion, a champion. The master said, 'Yes, of course. Go with God. And take good care of my horse.'"

It was only while Vince was describing the servant climbing onto the horse—recounting it so well, remembering every detail, as if he'd seen it himself—that I finally realized he was telling me a centuries-old Arab tale that I'd read somewhere before.

"As he was mounting this magnificent horse," Vince said, "the servant said to his master, 'Pray for me. For when I turned and saw the woman that bumped me in the soukh, I recognized that she is Death. I will ride now to Samarra and avoid my fate. In Samarra, Death will not find me.' The servant dug his heels into the horse's flanks and away they went, galloping over hard-packed yellow sand beside the banks of the Tigris."

Vince stopped for a sip of wine, drawing the story out. "Then the rich businessman went down to the soukh to investigate. He found the woman in the crowd, stopped her. He asked her, 'Why did you make a threatening gesture to my servant this morning?' And the woman said, 'That was not a threatening gesture. It was a start of surprise. I was shocked to see him in Baghdad, for I have an appointment with him tonight in Samarra.'"

After a pause, Vince said, "Have you heard that story, Larry?"

"Yes, sort of." I nodded. "I think I read it somewhere."

He broke some bread and dabbed it in one of the trails of red sauce left on his plate. He took a bite, then said, "John O'Hara reprinted it, on a separate page, right before the start of his novel *Appointment in Samarra*."

"You mean," I said, "it was the epigraph. Maybe that's where I saw it. I don't remember."

I poured him some wine.

"Anyhow," Vince said, "I brought it up because I've been thinking about what you told me about your first encounters with Hirschfeld. You said they started out nicely enough but he ended up screaming at you. That's very unusual for Hirschfeld, you know. Almost everyone he ever met came away charmed by him."

I nodded.

"Even in all those newspaper stories that came out after his death," Vince said, "almost everyone had something good to say about him. Even the prosecutors who'd tried to put him away, and the Feds who'd tried to catch him. Even some of his victims talked as if it was almost an honor to have been conned by Richard Hirschfeld, and they wouldn't have missed it for the world."

"And yet," I said, "from the moment I first spoke with Hirschfeld,

I didn't like him or trust him. Maybe he thought I saw through him. Maybe that's why he ended our first few calls by screaming at me."

"Maybe," Vince said. "But I think it's even more than that."

"What?"

"I think that, from the beginning, in some dark corner of his soul, Richard realized that you were his destiny, that you would be his death, that you were his appointment in Samarra."

"I don't know about *that*," I said.

"The screaming was to drive you away. But you can't change fate."

"Last summer," I said, "while I was up all those nights doing all that work, making the choices I made, searching for a pattern in the chaos, flying off to New York to warn Kerry, it didn't feel like destiny. It felt like free will. Though I must admit, Vince, I don't really know what destiny feels like."

"Yes, you do. You do now."

"No. I really don't. But since you've put us on this tack, listen to this:

"A couple of weeks after Richard killed himself, or was killed, whatever really happened, I received an e-mail message from his son Kevin Hirschfeld. One of my first thoughts was 'How the fuck did they find me so soon?' So that was one of the first things I asked Kevin in the course of the conversation we had by e-mail over the next few weeks.

"I'd heard that Hirschfeld was reading my book in his cell. But Kevin said one of his brothers had found my book on the Internet. I don't know which story is true. Anyway, he said when they got the book and read the dustjacket they were struck by all the similarities between their father's story and mine. I got the feeling their first impression was 'Maybe this book was written by our father. Maybe Larry Kolb was just another one of his identities.'"

Vince leaned forward, eyes wide.

"I mean, think about it, Vince," I said. "Two American white boys who suddenly had high-level contacts all over the Muslim world, thanks to their close friendships with Muhammad Ali. Both of them are recruited by the CIA. Both of them end up in hiding in Florida.

"Well, I'd never really thought about that," I continued, "but I had to admit Kevin had a point. There *was* a certain synchronicity to it all. And I can only imagine what Kevin and his brother thought when they read the second sentence of Chapter One. I can't remember it exactly, but it says I was born in Norfolk, Virginia. Which is where Richard grew up. I knew that much. But I didn't know where he was born. I couldn't get that information out of the Virginia authorities. All the states have cracked down on birth certificates and things like that since 9/11."

"Yes. I know," Vince said.

"So I asked Kevin, 'Where was your father born?' And Kevin wrote back, 'Norfolk.'"

Vince reached for his wine, without taking his eyes off of me.

"So then I wrote Kevin again and said, 'Where in Norfolk?' And he wrote me back, 'Norfolk General Hospital.'

"Well, damn it, Vince! That's where I was born. So then I called the hospital and asked them if the hospital had moved between 1947, when Richard was born, and 1953, when I was. 'No.' So I asked how many delivery rooms they had back then. 'One.' Then I asked if by any chance the delivery room had been moved between those years. 'No.' I don't know what to make of it, Vince, but Richard Hirschfeld and I were born in the same room!"

"Jesus!" Vince said. "Jesus! It was fate."

The rain had died down. Three damp people arrived. Several

people left. Then the three damp people finished scanning the menu and left too.

A few minutes later, Vince announced: "There are now more waiters than customers in here. And they'd better get used to it. Jesus! Would you look at that rain!"

It was pouring again.

"By the way," I said, "I've now discovered that way back in 1983, Hirschfeld tried to take Seriani's lens business public. He and Seriani were working together at least ten years earlier than I'd originally learned. I don't know if you remember, but back when Engin and his partner Yali were convicted, in 1990, the prosecutors recommended probation. No jail time. Instead, the judge sentenced them to six years in prison. Meanwhile, the drug dealer who actually sold the cocaine got three years. There was something very odd about that. Now that I know Hirschfeld was already Seriani's silent partner back then, and knowing what we know about Hirschfeld's M.O., I don't have much doubt Hirschfeld was behind all of Engin's troubles with the government, from the date of his sentencing on."

"In other words," Vince said, "if it weren't for Hirschfeld orchestrating behind the scenes, Engin never would've even gone to prison."

"Exactly."

Vince sighed. "This whole thing's shocking," he said. "The corruption and crudeness. It could undermine your faith in elected officials and public servants. Unless you happen to have spent half your life in Washington, like I have, in which case there's no such faith to undermine. Are you sure you won't have some wine?"

"I'll have a sip," I said. "Just a taste. How is it, anyway?"

"It's great," Vince said, pouring a glass for me.

We'd recently learned Hirschfeld had written and mailed a pair of long, lugubrious suicide letters before he shuffled off his mortal coil.

Or someone shuffled it off for him. Vince's latest theory was that Hirschfeld had agreed to stage a suicide attempt that would get him out of jail and ultimately out of the country. But he'd been double-crossed and, once he was out of the jail, someone had helped him complete his suicide. As Vince wound up his explanation of this, he asked me, "What do you think?"

"I think he killed himself," I said. "I think it was one last self-indulgent act. But you may be right. There's a secret world out there, it's all around us. We'll never know the real story."

Outside, it was thundering now. Rain was spinning in the arc lights and dancing on the sidewalks. We wouldn't be leaving any-time soon.

Vince finished his wine, then settled back into his chair. "You're right," he said. "We'll never know the whole story." Then he smiled at me and closed his eyes, as if to sleep.

"No," I said. "And I'm not sure we want to. Might be dangerous."

Not as dangerous, though—I thought while we sat there waiting for the storm to pass—as the fact that our best law enforcement and counterintelligence services could not, or would not, track down or even I.D. Richard Hirschfeld. And that the highest-level Republicans in America today seem more than willing to keep jumping into bed with criminals. There are some very strange things going on in the night. Meanwhile, our government has spent trillions turning Iraq into the world's largest terrorist training camp, while pursuing poli-cies guaranteed to keep at least a billion people around the world intensely pissed off at us. Our military forces are so overstretched that, if any real threat emerges, we will risk being seen as a paper tiger. And in spite of all the blue-ribbon panels and commissions, and the new layer of bureaucracy called the Department of Homeland Se-curity, the hundreds of billions of dollars spent to make us safe at home, America is less safe now from terrorism and cataclysm than it ever was.

If you doubt that, think back to the year of two popes, and the second inauguration of the second President Bush—and nearly a thousand more Americans dead in Iraq. It was another year of optimistic generals and no victory, of waterboarding and rendering, but no Osama. It was the year Richard Hirschfeld did or did not die, and the year more than half of the American people finally lost faith in our president. It was the year we watched New Orleans drown, and saw for ourselves that the summer is over, the harvest is in, and we are not saved.

AUTHOR'S NOTE

Several persons who played significant roles in the events recounted in this book—including Vince Messina, Gary Messina, Dave Kindred, Arik Meimoun, Effi Yeoshoua, Dan Schwartz, Steve Kroft, John Alexander, Dave Morrison, Sarah-Jane Wilde, and Bill Dewey—have read either the entire text of this book or, in a few cases, only those portions of the text that describe events and conversations in which they were involved. Each of them has agreed that the text faithfully reflects their recollections of the circumstances and events described in the book. Robert Sensi and Jerris Leonard, who also play significant roles in this story, were invited by me to answer one hundred thirty-three questions, which I submitted to them in writing; but, for the most part, they declined.

It was with documentary evidence, most of it available—though often thoroughly obscured—in the public record, that, in late May and early June of 2004, I pieced together the story of Hirschfeld and Sensi, and then figured out what they were really up to. All of the documents I used then, and several other relevant documents that I have found since, are listed in the Bibliography section of this book. Many of the source materials I found most significant or useful are also identified, chapter by chapter and fact by fact, in the Notes section of this book.

Most of the conversations quoted in this book were not recorded and have been re-created. As re-created, they faithfully represent my recollections or the recollections of the persons who told me, first-hand, about the conversations. When quoting written material, I have in a few cases made minor edits for the sake of clarity and brevity, while endeavoring to avoid changing the substance of any written source. To protect the identity of a friend who works in a covert capacity for an American intelligence service, I have altered, by just one day, the chronology of events as it relates to precisely when and how I met and spoke with him concerning the curious case of Messrs. Hirschfeld and Sensi; that change in no way alters anything he told me, as recounted in this book. Toward keeping my promise not to reveal the identity of the person I have called the Gray Eminence, I have changed certain details regarding the location of his office, which is indeed in New York. With that exception, everything I have written about my conversations and correspondence with the Gray Eminence is completely factual. The story told in this book is true.

ACKNOWLEDGMENTS

I acknowledge with gratitude the help of many people who generously assisted me with this book. André Verløy searched through the archives, document boxes, filing cabinets, dumpsters, databases, and cesspools of Washington for me, turning up material most would've thought, and some certainly would've hoped, had been lost forever. Vince Messina, Gary Messina, Engin Yesil, Ayesha Yesil, Arik Meimoun, Effi Yeoshoua, Nat Bynum, and Dave Kindred kindly shared with me many memories they would probably have preferred to forget. There are others, including friendly spirits working inside our intelligence community, who provided me with very useful information relating to this matter but who would be embarrassed if I mentioned them here.

James Ellroy, Richard Lourie, and Michael Connelly showed me extraordinary courtesy, spoiling me with encouragement and sage advice on how to turn my often-fragmented memories of a difficult season into a coherent narrative. Dan Barber, Robert Marx, Michael Woodhead, Malcolm Venville, Daniel Raymont, and Lynwood Spinks read early drafts of this book, and along the way pointed out several black holes in my thinking. Bernard Cohen put up with my many questions and translated more than a few passages from French into English for me. Pascal Riché learned the story told in this book over a year ago, while writing a profile of me for the French newspaper *Libération,* and then kept his word by keeping the story under his hat until I had finished writing it.

Joel Gotler, Justin Manask, and Maria Ruvalcaba Hackett, of Intellectual Property Group, represented me well in New York and Hollywood. Kathy Kennedy, and her colleagues Gregg Taylor and Mike Schneider, of the Kennedy/Marshall Company, read drafts of the beginning of this story even before the election of 2004, and after that were always available to share with me their advice and wisdom as I wrote this book. Sean McDonald, Larissa Dooley, and Molly Barton, of my publisher, Riverhead Books, gave me much encouragement and good advice. David Shanks and Alexander Gigante, of Riverhead's parent, Penguin Group (USA) Inc., ably fought off those who sought to prevent publication of this book.

For more than a year, Judith McNally worked by day for Norman Mailer, helping him turn out his next great novel, and by night for me, an untrained writer working on only his second book. This would not be the book it is if not for Judith. She contributed research, ideas, and stern but incisive editing. In the week before I wrote these acknowledgments, Judith died of a sudden illness. She went quickly and, I am certain, with courage. She is missed.

GLOSSARY OF ABBREVIATIONS AND ACRONYMS

BCCI	Bank of Credit and Commerce International
BCIS	Bureau of Citizenship and Immigration Services
BICE	Bureau of Immigration and Customs Enforcement
BIS	Bezpečnostní Informační Služba (Czech for "Security Information Service")
CAT	Civil Air Transport
CBS	Columbia Broadcasting System
CCTV	closed-circuit television
CIA	Central Intelligence Agency
CIO	Chief Information Officer
DARPA	Defense Advanced Research Projects Agency
DCI	Director of Central Intelligence
DEA	Drug Enforcement Administration
DIA	Defense Intelligence Agency
DOD	Department of Defense
FBI	Federal Bureau of Investigation
FEMA	Federal Emergency Management Agency
FUBAR	fucked up beyond all repair
GRU	Glavnoye Razvedyvatel'noye Upravleniye (Russian for "Chief Intelligence Directorate")

hazmat	hazardous materials
HUAC	House Committee on Un-American Activities
IED	improvised explosive device
INP	Israel National Police
INS	Immigration and Naturalization Service
IRS	Internal Revenue Service
JPEG	compressed digital image file
K-7th	kindergarten through seventh grade
KGB	Komitet Gosudarstvennoy Bezopastnosti (Russian for "Committee of State Security")
K-O	knockout
LAX	Los Angeles International Airport
LLC	limited liability company
M&A	mergers and acquisitions
MBA	Master of Business Administration
M.O.	modus operandi
Mossad	Ha-Mossad Ha-Merkazi Le-Modi'in Ve-Tafkidim Meyuchadim (Hebrew for "The Central Institute for Intelligence and Special Tasks")
MRE	meal ready to eat
MS	Microsoft
Nasdaq	National Association of Securities Dealers Automated Quotation System
NSA	National Security Agency
OC	organized crime
Op	operation
OSS	Office of Strategic Services
PI	private investigator
PLO	Palestine Liberation Organization
RAF	Royal Air Force

RICO	Racketeer Influenced and Corrupt Organizations Act
RNC	Republican National Committee
RPG	rocket-propelled grenade
S.A.	*société anonyme* (French for "corporation")
satphone	satellite telephone
SBU	Sluzhba Bezpeky Ukrayiny (Ukrainian for "Security Service of Ukraine")
SEC	Securities and Exchange Commission
Stasi	Staatssicherheitsdienst (German for "State Security Service")
SUV	sport-utility vehicle
TWA	Trans World Airways
UPS	United Parcel Service
Wi-Fi	wireless local area network
WQNI	WorldQuest Networks, Inc.

NOTES

1. HOW I SPENT MY SUMMER VACATION

1 **That book,** *Overworld:* Larry J. Kolb, *Overworld: The Life and Times of a Reluctant Spy* (New York: Riverhead Books, 2004).

2 **Miles Copeland had engineered the CIA's first coup d'état:** Copeland's role in the CIA's first coup d'état is detailed in Miles Copeland, *The Game Player: Confessions of the CIA's Original Political Operative* (London: Aurum Press, 1989) 88–109; and in Miles Copeland, *The Game of Nations* (New York: Simon & Schuster, 1969), 34–56. Copeland's relationship with Shah Reza Pahlavi is mentioned, in passing, in *The Game Player,* 190–191. Most of what I know about Copeland's relationship with the Shah, Copeland told me himself during the 1980s. Copeland's relationship with Nasser is the subject of much of *The Game of Nations.*

2 **In the 1960s, when Miles wrote a bestseller:** As to Philby's life and career, see Kim Philby, *My Silent War* (New York: Grove Press, 1968). See also Phillip Knightly, *The Master Spy: The Story of Kim Philby* (New York: Knopf, 1988).

2 **"I've known that intriguer for twenty years":** The quotation of Philby's remark on Radio Moscow is taken from a dustjacket of Copeland, *The Game of Nations.* Copeland was the last Western intelligence officer to see Philby on our side of the Iron Curtain.

6 **It took, they say, only the taste of a single cookie:** The first to say this was Proust himself. See Marcel Proust, *In Search of Lost Time: Volume I: Swann's Way,* translated by C. K. Scott Moncrief and Terence Kilmartin (New York: Modern Library Classics, paperback edition, 2004), 60–64.

6 **Gary was one of the highest-ranking officers:** Gary Messina was, as of my May 27, 2004, lunch with Vince Messina, the Chief Information Officer of the Bureau of Citizenship and Immigration Services, a division of the Department of Homeland Security. Prior to the formation of the Department of Homeland Security, Gary Messina served as the Assistant Commissioner of the Immigration and Naturalization Service.

7 **It was all fresh in my mind:** Kolb, *Overworld,* 205–229, 289.

7 **Early in 1985:** For a more detailed account of the meeting, see *Overworld,* 204–206.

7 **Sensi's primary mission for the CIA:** Sensi told me this on various occasions during 1985 and 1986. See also Deposition of Robert M. Sensi, conducted October 10–11, 1987, in Washington, D.C., filed March 25, 1988, in re *Kuwait Airways Corporation v. American Security Bank, N.A., and First American Bank, N.A.,* Civil Action No. 86-2542 (U.S. District Court, District of Columbia), 251–274.

7 **His primary mission for the Republican Party:** Sensi told me this during 1985 and 1986.

8 **Over the next few weeks, Sensi orchestrated meetings:** For a more detailed account of the London meetings, see *Overworld,* 208–211.

8 **But they seemed to be representatives:** Since 1985, I had believed that the white house in Belgravia, and the company it served as an office for, Cyrus International, were fronts for an Iranian intelligence service. Sensi told me as much during 1985. However, in 2005, while doing research for this book, I learned that Cyrus International was actually a CIA front, paid for by Sensi out of funds he obtained from Kuwait Airways. Sensi Deposition, 284.

8 **After several meetings in London:** For a detailed account of the trip to Beirut, see *Overworld,* 211–229.

8 **Months later, Sensi was arrested**: Martin Weil, "D.C. Man Arrested in London," *Washington Post,* August 26, 1986, B3.

8 **Sensi's defense was that he worked for the CIA:** Nancy Lewis, "Ex-Kuwait Airways Official Testifies of CIA Ties," *Washington Post,* October 21, 1987, A28, and "Testimony Details 1983 CIA Operation on Iran Moderates," *Washington Post,* March, 17, 1988, A24.

8 **Sometime after his release:** U.S. Department of Justice Press Release 94-585, "Federal Grand Jury Indicts Seven in International Money Scam," October 7, 1994.

9 **So I already liked these guys a lot:** Michael Fleming, "Atmosphere to Engulf 'Overworld': Canton, Goldmann to Produce Spy Pic," *Variety,* June 14, 2004.

2. PULP NONFICTION

15 **The CIA was:** Sensi Deposition, 251–274, and *Overworld,* 204–206.

17 **After that, the only other time:** The trip to Cairo is mentioned in *Overworld,* 430–431.

18 **In Jiddah, I'd once waited with Muhammad:** *Overworld,* 135–138.

18 **One day while we waited:** The telephone call from Ferdinand Marcos is mentioned in *Overworld,* 430–431.

19 **Three simple tasks:** House Committee on Foreign Affairs, Subcommittee on Asian and Pacific Affairs. *Plan to Invade the Philippines,* Report on Hearing of July 9, 1987, 100th Congress, 1st session, Washington, D.C., U.S. Government Printing Office, 1987, 16–21.

20 **He set up a complex deal:** *Plan to Invade the Philippines,* 30.

20 **In the end, Marcos wouldn't receive a single dime:** *Plan to Invade the Philippines,* 31.

20 **The People Power government:** In *Plan to Invade the Philippines,* 34–35, Hirschfeld states that the government of the Philippines agreed "to provide some reward for the efforts we made." Contemporaneously, Muhammad Ali informed me that, according to Hirschfeld, it had been agreed that the reward would be a five-percent commission.

21 **But he also kept leaning closer and closer:** *Plan to Invade the Philippines,* 63.

21 **During the trial of Adnan Khashoggi:** My wife, Kim Patrick, is Adnan's Khashoggi's stepdaughter.

22 **He developed a particularly close friendship:** Dave Kindred, "The Man and the Voice: Part Two: Ali-Hirschfeld Relationship Steeped in Curiosities, Intrigue," *Atlanta Journal-Constitution,* December 12, 1988, A1.

22 **Night after night, he called senator after senator:** For more detailed accounts of Hirschfeld's telephone impersonations of Ali, see Dave Kindred, "The Man and the Voice" (3-part series), *Atlanta Journal-Constitution,* December 11, 12, and 13, 1988, A1, and *Washington Post,* "'Muhammad Ali Calling'—Or Is It?" December 11, 1988, A8.

25 **Next I pulled from the SENSI file:** Anonymous, unattributed background report on "Robert Mario Sensi. Born November 22, 1950, in Blue Island, Illinois," transmitted by telecopier by Miles A. Copeland to Larry J. Kolb, c. 1985.

27 **With his olive skin:** When I knew him, during the eighties, Sensi's skin was either olive or deeply tanned, and his hair and mustache were dark brown. Reporter Robert Parry, who knew Sensi in the eighties, said Sensi "looks a bit like Saddam Hussein except a lot less sinister." Parry, *Fooling America: How Washington Insiders Twist the Truth and Manufacture the Conventional Wisdom,* New York, William Morrow & Co., 1992, 140. But two people who believe they met Sensi as recently as 2003 and 2004 have told me "Sensi is fair and blond."

28 **We'd been to a charity dinner with Muhammad:** The dinner was the American Academy of Achievement's Twenty-fifth Annual Banquet of the Golden Plate, in Washington, D.C., on the night of Saturday, the twenty-eighth of June 1986.

28 **Deep-brown ultrasuede:** Or so I remember that room now. I have a poor memory for colors. As I write this, I could not confidently tell you what color socks I'm wearing without looking down to make sure.

29 **From the start of his tenure in Langley:** See Sworn Testimony of Robert Carter, trial transcript in re *United States v. Robert Mario Sensi,* Criminal Case No. 86-0318 (U.S. District Court, District of Columbia). See also Sensi Deposition.

29 **And the value of using Republican Party business:** Sensi apparently told much the same story to former CIA officer Frank Snepp. See Frank Snepp and Jonathan King, "GOP Had Secret Channels to Iran: Casey Aides Used Party Organization for Intelligence Activities in Mid-'80s," *Village Voice,* July 23, 1991, 30.

29 **And, of course, in this world:** Conversation with Sensi in 1986.

29 **Ratfucking, as the Republican operatives called it:** Bob Woodward and Carl Bernstein, *All the President's Men* (New York: Touchstone, 1994; orig. published 1974), 126, 128, 132.

30 **I was busy—to use the intelligence jargon:** *Overworld,* 233.

30 **Bob Sensi was arrested:** Parry, *Fooling America,* 135.

30 ***Wait just a goddamned minute!:*** The story Sensi told following his arrest in London is re-created, based on what Sensi told me, accounts of

others regarding what Sensi said to them while in jail in England, and the Sensi Deposition.

30 **Under arrest, the new and expanded Sensi libretto:** See Sensi Deposition. See also Lewis, "Ex-Kuwait Airways Official Testifies of CIA Ties," *Washington Post,* October 21, 1987, A28, and "Testimony Details 1983 CIA Operation on Iran Moderates," *Washington Post,* March, 17, 1988, A24.

31 **The Kuwaitis were scared shitless:** Sensi Deposition, 252–253.

31 **This is a Kuwaiti cover-up:** Sensi Deposition, 249, 268.

31 *I'm not going to be the fall guy:* In 1986, Muhammad Ali told me this was Sensi's position.

31 **So Sensi did time:** See U.S. Federal Bureau of Prisons, Federal Correctional Institution, Loretto, Pennsylvania, "Record of Voluntary Surrender of Robert Mario Sensi to F.C.I. Loretto on July 29, 1988," filed in U.S. District Court, District of Pennsylvania, August 23, 1988; and Lewis, "Kuwait Airways Ex-Aide Guilty in Theft Here," *Washington Post,* March 22, 1988, A19.

32 **A transcript of Hirschfeld's testimony:** Sworn testimony of Richard M. Hirschfeld. Court record of trial transcript of March 16, 1983, in re *United States v. Robert Mario Sensi,* Criminal Case No. 86-0318 (U.S. District Court, District of Columbia), 129–153.

33 **The original name of the county:** http://www.rootsweb.com/ ~flbreva2/History/1821-now.html (accessed February 4, 2006).

33 **Prehistoric-looking birds:** The birds in the twenty-acre wood include great egrets, great blue herons, tri-colored herons, and wood storks.

34 **Once when I was a kid:** *Overworld,* 36.

35 **Miles, too, had impressed upon me:** *Overworld,* 230, 235–238, 248–250.

35 **On my first try:** U.S. Department of Justice Press Release 94–585, "Federal Grand Jury Indicts Seven in International Money Scam," October 7, 1994.

36 **That was news to me:** Mark Conrad, "Ali Sues Former Co-Directors to Nullify 1988 Contract: Boxer Gave 40 Percent of His Rights to Life Story Without Any Payment." *SportsLaw News,* August 28, 1999. http://www .sportslawnews.com/articles/ articles%201999/alisuit.htm/.

36 **For the first time in years:** *Plan to Invade the Philippines.*

36 **He'd started out in the case:** Sworn testimony of Richard M. Hirschfeld, in re *United States v. Robert Mario Sensi,* 130.

36 **On the stand:** Hirschfeld's presentation is paraphrased here.

37 **Why, not long after I met Mr. Sensi:** Sworn testimony of Richard M. Hirschfeld, in re *United States v. Robert Mario Sensi,* 142–143.

38 **But even after his performance:** Sworn Testimony of Robert Carter. Court record of trial transcript in re *United States v. Robert Mario Sensi,* Criminal Case No. 86-0318 (U.S. District Court, District of Columbia) (Date of testimony unknown.)

38 **Mohamed Al-Fassi was not Saudi royalty:** Al-Fassi was born in Morocco into an upper-middle-class Moroccan family. He claimed to have later obtained Saudi Arabian citizenship. His sister married a Saudi prince, and it was on the basis of that connection that Al-Fassi and Hirschfeld staked their claim to Al-Fassi's status as a member of the Saudi royal family.

40 **Item: Faded Lexis/Nexis extract:** John H. Allan, "Virginia Bank Calls Off Unusual Stock Offering." *New York Times,* October 30, 1974, 74.

41 **Before he blew out of town:** I first heard this from Kindred.

41 **Item: Text of *The Washington Post* story:** Nina Martin, "SEC Deals Blow to Ali's Boxing Camp," *Washington Post,* October 29, 1984, Washington Business, 1.

41 **Item: Yellowed, torn, and slightly faded:** Ronald Smothers, "Carter Calls on Americans to Give Reagan 'Our Full Support,'" *New York Times,* June 22, 1985, A6.

42 **And that, as it happened:** Kindred's dual biography of Ali and Cosell has since been published, to excellent reviews. Dave Kindred, *Sound and Fury: Two Powerful Lives, One Fateful Friendship* (New York: Free Press, 2006).

42 **Elicitation, one of the core techniques:** *Overworld,* 256–258.

3. HOMELAND SECURITY

47 **Then all I had to do:** My father's need-to-know speech is recounted in *Overworld,* 30–31.

48 **I e-mailed Dave a scan:** Allan Sonnenschein, "Champ," *Penthouse,* September, 1984, 166.

48 **"That's going in the book":** But Kindred did not include the Jersey Joe Walcott story in *Sound and Fury.* When I asked him why, Kindred said, "I couldn't figure out a place to fit it in."

49 **The Rumble in the Jungle:** The best account of the fight is Norman Mailer's *The Fight* (Boston: Little, Brown and Company, 1975).

52 **This is Dashiell Hammett:** The quote is from Dashiell Hammett, "Bodies Piled Up" (a/k/a "The House Dick"), *Black Mask* (New York), December 1, 1923.

52 **He had a tape of Hirschfeld:** "Audio Recording of Telephone Conversation Between Dave Kindred and Richard Hirschfeld," 1988, and "Audio Recording of Telephone Conversation Between Dave Kindred and Richard Hirschfeld, Impersonating Muhammad Ali," 1988.

54 **By now, of course, Hirschfeld:** While telephonically masquerading as Ali, Hirschfeld told Kindred of "Ali's" telephone conversations not only with several U.S. senators but also with Vice President George Bush, and of a failed attempt by "Ali" to reach President Reagan by telephone. "Audio Recording of Telephone Conversation Between Dave Kindred and Richard Hirschfeld, Impersonating Muhammad Ali," 1988.

56 **How, in 1975, the Securities and Exchange Commission:** Nina Martin, "Tidewater Attorney's Life Has 'Gatsby-esque' Overtones," *Washington Post,* October 29, 1984, Washington Business, 33.

56 **How, in 1976, Hirschfeld's Lincoln Continental:** While I learned this from a separate source, it was confirmed by reporter Bill Burke in "Letter From the Grave—Chapter 2: The Early Years, " *Virginian-Pilot,* April 5, 2005.

56 **How, in 1977, Hirschfeld filed for bankruptcy:** John Mintz, "The Intriguing Richard Hirschfeld," *Washington Post,* May 18, 1989, C1.

57 **How, in 1981, Hirschfeld founded:** Martin, "SEC Deals Blow to Ali's Boxing Camp."

57 **How, in 1987, Hirschfeld allegedly took twelve million dollars:** William Scott Malone reports the story of Marcos's twelve-million-dollar payment intended for Reagan in "The Golden Fleece," *Regardies,* October 1988, 118–140. Malone's article does not state that Hirschfeld was the bagman who ended up with the money. But, around 1988, I was told that by a confidential source who, at the time, knew Hirschfeld well.

57 **How, in 1989, when Hirschfeld was arrested:** Carlos Santos, "Celebrity Days Bitter Reminder For Hirschfeld, " *Richmond Times-Dispatch,* May 26, 1991, A1.

57 **How, later in 1989, Hirschfeld's old friend:** Carlos Santos, "Hirschfeld Saga Continues to Unfold; Ex-Business Partner's Kin Sue U.S. Prosecutors Over Exhumation," *Richmond Times-Dispatch,* February 17, 1997, A1.

58 **How, in 1991, soon after his conviction:** See Santos, "Celebrity Days Bitter Reminder For Hirschfeld;" and "4th Circuit Panel Upholds Beach Lawyer's Convictions," *Richmond Times-Dispatch,* May 9, 1992, B3.

58 **How, in 1993, after a mountain of appellate briefs:** Joseph Cosco, "Imprisoned Lawyer Still Making Deals: But the Beach Lawyer's Efforts Now Center on Getting an Early Release," *Virginian-Pilot,* April 11, 1993, B1; "Optometrist Faces New Charges Related to His Letters to Judges," *Richmond Times-Dispatch,* March 15, 1996, B3; and my correspondence with Dr. Joe Seriani.

58 **How, in 1996, a federal indictment was unsealed:** Lynn Waltz, "Virginia Men Allegedly Plotted to Attack Judge: Hirschfeld Has Not Been Charged, but His Name Appears in an Indictment 25 Times," *Virginian-Pilot,* May 23, 1997, A1; and Carlos Santos, "Gaffney Pleads Guilty to Conspiracy Charge: Case Involves Plot to Get Judge Off Case," *Richmond Times-Dispatch,* July 2, 1997, B4.

62 **"The CIA can't find its ass":** Conversation with a well-informed and usually reliable U.S. government official, who asked not to be further identified.

62 **Messrs. Hirschfeld and Sensi had been keeping busy:** Conversations with U.S. government officials, who asked not to be further identified, and with Gary Messina, who consented to his identification in this book.

63 **And because we are living in an increasingly hectic and complex world:** Conversations with U.S. government officials, who asked not to be further identified, and with Gary Messina.

64 **"It's really very simple," Richard Marshall told them:** Conversation with Gary Messina.

64 **Take, for example, the dream journey:** A U.S. government official, who asked not to be further identified, first told me about Birshtein's trip to Washington and New York. Gary Messina confirmed it.

64 **According to an FBI report:** U.S. Federal Bureau of Investigation, Intelligence Section, Organizational Intelligence Unit, *Semion Mogilevich Organization: Eurasian Organized Crime* (Washington, D.C., 1996), 35–36.

66 **But I was sure it was through the second President Bush's father:** *Overworld,* 205.

68 *Did Sensi, or Hirschfeld, have anything at all:* For a more detailed account of my visits to Islamabad and Peshawar with Muhammad Ali in 1987, see *Overworld,* 281–289.

69 **Then, little by little, Gary and others:** I was told about Engin Yesil by Gary Messina, Vince Messina, and U.S. government officials who either asked not to be further identified, did not identify themselves to me, or used "work names," aliases, when identifying themselves to me.

72 **This made Radiant Telecom:** While I originally learned this from another source, it was confirmed by Gary Messina.

72 **Radiant . . . through an affiliated company:** In January 2006, Engin Yesil informed me this is not true. It is, he suggested, an example of the disinformation about Yesil and his business activities that was propagated by Hirschfeld in fabricated reports to the U.S. government.

72 **Unaware of the extent:** Conversation with Gary Messina.

73 **The previous year—in 2003:** GlobalNet Systems, Inc., "Letter to L. Paul Bremer, Chief Interim Civil Administrator, Coalition Provisional Authority, Ministry of Military Industries Building, Baghdad, Iraq," dated July 15, 2003 (archival records of Radiant Telecom). See also "GlobalNet Announces Mobile Phone Service Launched in Iraq; Free Calls for Troops Through Valentine's Day," *Business Wire,* January 5, 2004.

74 **And . . . in addition to its concerns:** These were employees of Next Communication, a company run by Arik Meimoun, an Israeli citizen who resides in Miami.

4. PATTERN RECOGNITION

78 **The great and mythical Muhammad Ali Motor Car Company:** Jack Norman, "Can You Believe Muhammad Ali Sports Cars Were Going to Be Built in This Caledonia Field? Many Folks Did," *Milwaukee Journal,* November 22, 1987.

78 **Bill Casey's secret channel to Iran:** Sensi Deposition, 251-274; Snepp and King, "GOP Had Secret Channels to Iran;" and conversation with Sensi on June 28, 1986.

78 **The Hirschfeld Bank of Commerce:** "Virginia Bank Calls Off Unusual Stock Offering."

78 **The curious death and exhumation:** Joe Jackson, "The Peculiar Case of the Life, Death, Burial and Reburial of Robert Chastain: Was Chastain's Death Faked So That He and His Business Partner, A Virginia Financier, Could Collect on Insurance? The FBI Seemed to Think So. An Exhumation Later, They May Not Be So Sure," *Virginian-Pilot,* October 31, 1994, A1.

78 **Hirschfeld and Ottimo Stabilimente Immobiliere:** U.S. District Court, Southern District of New York, "Findings of Fact and Conclusions of Law in re *Securities and Exchange Commission against Champion Sports Management, Inc., and Richard Hirschfeld,*" Case No. 84 Civ. 5778 (RJW), filed November 1, 1984.

79 **Hirschfeld and Pan Nordic Corporation:** "Findings of Fact and Conclusions of Law in re *Securities and Exchange Commission against Champion Sports Management, Inc., and Richard Hirschfeld.*"

79 **Industrias Cardoen Limitada:** See Justin Hibbard, "The Chilean Connection: Carlos Cardoen—arms dealer to Iraq, former friend of the U.S. government, and now fugitive—still lines his pockets with profits from our appetite for wine," *San Francisco Chronicle,* March 2, 2003.

79 **Inmate Richard Marshall Hirschfeld's prison friendship:** See, for example, Lynn Waltz, "Virginia Men Allegedly Plotted to Attack Judge: Hirschfeld Has Not Been Charged, but His Name Appears in an Indictment 25 Times," *Virginian-Pilot,* May 23, 1997, A1.

79 **FBI Intelligence Section report dated August 1996:** *Semion Mogilevich Organization: Eurasian Organized Crime.*

79 **"Defendant Sensi's Proposed Stipulation":** Robert M. Sensi, "Defendant's Proposed Stipulation Regarding CIA Witnesses and Classified Material," filed March 4, 1988, *United States v. Robert Mario Sensi,* Criminal Case No. 86-0318 (U.S. District Court, District of Columbia).

80 **Mahdi was an American black man:** For more about Mahdi and his relationship with Sensi, see *Overworld,* 209–229.

81 **Come to think of it, the last time:** Banquet of the Golden Plate, June 28, 1986.

81 **But my suspicion that he'd left the country:** While I learned of this telephonically in 2004, I later found public record confirmation that Mahdi was in prison. U.S. Court of Appeals, Ninth Circuit, Memorandum of the Court Regarding Disposition of Appeal in re *Abuwi Muhammad Mahdi v. MCI-Worldcom, et al.,* No. 03-56243 (District of Columbia), No. CV-00-

01518-IEG, filed January 13, 2005. The first seven words of the memorandum are: "Abuwi Muhammad Mahdi, a California state prisoner."

82 **"Semion Mogilevich attended a summit meeting":** *Semion Mogilevich Organization: Eurasian Organized Crime,* 35–36.

82 **"The BIS and SBU indicate that criminal groups":** *Semion Mogilevich Organization: Eurasian Organized Crime,* 25.

84 *January 1985.* **Behind closed doors:** *Overworld,* 205.

84 *July 1987.* **In Room 2172:** *Plan to Invade the Philippines,* 20.

84 **Mr. Leonard had been appointed by:** American League of Lobbyists, "Biography of Jerris Leonard, Chairman, The Leonard Group, LLP" (accessed online at www.alldc.org/leonardbio.htm/).

84 **Since leaving government:** By e-mail, Leonard informed me that, after leaving the government, during the Watergate investigations, he served as an attorney for both the Republican National Committee and its chairman, George H. W. Bush. For additional information on Leonard's career path, see American League of Lobbyists, "Biography of Jerris Leonard, Chairman, The Leonard Group, LLP," http://www.alldc.org/leonardbio .htm/.

84 **Hirschfeld also brought with him:** As to Chastain, see *Plan to Invade the Philippines,* 20, 34, 36–41. As to Sensi's presence at the hearing, I was informed of this by Muhammad Ali in 1987.

84 **In his testimony, Hirschfeld said:** *Plan to Invade the Philippines,* 21.

84 **Hirschfeld further testified:** *Plan to Invade the Philippines,* 16–17.

84 **When asked by the subcommittee chairman:** *Plan to Invade the Philippines,* 55–56.

85 *October 1987.* **In the civil matter of Kuwait Airways Corporation:** Sensi Deposition, 2.

85 *June 1988.* **In the netherworld:** See "The Man and the Voice," and " 'Muhammad Ali Calling'—Or Is It?"

85 *August 1988.* **In New Orleans:** "The Man and the Voice."

85 *December 1988.* **In Washington:** "The Man and the Voice."

85 **Judd Best: Republican partisan and problem-fixer:** Debevoise & Plimpton LLP, "Biography of Judah Best, Of Counsel," http://www .debevoise.com/attorneys/.

85 **Then, during Watergate:** *All the President's Men,* 327.

86 **"Add the name of Robert H. Bork":** Joseph Cosco, "Hirschfeld Law Team Includes Justice Reject," *Virginian-Pilot,* January 9, 1992, D5.

87 *1985:* **"Robert M. Sensi, Chairman":** *Overworld,* 205.

87 *2002:* **Robert M. Sensi, Boris Birshtein's ticket:** I first heard of this from a U.S. government official, who asked not to be further identified. Gary Messina confirmed the story, and added details to it.

87 **The deal had been announced:** *PRNewswire,* "WorldQuest Networks Announces Merger Agreement With Ntera Holdings: Transaction Will Give WorldQuest Access to a VoIP Network Capable of Handling 4 Billion Minutes a Month," March 17, 2004.

88 **And Robert Farmer was now the campaign treasurer:** George Washington University, "John Kerry Campaign Organization: Primary and Caucus Edition: A Sketch of the Kerry Organization in Early 2004."

88 **I went online and saw that:** WQNI website, as of June 5, 2004.

89 **The next thing I found on the Internet:** U.S. Federal Election Commission, "Schedule A: Itemized Receipts: Individual Contributions Arranged by Type, Given, then Recipient: Sensi, Robert, Kerry, John F., via John Kerry for President Inc., February 5, 2004; 1000," FEC Image 24990855987 (page 2545 of 3000).

89 **KINDRED: "What about the presidential thing?":** "Audio Recording of Telephone Conversation Between Dave Kindred and Richard Hirschfeld, Impersonating Muhammad Ali, " 1988.

5.   IN WHICH, POSSESSING A DARK AND DANGEROUS SECRET, I ATTEMPT TO SAVE THE WORLD

92 **He ignored the lessons of Mideast history:** As to stovepiped intelligence, see Seymour M. Hersh, "The Stovepipe: How Conflicts Between the Bush Administration and the Intelligence Community Marred the Reporting on Iraq's Weapons," *New Yorker,* print edition of October 27, 2003.

92 **Almost every foreign nation:** As to even the French, the actual *Le Monde* headline was: "*Nous sommes tous les Américains.*"

93 **"All of us have heard this term":** Jonathan Schell, "The Case Against the War, " *The Nation,* March 3, 2003.

93 **In 1917, just after Baghdad was occupied:** See Niall Ferguson, "Hegemony or Empire?" *Foreign Affairs,* September/October, 2003. See also Robert Fisk, "Liberating the Mideast: Why Do We Never Learn?" *Independent* (London), March 10, 2003.

94 **By early 1920, three years after Sir Stanley Maude's declaration:** For a fuller account, see Dan Murphy, "In Iraq, 'Lawrence' Is a Must Read," *Christian Science Monitor,* December 8, 2004. See also T. E. Lawrence, *Revolt in the Desert* (Garden City, NY: Doubleday, Doran & Co., 1927).

94 **"Analogy is fudge, anyhow":** "In Iraq, 'Lawrence' Is a Must Read."

95 **The FBI's computers don't work:** I first heard details of the inadequacy of the FBI's computers from Gary Messina. See also Michael Isikoff and Mark Hosenball, "FBI Computers: You Don't Have Mail," *Newsweek,* February 14, 2006; and Eric Lichtblau, "F.B.I. May Scrap Vital Overhaul of Its Outdated Computer System," *New York Times,* January 14, 2005, A1.

96 **And how he dressed himself up like a decorated-war-veteran fighter pilot:** CNN, "Bush Calls End to 'Major Combat.'" May 2, 2003. http://www.cnn.com/2003/ WORLD/meast/05/01/sprj.irq.main/.

97 **Iran *is* a democracy:** CIA, *The World Factbook: Iran.* http://www.odci.gov/cia/ publications/ factbook/ geos/ir.html.

97 **Meanwhile, in Iraq, the tales of African yellowcake:** As to the yellowcake, see Joseph Wilson, *The Politics of Truth: A Diplomat's Memoir: Inside the Lies That Led to War and Betrayed My Wife's CIA Identity* (New York: Carrol & Graf, 2004), 2, 5, 9, 23-25, 297, 325, 330–332, 478, 484. See also Mitch Frank, "Tale of the Cake: Since March, 2002, CIA Officials Had Known the Niger Tale Wasn't Credible. So Why Did It Resurface?" *Time,* July 13, 2003. As to the "confirmed sightings of mobile biological warfare production plants," see Joby Warrick, "Lacking Biolabs, Trailers Carried Case for War: Administration Pushed Notion of Banned Iraqi Weapons Despite Evidence to Contrary," *Washington Post,* April 12, 2006, A1. As to faulty intelligence concerning weapons of mass destruction, see Commission on the Intelligence Capabilities of the United States Regarding Weapons of Mass Destruction. *Report to the President of the United States* (Washington, D.C., March 31, 2005).

99 **The cover said:** Nielsen Media Research, "Hook Up With The Nielsen TV Ratings System: Help Us Measure Television Usage In Your Area," 2003.

103 **A typical day overseas with Muhammad:** For a fuller account of life on the road with Ali, see *Overworld,* 134–142.

106 **Adolf Hitler posited the Big Lie Theory:** Adolf Hitler (translated by James Murphy), *Mein Kampf: An Historical Document Describing the Aims and Development of the National Socialist Movement* (London: Hutchinson & Co., 1939), 134.

106 **"Think of the press," Goebbels said:** *Time,* "Scared to Death," March 27, 1933.

107 **But now, just a few months before the election:** *CNN.com,* "Kerry Takes New Fire Over Vietnam," February 12, 2004. http://www.cnn .com/2004/ALLPOLITICS/02/11/elec04.prez.kerry.fonda/.

114 **The Republican operatives called their sabotage operations:** *All the President's Men,* 115–128, 132.

114 **During the 1972 campaign, young Karl Rove:** John Saar, "GOP Probes Official as Teacher of 'Tricks,'" *Washington Post,* August 10, 1973, A16.

114 **Rove had been ratfucking for Republicans:** See James Moore and Wayne Slater, *Bush's Brain: How Karl Rove Made George W. Bush Presidential* (Hoboken, NJ: John Wiley & Sons, 2003). See also Joshua Green, "Karl Rove in a Corner," *Atlantic Monthly,* November 2004, 92–102.

117 **Then I remembered my training:** *Overworld,* 266.

6. MENDING WALL

120 **"Ask them," I said:** See, for example, BBC News, "Who star Townshend bailed," January 14, 2003. http://news.bc.co.uk/1/hi/ uk/2651871.stm.

122 **Tex again, while training:** *Overworld,* 261.

125 **But while the Gray Eminence and I spoke:** Williams & Connolly LLP, "Biography of Gregory B. Craig, Partner." http://www.wc.com/attorney .cfm?attorney_id=261/.

126 **When Bob Chastain left for Vienna:** Conversation with Kindred, and "The Peculiar Case of the Life, Death, Burial and Reburial of Robert Chastain."

127 **Chastain's ex-wife said:** Conversation with Nat Bynum, and "Hirschfeld Saga Continues to Unfold."

127 **Other than confirming:** "Hirschfeld Saga Continues to Unfold" and "The Peculiar Case of the Life, Death, Burial and Reburial of Robert Chastain."

128 **Dan Schwartz, once the general counsel:** Bryan Cave, "Biography of Daniel C. Schwartz, Partner." http://www.bryancave.com/files_bc/pdf/ SchwartzD%2DCorpCo.pdf/.

128 **Early in July, I went to Washington:** Bryan Cave's Washington address is 700 Thirteenth Street N.W.

130 **One of the first things he taught me:** *Overworld,* 194.

131 **"Well," Dan said:** Larry J. Kolb, "Privileged and Confidential Memorandum to the person referred to as 'the Gray Eminence' Headed 'Re: Our Discussion of 9 June 2004,'" dated June 14, 2004.

134 **Miles taught me to think of every car:** *Overworld,* 254–255.

136 **These two sentences:** *Bush's Brain,* 52.

137 **When you're on the run:** *Overworld,* 439.

137 **John is a painter of some renown:** See, for example, Eric Konigsberg, "Big Man on Canvas," *New York,* December 14, 1998, 42–48; Robert Hughes, "Weird and Beautiful Danger," *Men's Journal,* March 2000, 101–108; and Bob Colacello, "Studios by the Sea," *Vanity Fair,* August 2000, 138–154.

140 **In the morning the storm:** Weeks later, when an insurance adjuster finally appeared at my property, good Kremlinologist that he was, he said that on the night of Jeanne we'd been hit not only by the hurricane but also by a tornado. That, he said, was the only way to make sense of what he saw.

140 **Waiting in soup lines:** Thank you to FEMA, the American Red Cross, and the U.S. military for the soup, the sandwiches, the bread, the ice, the water.

141 **President Bush dropped in:** Bill Adair, "Hurricane Relief: Doughnuts, Water, President," *St. Petersburg Times,* September 9, 2004, A1.

142 **He'd bought the place about a month earlier:** As to the title to the property, see Broward County Tax Assessor, Broward Country, Florida, "Property Assessment Values Record for 1310 Brickell Dr., Fort Lauderdale, Colee Hammock 1-17 B Lot 20,21 E 25 BLK 36," recorded January 31, 2005. As to the financing of the purchase, see Broward County Commission, Broward County, Florida, "Mortgage Record, CFN # 103984904, or BK 37442, Pages 1836–1843," filed and recorded in Fort

Lauderdale, Florida, May 12, 2004; and "Second Mortgage Record, CFN # 103984905, or BK 37442, Pages 1844–1851," filed and recorded in Fort Lauderdale, Florida, May 12, 2004.

142 **"The articles of incorporation list Bob Sensi":** Florida Department of State, Division of Corporations, "Articles of Incorporation for Global Telesat Property Corp," filed and recorded in Tallahassee, Florida, May 10, 2004.

142 **At just before 3:30 in the afternoon of October 2004:** This account is drawn from a brief telephone conversation with Paul Russell, and from Jeff Stratton, "Mr. Big Shot: The Charismatic Lawyer and Power Broker Took One Last Lap in a New River Mansion During His Run from the Law," *New Times,* May 26, 2005. http://www.newtimesbpb.com/Issues/2005-05-26/news/feature.html/.

143 **Russell crept down:** Hirschfeld's e-mail address was given to me by Arik Meimoun, and confirmed by Engin Yesil.

146 **Meanwhile, inside the George Bush Center for Intelligence:** See George Tenet, "DCI George Tenet's Introduction of President Bush, at the Dedication Ceremony for the George Bush Center for Intelligence, April 26, 1999," Central Intelligence Agency electronic archive. See also George H. W. Bush, "Remarks by George Bush, 41st President of the United States, at the Dedication Ceremony for the George Bush Center for Intelligence, April 26, 1999," Central Intelligence Agency electronic archive.

146 **Tenet was out:** Dana Priest and Walter Pincus, "Tenet Resigns as CIA Director: Intelligence Chief Praised by Bush, But Critics Cite Lapses on Iraq War," *Washington Post,* June 4, 2004, A1.

146 **Good Republican Goss was in:** BBC News, "Bush Man Confirmed As CIA Boss: The U.S. Senate has confirmed the appointment of Porter Goss as head of the Central Intelligence Agency," September 23, 2004. http://news.bbc.co.uk/1/hi/world/americas/3681946.stm.

147 **When Bob Woodward asked our current president:** Bob Woodward, *Plan of Attack* (New York: Simon & Schuster, 2004), 421.

147 **My friend said there was a lot of snickering:** I was told this by a well-informed private individual who does not wish to be further identified.

7. THE FATAL SHORE

153 **Within days of his arrest, Hirschfeld:** I was informed of Hirschfeld's use of three separate teams of lawyers—and of much of the additional informa-

tion in this passage about things Hirschfeld did, instructed, or disclosed, while he was in federal custody in Miami—by a friend from Washington who seemed to be in a position to receive reports from officials monitoring Hirschfeld in jail. Much of what my friend told me while Hirschfeld was in jail in Miami was subsequently corroborated by reporter Bill Burke in "Letter From the Grave—Chapters 1–7," *Virginian-Pilot,* April 4–10, 2005. Burke and Hirschfeld had known each other for years, and Hirschfeld reportedly communicated with Burke from jail in Miami. Some of the information I obtained while Hirschfeld was jailed in Miami may be supplemented here by information contained in Burke's "Letter From the Grave."

153 **His three teams of advocates:** According to my source, who seems to have been corroborated by Burke in "Letter From the Grave," the three teams of lawyers Hirschfeld initially retained to represent him were a Florida team led by Fort Lauderdale criminal attorney Alvin Entin, a Virginia team led by Nina J. Ginsberg, and a Washington team led by Jerris Leonard. Both my source and subsequently published reports state that C. Boyden Gray, former White House counsel to the first President Bush, was later retained by Hirschfeld to ask for presidential clemency for Hirschfeld. As to Ginsberg, see DiMuroGinsberg, PC, "Biography of Nina J. Ginsberg, Founding Partner." http://www. dimuro.com/ attorneys/attginsberg.html. As to Leonard, see American League of Lobbyists, "Biography of Jerris Leonard." As to Gray, see Wilmer Cutler Pickering Hale and Dorr, LLP, "Biography of C. Boyden Gray, Partner." http://www.wilmerhale.com/boyden_gray/ htm (accessed April 8, 2005).

154 **Hirschfeld went to Washington:** I was informed of Hirschfeld's visit to Hatch, Hatch's refusal to help Hirschfeld, Hirschfeld's decision to flee U.S. jurisdiction, and Hirschfeld's last visit to his father, by the source from Washington while Hirschfeld was in federal custody in Miami. The account was confirmed by Bill Burke, "Letter From the Grave—Chapter 4: Thwarting a Marcos Revolt," *Virginian-Pilot,* April 7, 2005.

155 **"That was the most devastating experience":** Burke, "Letter From the Grave—Chapter 4."

155 **But the FBI had no clue where he was:** See Lynn Waltz, "Spanish Police Arrest Fugitive from Norfolk: Federal Authorities Will Seek Extradition of Hirschfeld from Canary Islands," *Virginian-Pilot,* January 31, 1997, B1, which includes the following: "The only reason Virginia officials even knew Hirschfeld was in the Canary Island chain was that he stopped by the Associated Press office in Madrid in December to proclaim he was being persecuted by authorities in Virginia, according to

sources. Virginia officials saw the news article, carried in this country's newspapers, and contacted Spanish authorities, who began a search, sources said."

156 **On the twenty-ninth of January 1997:** See Waltz, "Spanish Police Arrest Fugitive From Norfolk." As to the date of Hirschfeld's arrest in Spain, see Stratton, "Mr. Big Shot."

156 **He put up thirty-five thousand dollars:** Lynn Waltz, "Ex–Beach Lawyer, Arrested as Fugitive, Leaves Spanish Jail," *Virginian Pilot,* May 30, 1997, B4.

156 **For the next few months, he drove around Spain:** See Burke, "Letter From the Grave—Chapter 5: In Castro's Circle," *Virginian-Pilot,* April 8, 2005.

156 **This time, they indicted Hirschfeld for plotting:** See Burke, "Letter From the Grave—Chapter 7: Facing Extradition, Abandoning Hope," *Virginian-Pilot,* April 10, 2005. See also Laura Lafay, "Ex-Con Pleads Guilty in Plot on Judge: Court Document Says the Plan Was to Get the Jurist Off the Hirschfeld Case," *Virginian-Pilot,* July 1, 1997, B2.

157 **When his flight landed at José Marti:** For more detailed accounts of Hirschfeld in Cuba, see Burke, "Letter From the Grave—Chapter 5," and Stratton, "Mr. Big Shot." Arik Meimoun provided me a firsthand account of his experiences with Hirschfeld in Cuba.

158 **So claimed Hirschfeld from the jail cell:** As to claims about Cuba made by Hirschfeld while he was in jail in Miami, see Burke, "Letter From the Grave—Chapter 5." Some of what Hirschfeld told Burke seems to have been corroborated by attorney Dale Cooter in Stratton, "Mr. Big Shot." As to Hirschfeld's apartment in Havana, his Cadillac, his claim to have both a condo on Varadero Beach and a yacht at Marina Hemingway, all of these were confirmed to me by Arik Meimoun.

158 **He first met Castro at a wedding:** For more on the wedding, see Burke, "Letter From the Grave—Chapter 5."

159 **When Dale Cooter, an attorney from Washington:** I do not know how or when Hirschfeld met Cooter. But, during the Sensi Deposition, which took place in Washington on the tenth and eleventh of October 1987, in re *Kuwait Airways Corporation v. American Security Bank, N.A., and First American Bank, N.A.,* Civil Action No. 86-2542 (U.S. District Court, District of Columbia) , Cooter represented the defendant, for whom Sensi testified. Sensi was represented at the deposition by Jerris Leonard and Daniel J. McGuan.

159 **"I never really understood why"**: The quote is from "Letter From the Grave—Chapter 5." Hastert, as I write this, is the Speaker of the U.S. House of Representatives.

161 **"P.S. I almost forgot the most important thing"**: I have made minor edits to Bynum's e-mail messages to me, for the sake of brevity. Nothing of material importance to the information about Hirschfeld that Bynum provided me has been deleted or changed.

169 **The WQNI-Ntera merger had been called off:** WorldQuest Networks, Inc., "WorldQuest Networks Announces Termination of Merger Agreement with Ntera Holdings," Press Release dated September 2, 2004.

169 **I learned that in August 2000:** See Burke, "Letter From the Grave—Chapters 5 and 6," April 8 and 9, 2005.

170 **One day, I received a handwritten letter:** The letter was forwarded to me by Nat Bynum. Eugene, Fischer, "Letter Regarding Fraud Perpetrated on Anneliese Fischer by Richard Hirschfeld, Robert Sensi, and Guillermo Olle," Atlanta, Georgia, March 3, 1996.

171 **But it wasn't until sometime later:** See Sensi Deposition. On page 452 of the deposition transcript, Sensi identifies Jackson as "a retired major general from the U.S. Army and former chief of federal probation for the United States Courts." On page 386 of the deposition, Sensi states that he, Jerris Leonard, General Jackson, and others, had at one time served together on the board of directors of the Cariari Hotel, a business venture that failed. See also Sensi's "Summary of Checks Drawn on 640 Account," Court record of filing on March 4, 1991, in re *Kuwait Airways Corporation v. Robert M. Sensi,* Civil Action No. 89-2251 (U.S. District Court, District of Columbia).

173 **His new attorney, it seemed:** See "Biography of C. Boyden Gray, Partner."

173 **Gray went to the White House:** See Burke, "Letter From the Grave—Chapters 1 and 7."

177 **"He was sitting talking with a woman"**: Several news reports, including Daniel Schweimler's "Cold War Foes Revisit Battle Scene," *BBC News Online,* March 25, 2001 (http://news.bbc.co.uk/1/low/world/americas/1241667.stm.), place the late President Kennedy's sister, Jean Kennedy Smith, in Cuba at about the same time that Meimoun said he saw her there with Hirschfeld.

178 **Arik told me how:** Weeks after our first meeting, Meimoun sent me a copy of the share certificate. It recites that, under Certificate No. 98,

Meimoun received from the allotment of Alejandro Castro, "100 COM-MON Class 'A' Voting Shares," without par value, of Cohiba Rum Distributors Ltd., a limited liability company incorporated in the Canadian province of British Columbia. The certificate was apparently backdated by Hirschfeld, because it indicates that the shares were issued to Meimoun on July 7, 2000.

179 **In the lexicon of con men:** As to the outsideman, see David W. Maurer, *The Big Con: The Story of the Confidence Men* (New York, Anchor Books, 1999), 299. As to the insideman, see *The Big Con*, 296.

180 **"Richard and Sensi were carrying around gold CIA badges":** Meimoun's statement that Hirschfeld and Sensi were using gold CIA badges, which I believe were fake, is consistent with what I was told by numerous other sources who said they saw the badges themselves. Other witnesses to Hirschfeld and Sensi's use of what purported to be CIA badges include Gary Messina, Vince Messina, Engin Yesil, and Effi Yeoshoua. In Chapter 6 of "Letter From the Grave," Burke reports: "Hirschfeld began flying regularly from Florida to Washington, where he met with U.S. intelligence officials, said Robert D. Thorell, a telecom specialist who says he worked with Hirschfeld and often accompanied him on the trips. Thorell said Hirschfeld traveled under the moniker Richard Marshall and carried a badge and a credit card issued by the CIA."

183 **"He got almost nine hundred thousand dollars":** Arik Meimoun, "Schedule of Payments Made by Arik Meimoun and His Companies to 'Richard Marshall' and His Affiliates" (undated).

8. BYZANTIUM

187 **Byzantium:** Stand in modern Istanbul and you stand atop a pile of three great cities—layered in order of seniority, the eldest at the bottom. Beneath Istanbul is all that's left of Constantinople, and beneath Constantinople lie the worldly remains of Byzantium.

187 **Engin Yesil had a very nice house:** Isabella Geist, "Home of the Week: Miami Price," *Forbes.com,* June 9, 2003. http://www.forbesimg.com/2003/06/09/cx_bs_0609how_print.html/ (accessed June 20, 2004).

190 **"And he represented each":** As to Leonard's representation of Sensi, see Sensi Deposition, 2. As to Leonard's representation of Hirschfeld, see, among many corroborating sources, *Plan to Invade the Philippines,* 20.

190 **"And my source is quite certain":** The source is a highly placed U.S. government official who asked not to be further identified. A second source,
who I believe is reliable, told me much the same story.

191 **"And everyone knows Hyde":** That Hyde and Sensenbrenner worked
together in the impeachment, and impeachment trial, of Clinton was
widely reported. See, for example, CNN, "House Managers Argue for
Clinton's Impeachment Conviction: Prosecution Stresses Need for Witnesses, Senators' Impartiality," January 14, 1999. http://www.cnn.com/
ALLPOLITICS/ stories/1999/01/14/impeachment/.

191 **"Well, Sensenbrenner's from Wisconsin":** James F. Sensenbrenner, Jr.,
"Biography of Congressman Sensenbrenner," House of Representatives.
http://www.house.gov/ sensenbrenner/bio.htm/.

191 **"As is Jerris Leonard":** American League of Lobbyists, "Biography of
Jerris Leonard."

191 **"Since Sensenbrenner was seventeen":** See T. R. Goldman, "The Man
With The Iron Gavel," *LegalTimes.com,* May 2, 2005. http://www
.legal times.com/ (accessed January 7, 2006).

196 **"For eight years, I fought it":** Yesil fought it all the way to the U.S.
Supreme Court. See U.S. Supreme Court, "Petition For A Writ Of Certiorari, *Janet Reno, et al., v. Saul Navas, et al.*" October Term, 1998, submitted by Seth P. Waxman, Solicitor General, dated December 1998.

199 **Kroll performed a comprehensive forensic audit:** Kroll Inc., "Letter
from Thomas V. Cash, Executive Managing Director, to Engin Yesil,
Chief Executive Officer, Radiant Holdings Inc., dated October 3, 2003,
regarding 'extensive forensic examination and review of Radiant Holdings, Inc.'"

200 **"They'd included with his transcript":** The documents mistakenly provided by the U.S. government to Aydin included: (i) "E-Mail Message
from Scott T. Boulia to John A. Lowell, Jayne A. Howell, Elizabeth M.
Gracon, and Yolanda Salazar at Department of Homeland Security,
Athens Office, Subject: Re: Investigation Request, Sent: Thursday, October 09, 2003, 8:01 P.M."; (ii) U.S. Department of State, "Case Note
Summary, Case Number 2003183 537 0010, Regarding Turkish National Applicant Korhan Aydin, Date/Time Prepared: 12/22/2003
12:54:24"; (iii) U.S. Department of State, "Refusal Worksheet, OF-194,
for Refusal on 02-Jul-2003 of Visa for Turkish National Subject Korhan
Aydin, Under Patriot Act Section 403, Signed by Jayne A. Howell, Refusing Officer, and John Lowell, Principal Officer, Designee or Chief Con-

sular Officer"; (iv) U.S. Department of Labor, Employment and Training Administration, "Labor Condition Application for H-1B Nonimmigrants, Form ETA Case Number: T-02275-00081, Form ETA 9035, OMB Approval: 1205-0310, Expiration Date: 31 August 2003, Applicant: Numind, Inc., Signed by Chief, Division of Foreign Labor Certificates, U.S. Department of Labor, Dated 10/02/2002"; (v) U.S. Federal Bureau of Investigation, Criminal Justice Information Services Division, "Fingerprint Identification Record for Turkish National Subject Korhan Aydin, Fingerprinted: 2003/07/22, USNHNVC1Z, Agency Case IST200318353710"; (vi) U.S. Immigration and Naturalization Service, "H Classification Supplement to Form I-129, Supplement H (12/10/01)Y, OMB No. 1115-0168, Petitioner: Numind, Inc., Beneficiary: Turkish National Ahmet Cem Payzin" (undated); (vi) "I-94 Departure Record, Departure Number 981851402 08, for Ahmet Cem Payzin, Admitted Miami July 15, 2002"; and several other documents including the university grade transcripts, in Turkish and English, described below. In the e-mail message of October 9, 2003, from Boulia, of the Department of Homeland Security, Boulia wrote: "The companies do exist, although under the umbrella of 'Radiant Holdings.' Most share the same address, but are separate entities. We have no evidence that these individuals are not reporting to work as directed. We have a cooperating individual who has verified their attendance. The case has recently taken a turn toward an IRS tax investigation. We have fraudulent applications, the basis being discrepancies between salaries paid and proposed salaries indicated on the petitions."

200 **"They talked to every one of my professors":** Aydin received with his transcript a copy of a transcript of grades from a Turkish technical university of another Turkish student who had once been employed by Yesil: T.C./YILDIZ TEKNiK üNiVERSiTESi/ELEKTRiK ELEKTRONiK FAKüLTESi BiLGiSAYAR MüH. BöLüMü/TRANSCRiPT/Fakülte No: 9311015, Tarih: 09/07/2002. Aydin also received a copy of an English translation of the transcript: Foundation for International Services, Inc., "English Translation of Transcript Issued by T.C./Yildiz Technical University, Faculty of Electric and Electronic Engineering, Computer Science Engineering Department, Faculty Number 9311015, Grades of Ahmet Cem Payzin, dated July 9th, 2002." In the e-mail message of October 9, 2003, Boulia, of the Department of Homeland Security, also wrote: "We were surprised to find that the vast majority of the diplomas were authentic, but greatly appreciate everyone's assistance in making this determination. I could use a copy of any summary report that is created, especially as it relates to the one fraudulent education claim. Thanks again for your help.

The IRS investigation will be lengthy, but we will add our fraud charges when they are ready."

201 **Of course he knew—at least, that McCollum:** See Baker & Hostetler LLP, "Bio of Bill McCollum, Partner." http://www.bakerlaw.com/professionals/bio.aspx?id=11145/.

204 **It was hidden inside an option agreement:** "Share Exchange Agreement Between Growth Enterprise Fund, S.A., GlobalNet Corporation, and Engin Yesil," dated March 9, 2004.

207 **"By the time Seriani came to Florida":** As to Seriani's record in Ohio and West Virginia, see *Optometric Management,* "Lens Express Denies Racketeering Charges," Norwalk, December, 1992, 3. See also Vicki McCash, "Mail-Order Company Says It Is Correcting A Stigma," *Sun-Sentinel* (Fort Lauderdale), February 22, 1993, Weekly Business, 9.

207 **"Joe Seriani was suing us for treble damages":** "Complaint For Damages, *Joseph S. Seriani v. Yalie Golan, Engin Kamil Yesil, Mordechai Golan and Lens Express, Inc.*," Case No. 92-22923, Florida Circuit Court, 11th Judicial Circuit, Dade County, Florida, filed October 26, 1992.

210 **It is recorded that, in that December of 2004:** Burke, "Letter From the Grave—Chapters 1 and 7."

210 **It is also recorded that Jerris Leonard:** Burke, "Letter From the Grave—Chapter 6."

210 **Pat Robertson also declined:** Burke, "Letter From the Grave—Chapter 6."

210 **But Jerris Leonard kept working:** Burke, "Letter From the Grave—Chapter 1."

211 **The DOD report:** Burke, "Letter From the Grave—Chapter 6."

211 **According to Leonard, DOD officials:** Burke, "Letter From the Grave—Chapters 1 and 6."

211 **Thomas E. Mooney, Sr., staff director and general counsel:** The quotations of Mooney are from Burke, "Letter From the Grave—Chapter 1."

212 **A published account says:** Burke, "Letter From the Grave—Chapter 7."

212 **The few published references to the secret war:** These include Burke's seven-part series "Letter From the Grave" and Stratton, "Mr. Big Shot."

212 **One newspaper account says the DOD report:** Burke, "Letter From the Grave—Chapters 1 and 6."

212 **I called him because I had just read a news story:** Dick Thornburgh and Louis D. Boccardi, *Report of the Independent Review Panel on the September 8, 2004, 60 Minutes Wednesday Segment "For the Record" Concerning President Bush's Texas Air National Guard Service,* Kirkpatrick & Lockhart Nicholson Graham, LLP, Counsel to the Independent Review Panel, Washington, D.C.: January 5, 2005.

213 **"Hirschfeld's dead":** Catherine Wilson, "Richard Hirschfeld, Confidant of Ali, Kills Himself in Jail," Associated Press, January 11, 2005.

214 **Newspaper reports said prison telephone transcripts:** The newspaper reports that quote Hirschfeld's last telephone conversation with his wife include Stratton, "Mr. Big Shot."

214 **Certain newspapers reported he then:** These include Burke, "Letter From the Grave—Chapter 7."

214 **But *The Washington Post* reported:** Matt Schudel, "Flashy Fugitive Richard Hirschfeld Dies," *Washington Post,* January 13, 2005, B7.

214 **And another account said:** Stratton, "Mr. Big Shot."

215 **"You only made reference to him":** As I pointed out to Kevin Hirschfeld in one of my e-mail messages to him, Richard Hirschfeld is actually mentioned twice in *Overworld,* on pages 217 and 431.

216 **I could've told him a friend of mine:** That friend of mine was Kindred.

9. APPOINTMENT IN SAMARRA

221 **He took a bite, then said:** John O'Hara, *Appointment in Samarra* (New York: Vintage Books, 2003; orig. 1934).

221 **"You mean," I said:** The quote O'Hara used as an epigraph is from W. Somerset Maugham, *Sheppey* (London: William Heinemann Ltd., 1933).

224 **"By the way," I said:** While it was early in 2005 that I first got wind of Hirschfeld's attempt to take Seriani's lens business public in the early 1980s, Seriani himself confirmed it to me in a series of e-mail messages he sent me in March 2006.

224 **Instead, the judge sentenced them:** Yesil appealed his six-year sentence and it was reduced to time served, which was twenty-one months, with no requirement of probation after his release. It may be significant that

Yesil won his appeal, and his sentence was reduced, while Hirschfeld was in prison and presumably unable to influence Yesil's case.

224 **We'd recently learned Hirschfeld had written:** Burke, "Letter From the Grave—Chapters 1–7."

225 **Meanwhile, our government has spent trillions:** See Dana Priest and Josh White, "Iraq War Helps Recruit Terrorists, Hill Told: Intelligence Officials Talk of Growing Insurgency," *Washington Post,* February 17, 2005, A1. See also Douglas Jehl, "U.S. Panel Sees Iraq as Terrorist Training Area," *New York Times,* February 14, 2005, A14.

225 **Our military forces are so overstretched:** See Ann Scott Tyson, "Two Years Later, Iraq War Drains Military: Heavy Demands Offset Combat Experience," *Washington Post,* March 19, 2005, A1. See also Will Dunham, "U.S. General Warns Army Reserve Is Being 'Broken,'" Reuters, January 6, 2005.

BIBLIOGRAPHY

Adair, Bill. "Hurricane Relief: Doughnuts, Water, President." *St. Petersburg Times,* September 9, 2004, A1.

Allan, John H. "Virginia Bank Calls Off Unusual Stock Offering." *New York Times,* October 30, 1974, 74.

Allen, Vicky. "Wolfowitz Says No Nationalist Insurgency in Iraq." Reuters, February 3, 2005.

American Academy of Achievement. *1986 Banquet of the Golden Plate.* Washington, D.C., 1986.

American League of Lobbyists. "Biography of Jerris Leonard, Chairman, The Leonard Group, LLP." http://www.alldc.org/leonardbio.htm/ (accessed February 2, 2006).

Anderson, John Lee. *The Fall of Baghdad.* New York: Penguin Press, 2004.

Anderson, John Ward. "A Gruesome Find, With A Difference." *Washington Post,* March 19, 2005, A16.

Anonymous. Unattributed background report on "Robert Mario Sensi. Born November 22, 1950, in Blue Island, Illinois," transmitted by telecopier by Miles A. Copeland to Larry J. Kolb, c. 1985.

Anonymous [Michael Scheuer]. *Imperial Hubris: Why the West Is Losing the War on Terror.* Washington, D.C.: Brassey's, 2004.

Arab News. "Ali on Mission to Free Hostages." February 17, 1985.

Arnone, Michael. "FBI CIO: You Get What You Pay For." FCW.Com (Falls Church, Virginia), March 23, 2006. http://www.fcw.com/article92718 -03-23-060-Web/ (accessed April 5, 2006).

Arvedlund, Erin E. "Two Fugitives from Russia at Bush Event." *New York Times,* February 6, 2005, Section 1, 12.

Associated Press. "Fingerprint Database: Roadblocks to Unified System: Infighting Between Government Agencies Has Kept the U.S. from Fully Screening Visitors at Points of Entry." December 30, 2004.

Baker & Hostetler LLP. "Bio of Bill McCollum, Partner." http://www.bakerlaw .com/professionals/bio.aspx?id=11145/ (accessed January 22, 2006).

Bamford, FBI Special Agent. "Sworn Testimony of FBI Special Agent Bamford." Fragment of court record of trial transcript in re *United States v. Robert Mario Sensi.* Criminal Case No. 86-0318 (U.S. District Court, District of Columbia) (undated).

Bamford, James. *A Pretext for War: 9/11, Iraq, and the Abuse of America's Intelligence Agencies.* New York: Doubleday, 2004.

Basapress News Agency. "Moldovan President Vladimir Voronin has proposed that the parliament remove article 170 from the Moldovan Penal code." BBC Monitoring Service, August 19, 2003.

BBC News. "Bush Man Confirmed as CIA Boss: The U.S. Senate has confirmed the appointment of Porter Goss as head of the Central Intelligence Agency." September 23, 2004. http://news.bbc.co.uk/1/hi/world/ americas/3681946.stm.

———. "Who star Townshend bailed," January 14, 2003. http://news.bbc .co.uk/1/hi/uk/2651871.stm.

Belson, Ken. "The Call Is Cheap. The Wiretap Is Extra." *New York Times,* August 23, 2004, C1.

Bin Laden, Osama (translated by James Howarth). *Messages to the World: The Statements of Osama Bin Laden.* New York: Verso, 2005.

Blix, Hans. *Disarming Iraq: The Search for Weapons of Mass Destruction.* London: Bloomsbury, 2004.

Blomquist, Brian. "'Terrorist' Was a Regular in Adams Morgan Bar." *Washington Post,* July 24, 1997, District Weekly, 1.

Bocchichio, Anthony R. "Statement Before the House Judiciary Committee, Subcommittee on Crime, Regarding the Problems Posed to Law Enforcement by Cloned Cellular Phones." September 11, 1997. *U.S. Drug Enforcement Administration Publications.* http://www.dea.gov/pubs/cngrtest/ ct970911.htm (accessed March 2, 2006).

Boulia, Scott T. "E-Mail Message to John A. Lowell, Jayne A. Howell, Elizabeth M. Gracon, and Yolanda Salazar at Department of Homeland Security, Athens Office, Subject: Re: Investigation Request, Sent: Thursday, October 09, 2003, 8:01 P.M."

Bowden, Mark. *Road Work: Among Tyrants, Heroes, Rogues, and Beasts.* New York: Atlantic Monthly Press, 2004.

Bowers, Faye. "U.S. Unready for Rising Threat of 'Moles': A Recent Report on U.S. Intelligence Harshly Critiqued Counterspy Efforts." *Christian Science Monitor,* April 8, 2005.

Branigin, William. "Bush Nominates Negroponte to New Intel Post: Iraq Ambassador Will Return to Washington." *Washington Post,* February 17, 2005, A1.

Broward County Commission, Broward County, Florida. "Mortgage Record, CFN # 103984904, or BK 37442, pages 1836–1843." Filed and recorded in Ft. Lauderdale, Florida, May 12, 2004.

———. "Second Mortgage Record, CFN # 103984905, or BK 37442, pages 1844–1851." Filed and recorded in Ft. Lauderdale, Florida, May 12, 2004.

Broward County Tax Assessor, Broward Country, Florida. "Property Assessment Values Record for 1310 Brickell Dr., Fort Lauderdale, Colee Hammock 1-17 B Lot 20,21 E 25 BLK 36." Recorded January 31, 2005.

Brown, Mark. "What If Bush Has Been Right About Iraq All Along?" *Chicago Sun-Times,* February 1, 2005, Opinion.

Bryan Cave. "Biography of Daniel C. Schwartz, Partner." http://www.bryancave .com/files_bc/pdf/SchwartzD%2DCorpCo.pdf/ (accessed March 4, 2004).

Bryce, Robert. "Gas Pains: One of the U.S. Military's Greatest Vulnerabilities in Iraq Is Its Enormous Appetite for Fuel. The Insurgents Have Figured This Out." *Atlantic Monthly,* May 2005.

Buckley, Priscilla L. "Miles Copeland, R.I.P." *National Review,* February 11, 1991.

Buckley, William F. "It Didn't Work." *National Review,* February 24, 2006.

Budiansky, Stephen. "Losing the Code War: The Great Art of Code Breaking Is Over—and With It Much of Our Ability to Track the Communications of Our Enemies." *Atlantic Monthly,* February 2002.

———. "Truth Extraction: A Classic Text on Interrogating Enemy Captives Offers a Counterintuitive Lesson on the Best Way to Get Information." *Atlantic Monthly,* June 2005.

Bull, Chris. "Farming for Dollars: Bull's-Eye Target: Bob Farmer." *PlanetOut,* Money and Careers, September 18, 2004.

Bumiller, Elisabeth. "System Using Fingerprints Is Delayed, Report Finds: Infighting Over Prints." *New York Times,* December 30, 2004, A20.

Burke, Bill. "Letter From the Grave—Chapter 1." *Virginian-Pilot,* April 4, 2005.

———. "Letter From the Grave—Chapter 2: The Early Years." *Virginian-Pilot,* April 5, 2005.

———. "Letter From the Grave—Chapter 3: In the Champ's Corner." *Virginian-Pilot,* April 6, 2005.

———. "Letter From the Grave—Chapter 4: Thwarting a Marcos Revolt." *Virginian-Pilot,* April 7, 2005.

———. "Letter From the Grave—Chapter 5: In Castro's Circle." *Virginian-Pilot,* April 8, 2005.

———. "Letter From the Grave—Chapter 6: Aiding Saddam's Capture?," *Virginian-Pilot,* April 9, 2005.

———. "Letter From the Grave—Chapter 7: Facing Extradition, Abandoning Hope," *Virginian-Pilot,* April 10, 2005.

Burns, John F. "Across Baghdad, Security Is Only an Ordeal." *New York Times,* January 27, 2005, A13.

———. "Threats and Responses: Reporter's Notebook: Iraq's Thwarted Ambitions Litter an Old Nuclear Plant." *New York Times,* December 27, 2002, A1.

Bush, George H. W. "Remarks by George Bush, 41st President of the United States, at the Dedication Ceremony for the George Bush Center for Intelligence, April 26, 1999." Central Intelligence Agency electronic archive.

Bush, George W. "State of the Union Address: Full Text." BBC News, January 29, 2003. http://news.bbc.co.uk/2/hi/americas/2704365.stm/ (accessed November 19, 2005).

Business Wire. "GlobalNet Announces Mobile Phone Service Launched in Iraq; Free Calls for Troops Through Valentine's Day." January 5, 2004.

Bynum, Nat. "E-Mail Messages in Chron File of Messages from Nat Bynum to Kolb of November 1, 2004 to December 31, 2005."

Campbell, Tom. "Lawyer Arrested in Canary Islands: Ex-Va. Attorney Sought Asylum There." *Richmond Times-Dispatch,* January 31, 1997, B1.

Carl, Leo D. *International Directory of Intelligence.* McLean, VA: Maven Books, 1990.

Carter, Robert. "Sworn Testimony of Robert Carter." Court record of trial transcript in re *United States v. Robert Mario Sensi.* Criminal Case No. 86-0318 (U.S. District Court, District of Columbia).

Casey, William J. "Letter from Director of Central Intelligence to William French Smith, Attorney General of the United States, dated March 2, 1982, concerning understanding of new procedures to 'strike the proper balance between enforcement of the law and protection of intelligence sources and methods.'"

Clarridge, Duane R., with Digby Diehl. *A Spy For All Seasons: My Life in the CIA.* New York: Scribner, 1997.

Clark, Matthew. "Shifting Roles of U.S. Spies and Special Forces: Pentagon Takes Over Some CIA Spy Operations While U.S. 'Super-secret' Commandos Get Duty on U.S. Soil." *Christian Science Monitor,* January 25, 2005.

Clarke, Richard A. *Against All Enemies: Inside America's War on Terror.* New York: Free Press, 2004.

Clover, Charles. "Questions over Kuchma's adviser cast shadows: The Ukrainian president's administration is facing serious allegations ahead of polls this weekend." *Financial Times,* October 30, 1999, World News, 5.

CNN. "Bush Calls End to 'Major Combat.'" May 2, 2003. http://www.cnn.com/2003/WORLD/meast/05/01/sprj.irq.main/.

———. "House Managers Argue for Clinton's Impeachment Conviction: Prosecution Stresses Need for Witnesses, Senators' Impartiality." January 14, 1999. http://www.cnn.com/ALLPOLITICS/stories/1999/01/14/impeachment/.

———. "Kerry Takes New Fire Over Vietnam," February 12, 2004. http://www.cnn.com/2004/ALLPOLITICS/02/11/elec04.prez.kerry.fonda/.

Cohiba Rum Distributors Ltd. "Share Certificate for One Hundred Common Shares of Capital Stock Representing Ten Percent of the Capitalization,

Issued in Favor of Arik Meimoun." Certificate No. 98. Date of Issue June 7, 2000 [*sic*].

Colacello, Bob. "Studios by the Sea." *Vanity Fair,* August 2000, 138–154.

Coll, Steve. *Ghost Wars: The Secret History of the CIA, Afghanistan, and Bin Laden, from the Soviet Invasion to September 10, 2001.* New York: Penguin Press, 2004.

Commission on the Intelligence Capabilities of the United States Regarding Weapons of Mass Destruction. *Report to the President of the United States.* Washington, D.C., March 31, 2005.

Commonwealth of Virginia, General Assembly, "House Resolution No. 839: Commending Edward S. Garcia." Bill as Passed House and Senate (HJ839ER). Recorded February 22, 2003.

Congress of the United States. *Report of the Congressional Committees Investigating the Iran-Contra Affair, With Supplemental, Minority and Additional Views.* Senate Select Committee on Secret Military Assistance to Iran and the Nicaraguan Opposition, and House Select Committee to Investigate Covert Arms Transactions with Iran. November 1987. S. Rept. No. 100-216. H. Rept. No. 100-433. 100th Congress, 1st Session. Washington, D.C.

Congress of the United States. *Report of the Joint Inquiry into the Terrorist Attacks of September 11, 2001—By the House Permanent Select Committee on Intelligence and the Senate Select Committee on Intelligence.* Washington, D.C.: U.S. Government Printing Office, 2002.

Conrad, Mark. "Ali Sues Former Co-Directors to Nullify 1988 Contract: Boxer Gave 40 Percent of His Rights to Life Story Without Any Payment." *SportsLaw News,* August 28, 1999. http://www.sportslawnews .com/archive/articles%201999/alisuit.htm/.

Copeland, Miles. *The Game of Nations.* New York: Simon & Schuster, 1969.

———. *The Game Player: Confessions of the CIA's Original Political Operative.* London: Aurum Press, 1989.

———. *Without Cloak or Dagger: The Truth About the New Espionage.* New York: Simon & Schuster, 1974.

Cosco, Joseph. "Hirschfeld Law Team Includes Justice Reject." *Virginian-Pilot,* January 9, 1992, D5.

————. "Imprisoned Lawyer Still Making Deals: But the Beach Lawyer's Efforts Now Center on Getting an Early Release." *Virginian-Pilot,* April 11, 1993, B1.

Daily Report for Executives. "SEC Charges Fraud in Stock Sale by Firm Chaired by Muhammad Ali to Train Boxers." August 20, 1984.

Danner, Mark. "The War on Terror: Four Years On; Taking Stock of the Forever War." *New York Times,* September 11, 2005, Section 6, 45.

Davidson, Lee. "Lie to Reporter Led to Impersonation Charges, Ali Says." *Deseret News,* December 15, 1988, A6.

De Bellaigue, Christopher. *In the Rose Garden of the Martyrs: A Memoir of Iran.* New York: HarperCollins, 2004.

————. "Iran & the Bomb." *New York Review of Books,* April 27, 2006.

De Borchgrave, Arnaud. "Head in Sand Saw No Evil." *United Press International,* June 18, 2004.

————. "Iran's Strategy in Iraq." *Washington Times,* September 7, 2005.

Debevoise & Plimpton LLP. "Biography of Judah Best, of Counsel." http://www.debevoise.com/attorneys/ (accessed August 30, 2004).

Deming, Angus, with Rod Norland. "Ali's Rope-a-Dope Diplomacy." *Newsweek,* March 4, 1985, 37.

DiMuroGinsberg, PC. "Biography of Nina J. Ginsberg, Founding Partner." http://www.dimuro.com/attorneys/attginsberg.html.

Dobbs, Michael, and Steve Coll. "Ex-Communists Are Scrambling for Quick Cash." *Washington Post,* February 1, 1993, A1.

Doggart, Caroline. *Tax Havens & Their Uses.* London: Economist Intelligence Unit, 1997.

Dulles, Allen. *The Craft of Intelligence.* New York: Harper & Row, 1963.

Dunham, Will. "U.S. General Warns Army Reserve Is Being 'Broken.'" Reuters, January 6, 2005.

Eichhorn, Betty. "Brevard County Boundaries: 1821–Present." *Brevard GenWeb.* http://www.rootsweb.com/~flbreva2/History/1821-now.html (accessed February 4, 2006).

Eisenhower, Dwight D. *Crusade in Europe: A Personal Account of World War II.* New York: Doubleday, 1948.

Eggen, Dan. "Pre 9/11 Missteps by FBI Detailed: Report Tells of Missed Chances to Find Hijackers." *Washington Post,* June 10, 2005, A1.

Ehrlichman, John D. "Memorandum dated November 18, 1970, directing U.S. Attorney General John Mitchell to instruct Jerris Leonard to understand the federal government will not request a special grand jury to investigate the Kent State shootings." National Archives. 220-CU-MF, Records of the President's Commission on Campus Unrest, Main File, Box 122, Office Files of the Chairman.

Eisen, Jack. "Muhammad Ali, former world heavyweight boxing champion, has contributed $1,000 to Gene W. Hirschfeld Scholarship Fund." *Washington Post,* February 26, 1982, B3.

Eisenberg, Daniel. "Bush's New Intelligence Czar: John Negroponte faces intrigue, subterfuge and shadowy fighters. And that's just in Washington." *Time,* February 28, 2005, 32–35.

Fallows, James. "Why Iraq Has No Army: We Can't Leave Until the Iraqis Have One, the Bush Administration Says—and They're Not Even Close. So Now What?" *Atlantic Monthly,* December 2005, 60–77.

———. "Will Iran Be Next?: Soldiers, Spies and Diplomats Conduct a Classic Pentagon War Game—with Sobering Results." *Atlantic Monthly,* December 2004, 99–110.

Farmer, Robert A. "Telecopier Transmission to Unknown Recipient Containing Redacted Facsimile of Privileged & Confidential memorandum from Larry J. Kolb to the person referred to as 'the Gray Eminence,' with telecopier header dated June 21, 2004, 1:18 A.M."

FedEx. "U.S. Airbill, FedEx Tracking Number 846710896892, for Priority Overnight Delivery to 'Richard Marshal, 3832 Elijah Baum Road, Kitty Hawk, NC 27949.'" Dated June 14, 2004.

Ferguson, Niall. "Hegemony or Empire?" *Foreign Affairs,* September/October, 2003.

Fischer, Eugene. "Letter Regarding Fraud Perpetrated on Anneliese Fischer by Richard Hirschfeld, Robert Sensi, and Guillermo Olle." Atlanta, Georgia, March 3, 1996.

Fisk, Robert. *The Great War For Civilisation: The Conquest of the Middle East.* New York: Knopf, 2005.

———. "Liberating the Mideast: Why Do We Never Learn?" *Independent* (London), March 10, 2003.

Fitzgerald, Mary. "Survey Finds Border Agents Critical of Training, Resources." *Washington Post,* August 24, 2004, A15.

Fleming, Michael. "Atmosphere to Engulf 'Overworld': Canton, Goldmann to Produce Spy Pic." *Variety,* June 14, 2004. http://www.variety.com/article/VR1117906396?categoryid=1238&cs=1/ (accessed June 14, 2004).

Florida Department of Motor Vehicles. "Florida Vehicle Registration for VIN: WDBRN47JX2A274641, TC: 84630906, YR/MK: 2002 MERZ." Date issued: April 30, 2004. L#: 565826. T#: 382509706. B#: 446827. R#: 382509706.

Florida Department of State, Division of Corporations. "Articles of Amendment to Articles of Incorporation of Global Telesat Property Corp. P04000075477." Filed and recorded in Tallahassee, Florida, March 7, 2005.

———. "Articles of Incorporation for Global Telesat Property Corp." Filed and recorded in Tallahassee, Florida, May 10, 2004.

———. "Articles of Incorporation for Nextcom Investors, Inc." Filed and recorded in Tallahassee, Florida, May 10, 2004.

———. "Articles of Incorporation for Transition Services LLC." Filed and recorded in Tallahassee, Florida, April 11, 2002.

Forbes. "How the Hottest Issues Fared." December 2, 1985.

Foundation for International Services, Inc. "English Translation of Transcript Issued by T.C./Yildiz Technical University, Faculty of Electric and Electronic Engineering, Computer Science Engineering Department, Faculty Number 9311015, Grades of Ahmet Cem Payzin, dated July 9th, 2002."

———. "Evaluation Report Regarding Turkish National Subject Ahmet Cem Payzin, Purpose of Evaluation: Immigration, Ref: 173064/MKL, Signed by Megan A. Mittelstaedt, Evaluator, Dated September 17, 2002."

———. "Vita of Megan A. Mittelstaedt" (undated).

Frank, Mitch. "Tale of the Cake: Since March, 2002, CIA Officials Had Known the Niger Tale Wasn't Credible. So Why Did It Resurface?" *Time,* July 13, 2003.

Gawel, Richard. "Iraq Enters the Wireless Age." *Electronic Design,* February 2, 2004.

Geist, Isabella. "Home of the Week: Miami Price." *Forbes.com,* June 9, 2003. http://www.forbesimg.com/2003/06/09/cx_bs_0609how_print.html/ (accessed June 20, 2004).

Gellman, Barton. "Secret Unit Expands Rumsfeld's Domain: New Espionage Branch Delving into CIA Territory." *Washington Post,* January 23, 2005, A1.

George Washington University. "John Kerry Campaign Organization: Primary and Caucus Edition: A Sketch of the Kerry Organization in Early 2004." http://www.gwu.edu/~action/2004/kerry/kerrorg.html.

Gertz, Bill. *Breakdown: How America's Intelligence Failures Led to September 11.* Washington, D.C.: Regnery Publishing, 2002.

———. "Counterintelligence Posts Vacant: The top ranks of government counterintelligence agencies are empty due to resignations and retirements amid a dispute over the role of counterspying, U.S. intelligence officials say." *Washington Times,* February 10, 2006. http://www .washtimes.com/national/20060210-123648-8710r.htm/ (accessed February 10, 2006).

Glanz, James, and William Broad. "Looting at Weapons Plants Was Systematic, Iraqi Says." *New York Times,* March 13, 2005, A1.

Glasser, Susan B. "Probing Galaxies of Data for Nuggets: FBI Is Overhauled and Rolled Out to Mine the Web's Open-Source Information Lode." *Washington Post,* November 25, 2005, A35.

GlobalNet Systems, Inc. "Letter to L. Paul Bremer, Chief Interim Civil Administrator, Coalition Provisional Authority, Ministry of Military Industries Building, Baghdad, Iraq." Dated July 15, 2003. Archival Records of Radiant Telecom.

Golan, Yali. "Handwritten Notes on Relationship with Joseph Serian, a/k/a Joseph Seriani" (undated).

Goldberg, Jeffrey. "Breaking Ranks: What Turned Brent Scowcroft Against the Bush Administration?" *New Yorker,* October 31, 2005, 54–65.

Goldberg, Steve. "'Sting' Operation in Pacific Netted a Big Fish—Marcos." *Richmond Times-Dispatch,* July 10, 1987, A1.

Goldman, T. R. "The Man With The Iron Gavel." *LegalTimes.com,* May 2, 2005. http://www.legaltimes.com/ (accessed January 7, 2006).

Government of Italy. "Dossier Approfondito Cerved: SENSI ULISSE." Sezione Registro Imprese, recorded April 2, 2005.

Green, Joshua. "Karl Rove in a Corner." *Atlantic Monthly,* November 2004, 92–102.

Greenberg, David. "Fathers and Sons: George W. Bush and His Forebears." *New Yorker,* July 12 and 19, 2004, 92–98.

Growth Enterprise Fund, S.A. "Share Exchange Agreement Between Growth Enterprise Fund, S.A., GlobalNet Corporation, and Engin Yesil." Dated March 9, 2004. Archival records of Radiant Telecom.

———. "U.S. Securities and Exchange Commission, Schedule 13D, Report of Growth Enterprise Fund, S.A. Regarding Ownership of 2,310,841,329 shares of common stock of IDIAL Networks, Inc." Filed August 22, 2003.

Hall, Mimi. "Ex-Official Tells of Homeland Security Failures." *USA Today,* December 28, 2004.

Hamerly, David. "GlobalNet Corporation—Fact Sheet." *Hoovers Online,* August 21, 2004. http://www.gbne.net/.

Hammett, Dashiell. "Bodies Piled Up" (a/k/a "The House Dick"). *Black Mask* (New York), December 1, 1923.

Harding, Richard Allen. "Terrorism's Impact: New Laws Increase Power of Law Enforcement Agencies; Prepaid Regulation to Follow?" *Intele-Card News,* May 1, 2004.

Hauser, Thomas, with the cooperation of Muhammad Ali. *Muhammad Ali: His Life and Times.* New York: Touchstone, 1991.

Hersh, Seymour M. *Chain of Command: The Road from 9/11 to Abu Ghraib.* New York: HarperCollins, 2004.

———. "The Stovepipe: How Conflicts Between the Bush Administration and the Intelligence Community Marred the Reporting on Iraq's Weapons." *New Yorker,* print edition of October 27, 2003. http://www.newyorker .com/fact/content/?031027fa_fact/ (accessed October 21, 2003).

Hiatt, Fred. "Yeltsin Commission Accuses Vice President of Corruption." *Washington Post,* August 19, 1993, A20.

Hibbard, Justin. "The Chilean Connection: Carlos Cardoen—arms dealer to Iraq, former friend of the U.S. government, and now fugitive—still lines his pockets with profits from our appetite for wine." *San Francisco Chronicle,* March 2, 2003.

Hirsch, Jason. "Cashier's Check in Favor of 'Kerry for President' Drawn on Beach Bank, Miami, Florida, in the Amount of One Thousand and 00/100 Dollars." Issued January 22, 2004.

Hirschfeld Bank of Commerce and Richard M. Hirschfeld. "Consent to Entry of Final Judgment and Injunction Against the Hirschfeld Bank of Commerce." Dated February 12, 1975.

Hirschfeld, Kevin. "E-Mail Messages in Chron File of Messages from Kevin Hirschfeld to Kolb of January 1, 2005 to February 28, 2005."

Hirschfeld, Richard M. "Consent to Entry of Final Judgment and Permanent Injunction." Dated February 15, 1976.

———. "Sworn Testimony of Richard M. Hirschfeld Given on March 16, 1988." Court record of trial transcript in re *United States v. Robert Mario Sensi.* Criminal Case No. 86-0318 (U.S. District Court, District of Columbia).

Hirsh, Michael, Mark Hosenball, and John Barry. "Aboard Air CIA: The Agency Ran a Secret Charter Service, Shuttling Detainees to Interrogation Facilities Worldwide. Was It Legal? What's Next?" *Newsweek,* February 28, 2005.

Hitchens, Christopher. "Iran's Waiting Game." *Vanity Fair,* July, 2005, 46–54.

———. *A Long Short War: The Postponed Liberation of Iraq.* New York: Plume, 2003.

———. "Ohio's Odd Numbers." *Vanity Fair,* March, 2005, 214–218.

Hitler, Adolf (translated by James Murphy). *Mein Kampf: An Historical Document Describing the Aims and Development of the National Socialist Movement.* London: Hutchinson & Co., 1939.

Hockstader, Lee. "Ex-Kuwait Airways Official Gets 6 Months for Theft." *Washington Post,* July 2, 1988, A7.

Hougan, Jim. *Secret Agenda: Watergate, Deep Throat, and the CIA.* New York: Random House, 1984.

House Committee on Foreign Affairs, Subcommittee on Asian and Pacific Affairs. *Plan to Invade the Philippines,* report on hearing of July 9, 1987, 100th Congress, 1st session. Washington, D.C.: U.S. Government Printing Office, 1987.

House Committee on International Relations. "Markup of H.R. 695, 'The Security and Freedom through Encryption (SAFE) Act,' Consideration of a Motion to Authorize the Chairman to Make Motions on the House Floor Under Rule XX, Relative to H.R. 1757." 105th Congress, 1st Session. Washington, D.C. http://commdocs.house.gov/committees/intlrel/hfa50111.000/hfa50111_0.HTM (accessed November 14, 2005).

House October Surprise Task Force, "Executive Session Depositions of John A. Rizzo and Charles G. Cogan, Monday, December 21, 1992, Washington, D.C." Stenographic Minutes, unrevised and unedited, Office of the Clerk, Office of Official Reporters, U.S. House of Representatives, Washington, D.C.: December 21, 1992.

Hughes, Robert. "Careerism and Hype Amid the Image Haze." *Time,* June 17, 1985, 78–83.

———. "Weird and Beautiful Danger." *Men's Journal,* March 2000, 101–108.

Hyde, Henry J. "Biography of Congressman Henry J. Hyde." House of Representatives. http://www.house.gov/hyde/Biography.htm/ (accessed July 9, 2004).

Isikoff, Michael, and Mark Hosenball. "FBI Computers: You Don't Have Mail." *Newsweek,* February 14, 2006.

Jackson, Joe. "Chastain Exhumation Returns to Haunt Officials." *Virginian-Pilot,* December 15, 1995, B3.

———. "Justice or Vendetta?: Financier Hirschfeld, Out of Prison, Fights to Clear His Name." *Virginian-Pilot,* October 20, 1995, B1.

———. "The Peculiar Case of the Life, Death, Burial and Reburial of Robert Chastain: Was Chastain's Death Faked So That He and His Business Partner, a Virginia Financier, Could Collect on Insurance? The FBI Seemed to Think So. An Exhumation Later, They May Not Be So Sure." *Virginian-Pilot,* October 31, 1994, A1.

Jefferson Waterman International. "Business Card of Robert M. Sensi, Senior Counselor." Washington, D.C.

Jehl, Douglas. "2 CIA Reports Offer Warnings on Iraq's Path." *New York Times,* December 7, 2004.

———. "U.S. Panel Sees Iraq as Terrorist Training Area." *New York Times,* February 14, 2005, A14.

Jehl, Douglas, David Johnston, and Eric Schmitt. "U.S. Aides Cite Worry on Qaeda Infiltration from Mexico." *New York Times,* February 17, 2005, A16.

Jehl, Douglas, and Eric Schmitt. "The Struggle for Iraq: Intelligence; Prison Interrogations in Iraq Seen as Yielding Little Data on Rebels." *New York Times,* May 27, 2004, A1.

Johnston, David, and Douglas Jehl. "F.B.I.'s Recruiting of Spies Causes New Rift with C.I.A." *New York Times,* February 11, 2005, A19.

Kashar News (Kabul, Afghanistan). "The Untold Story of Operation Anaconda in Afghanistan." March 26, 2005.

Keegan, John. *Intelligence in War: Knowledge of the Enemy from Napoleon to al-Qaeda.* New York: Knopf, 2003.

Kindred, Dave. "Audio Recording of Telephone Conversation Between Dave Kindred and Richard Hirschfeld." 1988.

———. "Audio Recording of Telephone Conversation Between Dave Kindred and Richard Hirschfeld, Impersonating Muhammad Ali." 1988.

———. "E-Mail Messages in Chron File of Messages from Dave Kindred to Kolb of May 24, 2004 to December 31, 2004."

———. "The Man and the Voice: Part One: Talkative Ali Impostor Deceived Senators with Phone Calls." *Atlanta Journal Constitution,* December 11, 1988, A1.

———. "The Man and the Voice: Part Two: Ali-Hirschfeld Relationship Steeped in Curiosities, Intrigue." *Atlanta Journal Constitution,* December 12, 1988, A1.

———. "The Man and the Voice: Part Three: Ali, the Champ, Needs More Than Attention." *Atlanta Journal Constitution,* December 13, 1988, A1.

———. *Sound and Fury: Two Powerful Lives, One Fateful Friendship.* New York: Free Press, 2006.

Klein, Joe. "Saddam's Revenge: The Secret History of U.S. Mistakes, Misjudgments and Intelligence Failures That Let the Iraqi Dictator and His Allies Launch an Insurgency Now Ripping Iraq Apart." *Time,* September 26, 2005, 44–52.

Knightly, Phillip. *The Master Spy: The Story of Kim Philby.* New York: Knopf, 1988.

Kolb, Larry J. *Overworld: The Life and Times of a Reluctant Spy.* New York: Riverhead Books, 2004.

———. "Privileged and Confidential Memorandum to the person referred to as 'the Gray Eminence' Headed 'Re: Our Discussion of 9 June 2004.'" Dated June 14, 2004.

———. "Typescript of Notes of First Conversation with Richard M. Hirschfeld, August 8, 1983," with handwritten marginalia.

———. "When Ali Took On the Ayatollah." *Sunday Telegraph* (London), October 17, 2004, Review, 4.

Konigsberg, Eric. "Big Man on Canvas." *New York* magazine, December 14, 1998, 42–48.

Krim, Jonathan. "FBI Dealt Setback on Cellular Surveillance." *Washington Post,* October 28, 2005, A5.

Kroft, Steve. "E-Mail Messages to Larry Kolb in Chron File of Messages from Steve Kroft to Kolb of July 1, 2004 to December 31, 2004."

Kroll Inc. "Letter from Thomas V. Cash, Executive Managing Director, to Engin Yesil, Chief Executive Officer, Radiant Holdings Inc., dated October 3, 2003, regarding 'extensive forensic examination and review of Radiant Holdings, Inc.'"

Kroop & Scheinberg, P.A. "2003 For Profit Corporation Uniform Business Report (UBR)," Document No. 604759, Secretary of State, State of Florida, filing recorded January 23, 2003.

Kuwait Airways Corporation. "Memorandum of Points and Authorities in Support of Motion to Exclude Robert Sensi from Calling Witnesses Jerris Leonard, Robert Carter, Mohamed Sultan Abelcawad, and Representative of Central Intelligence Agency, et al., to Testify at Trial." Court record of filing on July 11, 1991, in re *Kuwait Airways Corporation v. Robert M. Sensi,* Civil Action No. 89-2251 (U.S. District Court, District of Columbia).

———. "Response to Defendant Robert Sensi's Request for Admissions." Court record of filing on June 17, 1991, in re *Kuwait Airways Corporation v. Robert M. Sensi,* Civil Action No. 89-2251 (U.S. District Court, District of Columbia).

Lafay, Laura. "Ex-Con Pleads Guilty in Plot on Judge: Court Document Says the Plan Was to Get the Jurist Off the Hirschfeld Case." *Virginian-Pilot,* July 1, 1997, B2.

Laquer, Walter. "The Geography of Terror." *National Geographic,* November, 2004, 72–81.

Laughlin, Meg, and Wanda J. DeMarzo. "A Bold Lawyer to the Famous Never Gave Up—Until the Very End." *Miami Herald,* January 23, 2005. http://www.miami.com/herald/ (accessed January 24, 2005).

Lawrence, T. E. *Revolt in the Desert.* Garden City, NY: Doubleday, Doran & Co., 1927.

———. *Seven Pillars of Wisdom.* London: Cape, 1935.

Leonard, Jerris. "Confidential Memorandum from Jerris Leonard to John Ehrlichman, 'Re Kent State University,' May 7, 1970." National Archives. 220-CU-MF, Records of the President's Commission on Campus Unrest, Main File, Box 122, Office Files of the Chairman.

Le Monde. "Nous sommes tous des Américains." (Paris) September 12, 2001, A1.

Lewis, Nancy. "Ali Still Has a 1-2 Punch with Words." *Washington Post,* June 9, 1988, A1.

———. "Defendant Backed in Kuwaiti Case: Royalty Allegedly Allowed Use of Fund." *Washington Post,* May 31, 1988, B3.

———. "Ex-Kuwait Airways Official Testifies of CIA Ties." *Washington Post,* October 21, 1987, A28.

———. "Kuwait Airways Ex-Aide Guilty in Theft Here." *Washington Post,* March 22, 1988, A19.

———. "Kuwait Airways Is Awarded $750,000 in Suit: Ex-Official of Carrier Testified That Most of Disputed Funds Were Spent on CIA Projects." *Washington Post,* October 21, 1987, A28.

———. "Testimony Details 1983 CIA Operation on Iran Moderates." *Washington Post,* March, 17, 1988, A24.

Lewis, Neil A. "U.S. Reported to Thwart a Marcos Coup Plot." *New York Times,* July 9, 1987, A5.

Lichtblau, Eric. "F.B.I. May Scrap Vital Overhaul of Its Outdated Computer System." *New York Times,* January 14, 2005, A1.

Lipton, Eric. "Audit Faults U.S. for Its Spending on Port Defense." *New York Times,* February 20, 2005, A1.

Long, Josh. "Unmasking Criminals: Would Congress Pass Law Requiring Prepaid Wireless ID Check to Aid Investigations?" *Phone+* magazine, April 2002.

McCash, Vicki. "Mail-Order Company Says It Is Correcting a Stigma." *Sun-Sentinel* (Fort Lauderdale), February 22, 1993, Weekly Business, 9.

McGeary, Johanna. "6 Reasons Why So Many Allies Want Bush to Slow Down: They Want More Proof, They Like Inspections, and They Don't Like Cowboy Bush. And Yes, There's More." *Time,* February 3, 2003, 34–39.

McNair, James. "Summit Technology Buys Lens Express and Is Named in Suit." *Miami Herald,* May 17, 1996, C3.

Madsen, Dick. "Letter to Bob Chastain Regarding Outstanding Debt and Richard Hirschfeld." Dated December 2, 1988.

Mailer, Norman. *The Fight.* Boston: Little, Brown and Company, 1975.

Malone, William Scott. "The Golden Fleece." *Regardies,* October 1988, 118–140.

Marek, Angie C. "A Post-Katrina Public Flaying: The First Reviews Are In on Washington's Response to the Storm—and They're Scathing." *U.S. News & World Report,* February 27, 2006, 62–64.

Margolick, David, Evgenia Peretz, and Michael Shnayerson. "The Path to Florida." *Vanity Fair,* October 2004, 310–369.

Martin, Nina. "Ali Attorney Sues to Bar SEC Probe." *Washington Post,* November 19, 1984, Washington Business, 3.

———. "SEC Deals Blow to Ali's Boxing Camp." *Washington Post,* October 29, 1984, Washington Business, 1.

———. "Tidewater Attorney's Life Has 'Gatsby-esque' Overtones." *Washington Post,* October 29, 1984, Washington Business, 33.

Maugham, W. Somerset. *Sheppey.* London: William Heinemann Ltd., 1933.

Maurer, David W. *The Big Con: The Story of the Confidence Men.* New York: Anchor Books, 1999 (originally published by Bobbs-Merrill, 1940).

Mayer, Mary. "DEA Looks to a Case-Tracking Application." *Government Computer News,* October 26, 1998. http://www.gcn.com/print/17_29/33010-1.html (accessed December 4, 2005).

McCain, John. "Torture's Terrible Toll: Abusive interrogation tactics produce bad intel, and undermine the values we hold dear. Why we must, as a nation, do better." *Newsweek,* November 21, 2005, 34–36.

Meimoun, Arik. "Schedule of Payments Made by Arik Meimoun and His Companies to 'Richard Marshall' and His Affiliates" (undated).

Melman, Yossi. "White House Hosts 2 Israeli-Russians Wanted By Moscow." *Haaretz* (Tel Aviv), February 3, 2005.

Messina, Gary S. "Curriculum Vitae of Gary S. Messina." June 21, 2004.

———. "E-Mail Messages in Chron File of Messages from Gary Messina to Kolb of May 24, 2004 to December 31, 2004."

Messina, Vincent J. "E-Mail Messages in Chron File of Messages from Vince Messina to Kolb of May 24, 2004 to December 31, 2004."

Miller, Judith. "Aftereffects: The Hunt for Evidence: Trailer Is a Mobile Lab Capable of Turning Out Bioweapons, a Team Says." *New York Times,* May 11, 2003, Section 1, 12.

Miller, Judith, and William J. Broad. "Aftereffects: Germ Weapons: U.S. Analysts Link Iraq Labs to Germ Arms." *New York Times,* May 21, 2003, A1.

Mintz, John. "Hirschfeld and the 'Assassination' Lure." *Washington Post,* May 18, 1989, C8.

———. "Infighting Cited at Homeland Security: Squabbles Blamed for Reducing Effectiveness." *Washington Post,* February 2, 2005, A1.

———. "The Intriguing Richard Hirschfeld." *Washington Post,* May 18, 1989, C1.

———. "Matching a Name to the 'Ali Voice.'" *Washington Post,* April 17, 1991, C1.

———. "Muhammad Ali's Unlikely Match: The Champ and His Controversial Lawyer and Friend." *Washington Post,* May 18, 1989, C1.

———. "Probe Faults System for Monitoring U.S. Borders." *Washington Post,* April 11, 2005, A1.

Minzesheimer, Bob. "Ali Says It Wasn't So." *USA Today,* December 15, 1988, A4.

Moldova Azi. "Report Says Cost of ID Issue Is Exaggerated." July 7, 2003. http://www.azi.md/news?ID=24788/ (accessed June 18, 2004).

Moore, James, and Wayne Slater. *Bush's Brain: How Karl Rove Made George W. Bush Presidential.* Hoboken, NJ: John Wiley & Sons, 2003.

Morrison, Dave. "E-Mail Messages in Chron File of Messages from Dave Morrison to Kolb of May 24, 2004 to December 31, 2004."

Moynihan, Daniel Patrick. *Secrecy.* New Haven, CT: Yale University Press, 1998.

Murphy, Dan. "In Iraq, 'Lawrence' Is a Must Read." *Christian Science Monitor,* December 8, 2004. http://www.csmonitor.com/2004/1208/p01s03-woiq .html/ (accessed December 9, 2004).

National Commission on Terrorist Attacks Upon the United States. *The 9/11 Commission Report.* Washington, D.C.: U.S. Government Printing Office, 2004.

Nielsen Media Research. "Hook Up with the Nielsen TV Ratings System: Help Us Measure Television Usage in Your Area." (Dunedin, Florida), 2003.

New York Times. "Ali Leaves Lebanon; Fails to Find 5 Captives." February 21, 1985, A3.

———. "Sheik Arranges Woolco Talks." September 29, 1982, D4.

Next Communication, Inc. "Letter to David R. Phipps, Attorney-in-Fact, Hisbro Foundation, Vaduz, Liechtenstein, dated 11th April 2001."

Noonan, Peggy. "Hearings Won't Make Us Safe: Sins of Omission and the 9/11 Commission." *Wall Street Journal,* March 25, 2004. http://www .opinionjournal.com/columnists/pnoonan/?id=110004864/ (accessed March 27, 2004).

Norman, Jack. "Can You Believe Muhammad Ali Sports Cars Were Going to Be Built in This Caledonia Field? Many Folks Did." *Milwaukee Journal,* November 22, 1987.

Numind, Inc. "Letter from Engin Yesil, President, to Department of Justice, Immigration & Naturalization Service, Texas Service Center, Re: H-1B Nonimmigrant Visa Petition on Behalf of Ahmet Payzin. Dated September 27, 2002."

O'Hara, John. *Appointment in Samarra.* New York: Vintage Books, 2003 (orig. 1934).

O'Harrow, Robert Jr., and Scott Higham. "U.S. Border Security at a Crossroads: Technology Problems Limit Effectiveness of US-VISIT Program to Screen Foreigners." *Washington Post,* May 23, 2005, A1.

O'Meara, Kelly Patricia. "Anti-Terror Technology." *InsightMag.com,* July 21, 2003. http://www.insightmag.com/news/2003/08/05/National/AntiTerror .Technology/ (accessed June 14, 2004).

Optometric Management. "Lens Express Denies Racketeering Charges." Norwalk, CT. December, 1992, 3.

Packer, George. *The Assassin's Gate: America in Iraq.* New York: Farrar, Straus & Giroux, 2005.

Pamuk, Orhan. *Istanbul: Memories and the City.* New York: Knopf, 2005.

Parry, Robert. *Fooling America: How Washington Insiders Twist the Truth and Manufacture the Conventional Wisdom.* New York: William Morrow & Co., 1992.

———. *Trick or Treason: The October Surprise Mystery.* New York: Sheridan Square Press, 1993.

Philby, Kim. *My Silent War.* New York: Grove Press, 1968.

Pinck, Charles T., and Dan Pinck. "The Best Spies Didn't Wear Suits." *New York Times,* Op-Ed, December 10, 2004, A41.

Pincus, Walter. "Analysts Behind Iraq Intelligence Were Rewarded." *Washington Post,* May 28, 2005, A1.

Pincus, Walter, and Peter Baker. "Dissent on Intelligence Is Critical, Report Says: Commission's Ideas Diverge from Planned Centralization." *Washington Post,* March 30, 2005, A1.

Pound, Edward T. "The Iran Connection." *U.S. News & World Report,* November 22, 2004.

Powell, Colin. "A Strategy of Partnerships." *Foreign Affairs,* January/February 2004.

———. "Full Text of the U.S. Secretary of State Colin Powell's Speech to the United Nations on Iraq." *Washington Post,* Special Report, February 5, 2003.

Powers, Thomas. *Intelligence Wars: American Secret History from Hitler to Al-Qaeda.* New York: NYRB Books, 2002.

———. "The Failure." *New York Review of Books,* April 29, 2004.

———. "The Vanishing Case for War." *New York Review of Books,* December 4, 2003.

Premier Motorsports. "Promotional Brochure for Next iP 2002 Ford Taurus, No. 66, Driver Todd Hirschfeld, Sponsored by Next iP, 1-800-PetMeds, Hooters, FlashFone, Stewart Warner, Jackaroo; United States Alliance Racing, Hooters Pro Cup Series" (undated).

PRNewswire. "WorldQuest Networks Announces Merger Agreement with Ntera Holdings: Transaction Will Give WorldQuest Access to a VoIP

Network Capable of Handling 4 Billion Minutes a Month." March 17, 2004.

Priest, Dana. "CIA Moves to Second Fiddle in Intelligence Work." *Washington Post,* February 27, 2005, A9.

———. "Iraq New Terror Breeding Ground: War Created Haven, CIA Advisers Report." *Washington Post,* January 14, 2005, A1.

Priest, Dana, and Josh White. "Iraq War Helps Recruit Terrorists, Hill Told: Intelligence Officials Talk of Growing Insurgency." *Washington Post,* February 17, 2005, A1.

Priest, Dana, and Walter Pincus. "Tenet Resigns as CIA Director: Intelligence Chief Praised by Bush, but Critics Cite Lapses on Iraq War." *Washington Post,* June 4, 2004, A1.

Proust, Marcel (translated by C. K. Scott Moncrief and Terence Kilmartin). *In Search of Lost Time: Volume I: Swann's Way.* New York: Modern Library Classics, 2004.

Pullella, Philip. "Vatican Says Anti-Kerry Lawyer Hoodwinked Them." Reuters, October 20, 2004.

Radio Free Europe. "Moldova News Agency, PPCD Leader Fined for Defamation." November 5, 2003.

Rayburn, Joel. "The Last Exit From Iraq: How the British Quit Mesopotamia." *Foreign Affairs,* March/April, 2006, 29–40.

Raymont, Daniel. "E-Mail Messages in Chron File of Messages from Daniel Raymont to Kolb of May 24, 2004 to December 31, 2004."

Remnick, David. "High Water: How Presidents and Citizens React to Disaster." *New Yorker,* October 3, 2005. http://www.newyorker.com/fact/content/articles/051003fa_fact/ (accessed November 8, 2005).

Republican National Lawyers Association. "Find A Republican Lawyer: Profile of Jerris Leonard." http://rnla.org/bio/BioDetail.asp?MemberID=335/ (accessed November 18, 2005).

Regan, Tom. "Three Years After 9/11, U.S. Agencies Infighting Foils Unified Effort." *Christian Science Monitor,* December 30, 2004.

Republicans Abroad. "Business Card of Robert M. Sensi, Chairman, The Ambassador's Club, Republicans Abroad c/o Republican National Committee." Washington, D.C.

———. "1983 Directory of Officers and Offices." Washington, D.C., 1983.

Rice, Condoleezza. "Campaign 2000: Promoting the National Interest." *Foreign Affairs,* January/February 2000.

Riché, Pascal. "Notre Agent à Miami: Larry Kolb, 51 ans, Américain. Fils d'espion et espion lui-même, ancien manager du boxeur Mohamed Ali. Il accumule comme un aimant les aventures et les coups tordus." *Liberation* (Paris), June 10, 2005, Portrait, back cover.

Richmond Times-Dispatch. "Court Denies Request for Reduced Sentence." January 25, 1994, B4.

———. "Court Rules That Lawyer Can Remain in Islands." December, 19, 1997, B4.

———. "FBI Seeks Lawyer in Fraud Scheme: Faked Letter Secured Release, Officials Say." November 24, 1996, C4.

———. "4th Circuit Panel Upholds Beach Lawyer's Convictions." May 9, 1992, B3.

———. "May Yet See Lens Refund." June 21, 1988, Metro, 19.

———. "Optometrist Faces New Charges Related to His Letters to Judges." March 15, 1996, B3.

Richtel, Matt. "Live Tracking of Mobile Phones Prompts Court Fights on Privacy." *New York Times,* December 10, 2005, A1.

Risen, James. *State of War: The Secret History of the C.I.A. and the Bush Administration.* New York: Free Press, 2006.

Roosevelt, Archie. *For Lust of Knowing: Memoirs of an Intelligence Officer.* Boston: Little, Brown, 1988.

Rothwell, Nicolas. "Iran and Syria Unite Against Threats." *Australian* (Sydney), February 18, 2005.

Saar, John. "GOP Probes Official as Teacher of 'Tricks.'" *Washington Post,* August 10, 1973, A16.

Safire, William. "Progress in Iraq." *New York Times,* May 31, 2004, Editorial, A17.

Salazar, Yolanda. "E-Mail Message from Assistant Officer in Charge, Department of Homeland Security, Athens, Greece, to John A. Lowell, Consular

Section Chief, U.S. Consulate General, Istanbul, Turkey, Subject: Investigation Request, Sent: Wednesday, October 08, 2003, 2:29 P.M."

Sampson, Anthony. *The Arms Bazaar: From Lebanon to Lockheed.* New York: Viking Press, 1977.

Santos, Carlos. "Celebrity Days Bitter Reminder for Hirschfeld." *Richmond Times-Dispatch,* May 26, 1991, A1.

————. "Contacts, Abilities Make Many Take an Interest in 'Ali's Lawyer.' " *Richmond Times-Dispatch,* December 25, 1988, C1.

————. "Ex-Adviser to Ali Kills Self in Jail: Richard Hirschfeld Was Facing 70 Years in Prison on Charges." *Richmond Times-Dispatch,* January 12, 2005.

————. "Gaffney Pleads Guilty to Conspiracy Charge: Case Involves Plot to Get Judge Off Case." *Richmond Times-Dispatch,* July 2, 1997, B4.

————. "Hirschfeld Lived the Good Life on the Run: Charlottesville Lawyer Now in Jail in Canary Islands." *Richmond Times-Dispatch,* February 1, 1997, B4.

————. "Hirschfeld Saga Continues to Unfold; Ex-Business Partner's Kin Sue U.S. Prosecutors Over Exhumation." *Richmond Times-Dispatch,* February 17, 1997, A1.

————. "Hirschfeld Says New Man Evolving from Prison Stay." *Virginian-Pilot,* June 7, 1993, D2.

————. "Hirschfeld's Name Included in Indictment." *Richmond Times-Dispatch,* May 24, 1997, B4.

————. "Hirschfeld's 'Simple Job' Led to Web of Intrigue." *Richmond Times-Dispatch,* July 12, 1987, E1.

————. "Prison Plays Attitude Jolter for Hirschfeld: Go-Go Operator Learns Go-Slow Virtues." *Richmond Times-Dispatch,* May 23, 1993, C1.

Saudi Gazette. "Ali May Visit Iran to Seek Americans' Release." February 16, 1985.

————. "Ali Pursues Efforts for Release of Americans." February 20, 1985.

————. "Did Ali Play any Role in Levin's Release?" February 19, 1985.

Scarborough, Rowan. "Cell Phone Technology an Explosive Tool for Insurgents." *Washington Times,* March 7, 2005.

————. "Wolfowitz Criticizes 'Suspect' Estimate of Occupation Force." *Washington Times,* February 28, 2003.

Schell, Jonathan. "The Case Against the War." *The Nation,* March 3, 2003.

Schmitt, Eric. "Threats and Responses: Military Spending; Pentagon Contradicts General on Iraq Occupation Force's Size." *New York Times,* February 28, 2003, A1.

————. "Threats and Responses: Rebuilding Iraq; U.S. Suggests Iraqi-Americans Will Help in Recovery Process." *New York Times,* February 24, 2003, A10.

Schmitt, Richard B., and Greg Miller. "FBI in Talks to Extend Reach: Some past and present CIA officials see the bureau's push to change the ground rules of intelligence gathering as a threat to their agency." *Los Angeles Times,* January 28, 2005, A1.

Schrader, Katherine. "Negroponte: Iraq May Spark Regional Fight." Associated Press, March 1, 2006.

Schwartz, Daniel C. "Letter to Larry Kolb, Re Legal Representation, dated July 29, 2004."

Schudel, Matt. "Flashy Fugitive Richard Hirschfeld Dies." *Washington Post,* January 13, 2005, B7.

Schulte, Bret. "Turf Wars in the Delta: Plotting a Future for the new New Orleans isn't just about urban design. Try money—and politics." *U.S. News & World Report,* February 27, 2006, 66–71.

Schwartz, John, and Lowell Bergman. "F.B.I. Sees Delay in New Network to Oversee Cases." *New York Times,* June 26, 2004, A1.

Senate Select Committee on Intelligence. *Report on the U.S. Intelligence Community's Pre-War Intelligence Assessments on Iraq,* Ordered Reported on July 7, 2004, 108th Congress, Washington, D.C.

Sensenbrenner, James F., Jr. "Biography of Congressman Sensenbrenner." House of Representatives. http://www.house.gov/sensenbrenner/bio .htm/ (accessed December 4, 2004).

Sensi, Robert M. "Affidavit of Robert M. Sensi Dated August 9, 1991." Court record of filing on August 12, 1991 in re *Kuwait Airways Corporation v. Robert M. Sensi,* Civil Action No. 89-2251 (U.S. District Court, District of Columbia).

————. "Defendant's List of Witnesses." Court record of filing on July 9, 1991, in re *Kuwait Airways Corporation v. Robert M. Sensi,* Civil Action No. 89-2251 (U.S. District Court, District of Columbia).

————. "Defendant's Proposed Stipulation Regarding CIA Witnesses and Classified Material." Filed March 4, 1988. *United States v. Robert Mario Sensi.* Criminal Case No. 86-0318 (U.S. District Court, District of Columbia).

————. "Defendant Robert M. Sensi's Supplemental Answers to Plaintiff's Interrogatories." Court record of filing on March 4, 1991, in re *Kuwait Airways Corporation v. Robert M. Sensi,* Civil Action No. 89-2251 (U.S. District Court, District of Columbia).

————. "Deposition of Robert M. Sensi Conducted October 10–11, 1987 in Washington, DC." Court record of filing on March 25, 1988, in re *Kuwait Airways Corporation v. American Security Bank, N.A., and First American Bank, N.A.,* Civil Action No. 86-2542 (U.S. District Court, District of Columbia).

————. "Summary of Checks Drawn on 640 Account." Court record of filing on March 4, 1991, in re *Kuwait Airways Corporation v. Robert M. Sensi,* Civil Action No. 89-2251 (U.S. District Court, District of Columbia).

Sensi, Ulisse. "U.S. Securities and Exchange Commission, Form 3, Statement of Beneficial Ownership of Securities of GlobalNet Corp." Dated January 5, 2004.

Serian, Joe. "The Dr. Joe Serian Story." *Global IndyMedia.* January 24, 2003. http://global.indymedia.org.au/front.php3?article_id=844&group=webcast/ (accessed January 15, 2005).

Seriani, Joseph S. "Complaint for Damages, *Joseph S. Seriani v. Yalie Golan, Engin Kamil Yesil, Mordechai Golan and Lens Express, Inc.*" Case No. 92-22923. Florida Circuit Court, 11th Judicial Circuit, Dade County, Florida. Filed October 26, 1992.

Sethi, Inder. "Affidavit of Inder Sethi Dated May 12, 1988." Court record of filing on March 4, 1991, in re *Kuwait Airways Corporation v. Robert M. Sensi,* Civil Action No. 89-2251 (U.S. District Court, District of Columbia).

Shane, Scott, and David E. Sanger. "Bush Panel Finds Big Flaws Remain in U.S. Spy Efforts." *New York Times,* April 1, 2005, A1.

Shaw, Andy. "Clinton Impeachment Was Retaliation for Nixon, Says Retiring Congressman." *ABC7Chicago,* April 21, 2005. http://abclocal.go.com/wls/news/042105_ns_hyde.html/ (accessed April 21, 2005).

Snepp, Frank, and Jonathan King. "GOP Had Secret Channels to Iran: Casey Aides Used Party Organization for Intelligence Activities in Mid-'80s." *Village Voice,* July 23, 1991, 30.

Smothers, Ronald. "Carter Calls on Americans to Give Reagan 'Our Full Support.'" *New York Times,* June 22, 1985, A6.

Solomon, John. "Terror Expertise Not Priority at FBI." Associated Press, June 19, 2005.

Sonnenschein, Allan. "Champ." *Penthouse,* September, 1984, 164–173.

Sophocles, translated into English by George Young. *Oedipus Rex.* New York: Dover Thrift Editions, 1991 (orig. c. 460 B.C.).

Stratton, Jeff. "Mr. Big Shot: The Charismatic Lawyer and Power Broker Took One Last Lap in a New River Mansion During His Run from the Law." *New Times,* May 26, 2005. http://www.newtimesbpb.com/Issues/2005-05-26/news/feature.html/ (accessed May 29, 2005).

Sunday Times (London). "Not So Repentant: Irving's Real Views." February 26, 2006. http://www.timesonline.co.uk/article/0,,2092-2058361,00.html/ (accessed March 1, 2006).

———. "The Secret Downing Street Memo." May 1, 2005.

T Mobile. "Schedule of Local Airtime, Long Distance and International Charges, Itemized Details for (202) 390-2900."

———. "Schedule of Local Airtime, Long Distance and International Charges, Itemized Details for (202) 390-5400."

T.C./YILDIZ TEKNiK üNiVERSiTESi'/ELEKTRiK ELEKTRONiK FAKüLTESi/BiLGiSAYAR MüH. BöLüMü/TRANSCRiPT/Fakülte No: 9311015, Tarih: 09/07/2002.

Tamayo, Juan O. "Castro's Family: Fidel's private life with his wife and sons is so secret that even the CIA is left to wonder." *Miami Herald,* October 8, 2000.

Taylor, Joe. "Lawyer Sentenced in Federal Tax Case." *Richmond Times-Dispatch,* May 18, 1991, 23.

Teicher, Howard. "Affidavit of Howard Teicher, Staff Member of U.S. National Security Council, Regarding 'Bear-Spares' Program for Iraq." Filed under seal in the U.S. District Court, Southern District of Florida, in re *United States of America v. Carlos Cardoen, Franco Safta, et al.*, Case No. 93-241-CR-Highsmith. Original dated January 31, 1995.

Tenet, George. "DCI George Tenet's Introduction of President Bush, at the Dedication Ceremony for the George Bush Center for Intelligence, April 26, 1999." Central Intelligence Agency electronic archive.

Thornburgh, Dick, and Louis D. Boccardi. *Report of the Independent Review Panel on the September 8, 2004* 60 Minutes Wednesday *Segment "For the Record" Concerning President Bush's Texas Air National Guard Service.* Kirkpatrick & Lockhart Nicholson Graham LLP, Counsel to the Independent Review Panel. Washington, D.C.: January 5, 2005.

Tifft, Susan. "Please Speak into the Microphone: Marcos' Bizarre Plans for Insurrection Are Uncovered." *Time,* July 20, 1987.

Time. "Building a Better Spy Network: Who reports to whom in the spy world's flow chart? Negroponte's first job is to figure that out." February 28, 2005, 34–35.

———. "Scared to Death." March 27, 1933.

Tyson, Ann Scott. "Two Years Later, Iraq War Drains Military: Heavy Demands Offset Combat Experience." *Washington Post,* March 19, 2005, A1.

———. "US Faces Gap in 'Intelligence War' in Iraq: As a Well-Funded Insurgency Stiffens, US Military Officials Worry About Lack of Inside Knowledge of Resistance Cells." *Christian Science Monitor,* November 5, 2004. http://csmonitor.com/2004/1105/p02s02-usmi.html/ (accessed November 6, 2004).

U.S. Central Intelligence Agency. *Symposium on Teaching Intelligence.* Washington, D.C.: Center for the Study of Intelligence, 1994.

———. *The Worldfactbook: Iran.* http://www.odci.gov/cia/publications/factbook/geos/ir.html.

U.S. Counterdrug Technology Assessment Center, Office of National Drug Control Policy. "Ten- Year Counterdrug Technology Plan and Development Roadmap."http://www.ncjrs.gov/ondcppubs/publications/scimed/10year_1998/contcons.html (accessed March 5, 2006).

U.S. Court of Appeals, Ninth Circuit. Memorandum of the Court Regarding Disposition of Appeal in re *Abuwi Muhammad Mahdi v. MCI-Worldcom, et al.*, No. 03-56243, D.C. No. CV-00-01518-IEG. Filed January 13, 2005.

U.S. Department of Justice, Office of the Inspector General, Evaluation and Inspections Division. "Follow-up Review of the Status of IDENT/IAFIS Integration." Report Number I-2005-001. December 2004.

U.S. Department of Justice, United States Attorney, District of Columbia. "Request for Certain Records Pertaining to Robert M. Sensi Obtained by Kuwait Airways Through Court-Ordered Discovery in *Kuwait Airways v. American Security Bank*." Letter to Thomas Whalen, Esq., dated March 3, 1988. University of Virginia Law Library, Charlottesville. Special Collection: The Papers of Judge Revercomb, Judge of the U.S. District Court, District of Columbia.

U.S. Department of Justice. "Federal Grand Jury Indicts Seven in International Money Scam." Press release, 94-585, October 7, 1994.

———. "Reinventing Crime Fighting Through Increased Efficiency." Press release, undated. http://govinfo.library.unt.edu/npr/library/status/sstories/jus1.htm (accessed January 15, 2006).

———. "2000 Calendar Year Report on Department of Justice Freedom of Information Act Litigation Cases in Which a Decision Was Rendered in 2000." http://www.usdoj.gov/04foia/00addendum.htm/.

U.S. Department of Labor, Employment and Training Administration. "Labor Condition Application for H-1B Nonimmigrants, Form ETA Case Number: T-02275-00081, Form ETA 9035, OMB Approval: 1205-0310, Expiration Date: 31 August 2003, Applicant: Numind, Inc., Signed by Chief, Division of Foreign Labor Certificates, U.S. Department of Labor, Dated 10/02/2002."

U.S. Department of State. "Case Note Summary, Case Number 2003183 537 0010, Regarding Turkish National Applicant Korhan Aydin, Date/Time Prepared: 12/22/2003 12:54:24."

U.S. Department of State. "Refusal Worksheet, OF-194, for Refusal on 02-Jul-2003 of Visa for Turkish National Subject Korhan Aydin, Under Patriot Act Section 403, Signed by Jayne A. Howell, Refusing Officer, and John Lowell, Principal Officer, Designee or Chief Consular Officer."

U.S. District Court, District of Columbia. "Civil Docket for Case No. 1:89-cv-02251-GAG, *Kuwait Airways Corp. v. Robert M. Sensi.*" Record filed in Washington, D.C., August 10, 1989.

———. "Judgment in Case No. 1:89-cv-02251-GAG, *Kuwait Airways Corp. v. Robert M. Sensi.*" Record filed in Washington, D.C., February 5, 1992.

————. "Memorandum and Order in re *United States of America v. Robert Mario Sensi.*" Cr. No. 86-0318. Filed May 1, 1987. University of Virginia Law Library, Charlottesville. Special Collection: The Papers of Judge Revercomb, Judge of the U.S. District Court, District of Columbia.

————. "Memorandum of Opinion in re *Virtual Defense and Development International, Inc. v. The Republic of Moldova.* Civil Action No: 98-161 (RMU)." http://www.dcd.uscourts.gov/98-161.pdf/ (accessed August 21, 2004).

————. "Order to Defendant Sensi to Surrender to the Custody of the Attorney General, *United States of America v. Robert Mario Sensi.*" Cr. No. 86-0318. Filed July 21, 1988.

————. "Transcript of Proceedings in *Kuwait Airways v. American Security Bank, N.A. et al.* Regarding FBI Investigation and Testimony of Representative of Central Intelligence Agency on October 8, 1987." Record filed in the U.S. Court of Appeals for the District of Columbia Circuit, Washington, D.C., January 10, 1989.

U.S. District Court for the Eastern District of Pennsylvania. "Final Judgment of Permanent Injunction in re *Securities and Exchange Commission v. Richard M. Hirschfeld and William N. Chapman.*" Civil Action No. 76 Civ. 3887. Filed December 21, 1976.

U.S. District Court for the Eastern District of Virginia, Norfolk Division. "Final Judgment in re *Securities and Exchange Commission v. Hirschfeld Bank of Commerce.*" Civil Action No. 74-533. Filed February 18, 1975.

U.S. District Court, Southern District of New York. "Findings of Fact and Conclusions of Law in re *Securities and Exchange Commission against Champion Sports Management, Inc., and Richard Hirschfeld.*" Case No. 84 Civ. 5778 (RJW). Filed November 1, 1984.

U.S. Federal Bureau of Investigation. "Arrest of Richard Marshall Hirschfeld." Press release dated October 4, 2004. http://norfolk.fbi.gov/pressrel/2004/10042004release2.htm.

U.S. Federal Bureau of Investigation, Criminal Justice Information Services Division. "Fingerprint Identification Record for Turkish National Subject Korhan Aydin, Fingerprinted: 2003/07/22, USNHNVC1Z, Agency Case IST200318353710."

U.S. Federal Bureau of Investigation, Intelligence Section, Organizational Intelligence Unit. *Semion Mogilevich Organization: Eurasian Organized Crime.* Washington, D.C., 1996.

U.S. Federal Bureau of Investigation, NCIC Section. "National Comprehensive Report on Richard M. Hirschfeld" (partially redacted) (date redacted).

———. "National Comprehensive Report on Robert M. Sensi" (partially redacted) (date redacted).

U.S. Federal Bureau of Prisons. Federal Inmate Locator record for Engin Kamil Yesil, "Inmate Register Number 28743-004, Released 04-12-1994."

———. Federal Inmate Locator record for Eugene Albert Fischer, "Inmate Register Number 32904-004. Location USP Coleman I."

———. Federal Inmate Locator record for Richard M. Hirschfeld, "Inmate Register Number 24226-083."

———. Federal Inmate Locator record for Robert M. Sensi, "Inmate Register Number 13322-016, Released 12-13-1996."

———. Federal Inmate Locator record for Yalie Golan, "Inmate Register Number 28742-004, Released 09-13-1993."

U.S. Federal Bureau of Prisons, Federal Correctional Institution, Loretto, PA. "Record of Voluntary Surrender of Robert Mario Sensi to F.C.I. Loretto on July 29, 1988." Filed in U.S. District Court, District of Pennsylvania, August 23, 1988.

U.S. Federal Election Commission. "Schedule A: Itemized Receipts: Individual Contributions Arranged by Type, Given, then Recipient: Sensi, Robert, Kerry, John F., via John Kerry for President Inc., February 5, 2004; 1000." F.E.C. Image 24990855987 (page 2,545 of 3,000).

U.S. Immigration and Naturalization Service. "H Classification Supplement to Form I-129, Supplement H (12/10/01)Y, OMB No. 1115-0168, Petitioner: Numind, Inc., Beneficiary: Turkish National Ahmet Cem Payzin" (undated).

———. "H-1B Data Collection & Filing Fee Exemption, Form I-129 (Rev. 12/18/00)N, OMB No. 1115-0225, Petitioner: Numind, Inc., Beneficiary: Turkish National Ahmet Cem Payzin" (undated).

———. "I-94 Departure Record, Departure Number 981851402 08, for Ahmet Cem Payzin, Admitted Miami July 15, 2002."

———. "Notice of Entry of Appearance as Attorney or Representative, Form G-28 (09-26-00)Y, for Beneficiary: Turkish National Ahmet Cem Payzin, and Petitioner: Numind, Inc." (undated).

————. "Petition for a Nonimmigrant Worker, Form I-129 (Rev. 12/10/01)Y, OMB No. 1115-0168, Petitioner: Numind, Inc., Beneficiary: Turkish National Ahmet Cem Payzin" (undated).

U.S. Securities and Exchange Commission. "Complaint: *Securities and Exchange Commission v. Leon Levy, et al., and Atlantic 1 Corp.*" U.S. District Court for the Northern District of Texas, Dallas Division, Civil Action No. 3-04-CV-0351-N, dated and filed February 2004.

————. Form 8-K filing of iDial Networks, Inc., Item 2, "Acquisition of the Assets of GBLK Communication, LLC." September 5, 2003.

————. Form 8-K filing of iDial Networks, Inc., Item 7c, Exhibit 10.6, "Promissory Note," dated August 21, 2003, payable by iDial Networks, Inc. to Growth Enterprise Fund, S.A. September 5, 2003.

————. "Form 8-K filing of WorldQuest Networks, Inc. (WQNI)." Recorded May 17, 2004.

————. "Initial Decision: In the Matter of Richard Hirschfeld, By Order of Warren E. Blair, Chief Administrative Law Judge." United States of America, Before the Securities and Exchange Commission, Administrative Proceeding File No. 3-6544, Entered July 19, 1985.

————. "SEC Announces $1.3 Million Settlement of Insider-Trading Charges Against Three Foreign Nationals." Litigation Release No. 19217. Fort Worth, TX, May 4, 2005.

U.S. Supreme Court. "Petition for a Writ pf Certiorari, *Janet Reno, et al., v. Saul Navas, et al.*" October Term, 1998. Submitted by Seth P. Waxman, Solicitor General, dated December 1998.

UVA Lawyer. "In Memoriam." Spring, 2005. http://www.law.virginia.edu/home2002/html/alumni/uvalawyer/sp05/memoriam.htm/ (accessed April 8, 2005).

Vick, Karl. "Insurgents Attacked, but Voters Persevered: Resolute Electorate, Blanket Security Thwarted Onslaught." *Washington Post,* February 1, 2005, A11.

Virginia State Bar Association. "Attorney Records Search: Disciplinary Actions Taken: Richard M. Hirschfeld." VSB Docket No. 91-000-0752, Filed July 11, 1991.

Virginia State Corporation Commission. "Corporate Data Inquiry Return for Global Telesat Corp., Corp. ID 0599750, Incorporated July 11, 2003." Web# 449, CISM0180.

Virginian-Pilot. "Sentence for Lawyer: Tax Fraud Trial Sentencing." January 25, 1994, D4.

Wall Street Journal. "Former Boxing Firm Head Is Sentenced to Probation." November 19, 1986.

Waller, Douglas. "The CIA's Secret Army: Because of past scandals, the agency had largely dropped its paramilitary operations. But the war on terrorism has brought it back into the business." *Time,* February 3, 2003, 22–31.

Waltz, Lynn. "Ex–Beach Lawyer, Arrested As Fugitive, Leaves Spanish Jail." *Virginian-Pilot,* May 30, 1997, B4.

———. "Lawyer Indicted in Jail Scam." *Virginian-Pilot,* November 23, 1996, B1.

———. "Spanish Police Arrest Fugitive from Norfolk: Federal Authorities Will Seek Extradition of Hirschfeld from Canary Islands." *Virginian-Pilot,* January 31, 1997, B1.

———. "Virginia Men Allegedly Plotted to Attack Judge: Hirschfeld Has Not Been Charged, but His Name Appears in an Indictment 25 Times." *Virginian-Pilot,* May 23, 1997, A1.

Ware, Michael. "Appointment in Samarra: Urban Warfare: An Eyewitness Account of the Vicious Battle to Retake the City of Samarra." *Time,* October 11, 2004, 46.

Warrick, Joby. "Lacking Biolabs, Trailers Carried Case for War: Administration Pushed Notion of Banned Iraqi Weapons Despite Evidence to Contrary." *Washington Post,* April 12, 2006, A1.

Washington Post. "A Development Company Headed by Muhammad Ali Wants to Build a $14 Million Hotel." December 31, 1984, Washington Business, 7.

———. "Ali Allegedly Aided Va. Lawyer's Lobbying." September 19, 1988, C7.

———. "Ali Says Calls Made by Him, Not An Imitator." December 15, 1988, A22.

———. "Corrections." June 4, 1988, A3.

———. "FBI Admits Mistakenly Giving Man Back Secret Files He Took." March 27, 2005, A12.

———. "Judge Rejects Bid to Halt Extradition from London: Suspect Held in $1.5 Million Embezzlement." September 12, 1986, C6.

————. "Marcos Requests Hearing to Review U.S. Ban on Travel." July 24, 1987, A18.

————. "'Muhammad Ali Calling'—Or Is It?" December 11, 1988, A8.

————. "New Incorporations: Virginia." November 8, 2004, E6.

————. "New Marcos Restrictions Discussed: Detention Possible if Plots Continue." July 10, 1987, A20.

————. "Tapes Reveal Marcos Plot to Depose, Capture Aquino." July 9, 1987, A1.

Watson, Russell, with Rod Norland. "Unchained at Last: A U.S. Hostage Goes Free in Lebanon." *Newsweek,* February 25, 1985, 25.

Weil, Martin. "D.C. Man Arrested in London." *Washington Post,* August 26, 1986, B3.

White, Josh. "For U.S. Soldiers, a Frustrating and Fulfilling Mission." *Washington Post,* January 2, 2005, A12.

Williams & Connolly LLP. "Biography of Gregory B. Craig, Partner." http:// www.wc.com/ attorney.cfm?attorney_id=261/ (accessed June 17, 2004).

Wilmer Cutler Pickering Hale and Dorr, LLP. "Biography of C. Boyden Gray, Partner." http://www.wilmerhale.com/boyden_gray/htm (accessed April 8, 2005).

Wilson, Catherine. "Richard Hirschfeld, Confidant of Ali, Kills Himself in Jail." Associated Press, January 11, 2005.

Wilson, Joseph. *The Politics of Truth: A Diplomat's Memoir: Inside the Lies That Led to War and Betrayed My Wife's CIA Identity.* New York: Carrol & Graf, 2004.

Wolff, Michael. "All Roads Lead to Rove." *Vanity Fair,* September 2005, 256–262.

Woodward, Bob. *Plan of Attack.* New York: Simon & Schuster, 2004.

Woodward, Bob, and Carl Bernstein. *All the President's Men.* New York: Touchstone, 1994 (orig. published 1974).

WorldQuest Networks, Inc. "WorldQuest Networks Announces Termination of Merger Agreement with Ntera Holdings." Press release dated September 2, 2004.

Wright, Evan. *Generation Kill: Devil Dogs, Iceman, Captain America and the New Face of American War.* New York: G. P. Putnam's Sons, 2004.

Wright, Robin, and Ellen Knickmeyer. "U.S. Lowers Sights on What Can Be Achieved in Iraq: Administration Is Shedding 'Unreality' That Dominated Invasion, Official Says." *Washington Post,* August 14, 2005, A1.

Yesil, Engin. "Letter to John E. Collingwood, Assistant Director, Federal Bureau of Investigation, Dated June 7, 2003." Archival records of Radiant Telecom.

————. "Uncorrected Typescript of Handwritten Notes Headed 'Growth Enterprise Fund Case.'" October 14, 2004.

Zernike, Kate, with Tim Golden. "The Struggle for Iraq: The Guards; Three Accused Soldiers Had Records of Unruliness That Went Unpunished." *New York Times,* May 27, 2004, A13.

Zucchino, David. *Thunder Run: The Armored Strike to Capture Baghdad.* New York: Atlantic Monthly Press, 2004.

INDEX